BASICS

CREATIVE PHOTOGRAPHY

03

Anna Fox
Natasha Caruana

RESEARCH PHOTOGRAPHY

BEHIND THE IMAGE

2nd edition

Routledge
Taylor & Francis Group
LONDON AND NEW YORK

Research in Photography: Behind the Image

First published 2021
by Routledge
2 Park Square, Milton Park, Abingdon, Oxon OX14 4RN

and by Routledge
52 Vanderbilt Avenue, New York, NY 10017

Routledge is an imprint of the Taylor & Francis Group, an informa business

Cover design: Eleanor Rose
Cover image © Shiho Kito
Original book design by Atelier: www.atelier.ie

First published in 2012 by AVA Publishing

British Library Cataloguing-in-Publication Data
A catalogue record for this book is available from the British Library

Library of Congress Cataloging-in-Publication Data
A catalog record has been requested for this book

ISBN: 978-0-367-55205-3 (hbk)
ISBN: 978-1-350-01049-9 (pbk)
ISBN: 978-1-003-09303-9 (ebk)

0.1

Title: from 'Ever After'

Artist: Wiebke Leister

Leister's project *Lovers, Liars and Laughter* extends her earlier research interest in the mouth and the photographic portrayal of laughing and smiling to look at the rather invisible and unattainable features of love and kissing. Leister works with a variety of media, including drawing, photography, collage, and writing (both academic and fiction).

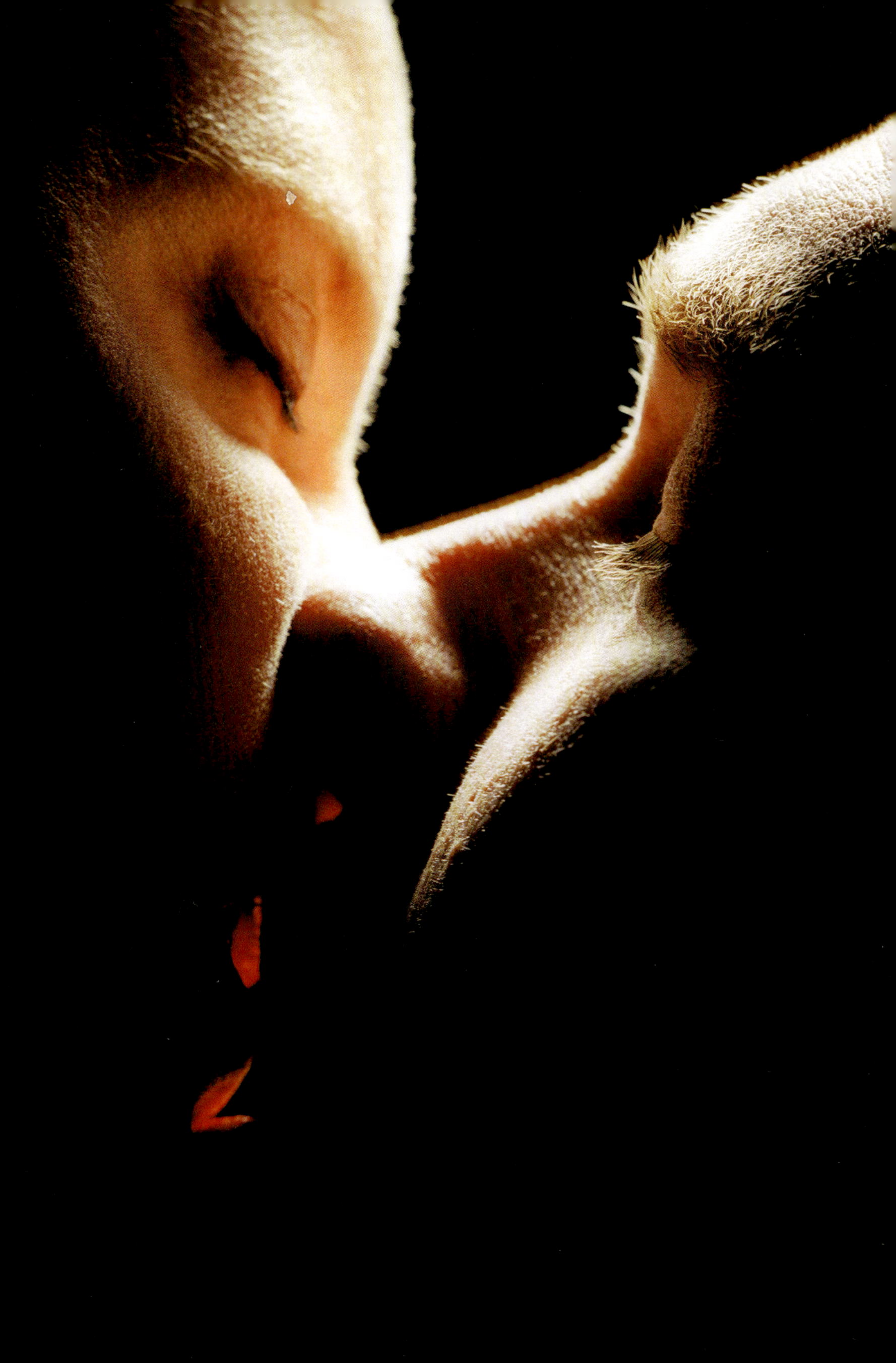

Introduction **6**

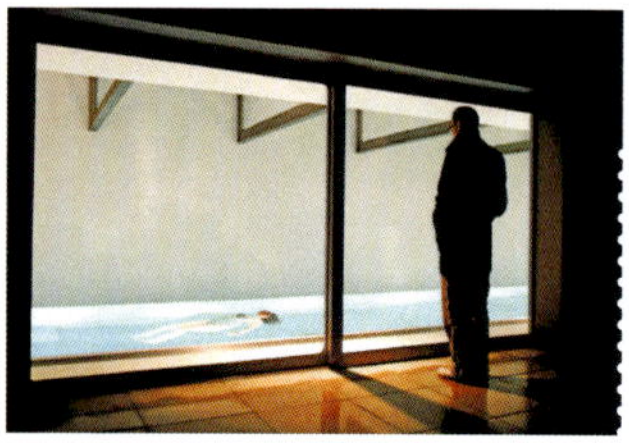

1

Planning **11**

A research proposal **12**

Being informed: History **22**

Being informed: Theory **26**

Case study 1: Shot at dawn **28**

Activity 1: Recording ideas **33**

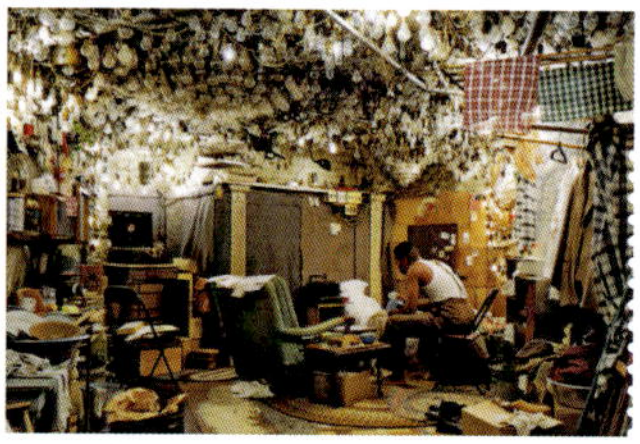

2

Developing ideas through research **35**

Where to do background research **36**

The Internet **46**

Archives **50**

Other interactive forms of research **56**

How research informs practice **60**

Case study 2: Flora **71**

Activity 2: An illustrated story **73**

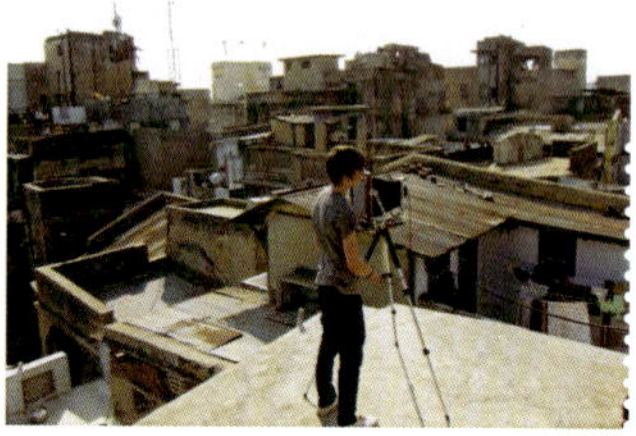

3

Practice as research – art-based photography **75**

What to do and why **76**

Studios **80**

Street photography **84**

Style, genre, medium and technique **92**

Post-production **102**

Applying research to practice **108**

Making judgements **114**

Compiling your research **116**

Blogging **120**

Storing your archive **124**

Case study 3: Melinda Gibson **127**

Activity 3: Pioneers of photography **131**

Contents

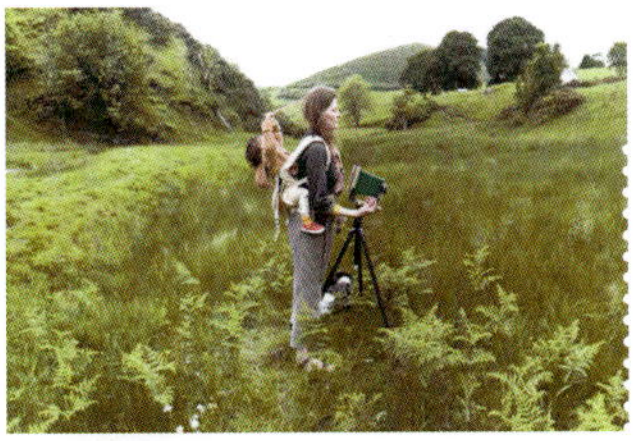

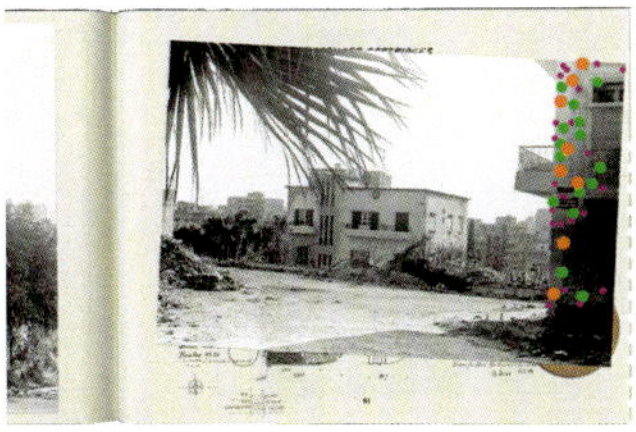

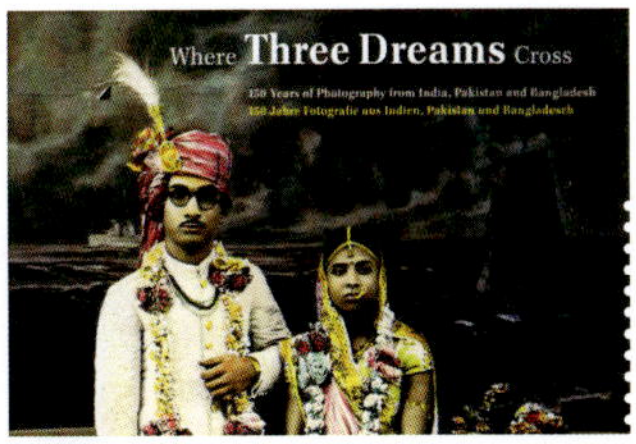

4

Practice as research – commercial photography **133**

Researching for commercial projects **134**

Starting points **140**

Directing the idea **148**

Types of commercial photography **154**

Case study 4: Nik Adam and Luke Norman **161**

Activity 4: Making a mood board **164**

5

Research and practice **167**

Testing the relevance of what you are doing **168**

Audience and context **170**

Revisiting past research **172**

Thinking time **174**

Modifying a plan **180**

Final production **182**

Case study 5: Clare Strand **189**

Activity 5: Context and meaning **191**

6

The impact of research **193**

The bigger picture: Reflection **194**

Photographers' archives **202**

Putting research into context **204**

Case study 6: Hashem el Madani **207**

Activity 6: Booklet **209**

Conclusion **211**

Glossary **212**

Bibliography and webography **214**

Index **215**

Acknowledgments and picture credits **219**

Research and exploration are vital elements of the photographer's practice; together they form part of the process of making photographic projects. Photographers can carry out their research in many different ways, but essentially a body of photographic work is developed through knowledge gained in exploring the medium: investigating histories and theories of photography, observing the world, reading and listening, taking part in debate, critical reflection, and numerous other activities. This book introduces a range of research methods for photography and suggests new ways of thinking about the medium.

Finding out how other photographers work, what informs them, why they are passionate about the work they do, and how they produce their photographs is a truly exciting part of the research process. Photographers model the way they work on the knowledge they have gained about how others operate. There is really no such thing as an 'original' idea: all ideas have been informed by looking at or studying other things as well as experimenting with the medium.

It can be tempting to think that research is not relevant to your work, but if you think carefully and spend some time reflecting on a recent project, you can trace how it evolved. What were its influences? How did the project start? Were you reading a particular book, viewing a website, listening to specific music, or experiencing something else that affected you? What was happening in the world at the time you worked on the project? These questions can reveal the development of a body of work.

Your everyday life and where you live also affects the development of your work. Once you understand the value of research and what it can be, it makes sense to start recording the research process. Documenting the process for the future enables critical reflection; evaluating what you have done helps you decide where to go next.

A body of photographic work is developed through knowledge gained in exploring the medium.

Planning

The first chapter takes a close look at the initial stages of the research process: planning your project, researching historical contexts and exploring relevant theory. It encourages you to consider the reasons you have for making your work. The importance of considering and articulating what you want to do and why is introduced in the context of proposal writing. Budget preparation and timetabling are discussed as part of the written proposal.

Developing ideas through research

The second chapter investigates a range of potential research tools, places to visit and things to do as part of the research process. The value of the widest range of resources is considered, as well as how to get the most out of each one. The chapter looks at where to find what you need and how to develop a framework for research. The value of archives, museums and the Internet is discussed, along with conducting interactive research.

Practice as research – art-based photography

What does practice-based research mean? Having looked at the early stages of planning, this chapter concentrates on exploring practice and looks at how it relates to other forms of research. Genre and style are explored, and editing is brought into the discussion as a way of analyzing practice. This chapter also examines how continuous evaluation informs the development of a body of work and shows that critical reflection is valuable at every stage. Consider compiling your research; making a record of your research is invaluable. To make the most of the work you have done, it is vital to find ways of bringing order to your research materials. There are many different ways of doing this, and there is scope to develop your own personal method. This chapter looks at some of the available methods for compiling your research, including workbooks, sketchbooks, archives and blogs.

Practice as research – commercial photography

If you are planning to work in the commercial sectors of photography, you will also need to engage with a research process. Picture editors and art directors will ask for a range of materials to evidence your thinking. These might include proposals and mood boards as well as test shots. This chapter looks at the various forms of research that a commercial photographer undertakes, how they use it, and how they record their processes.

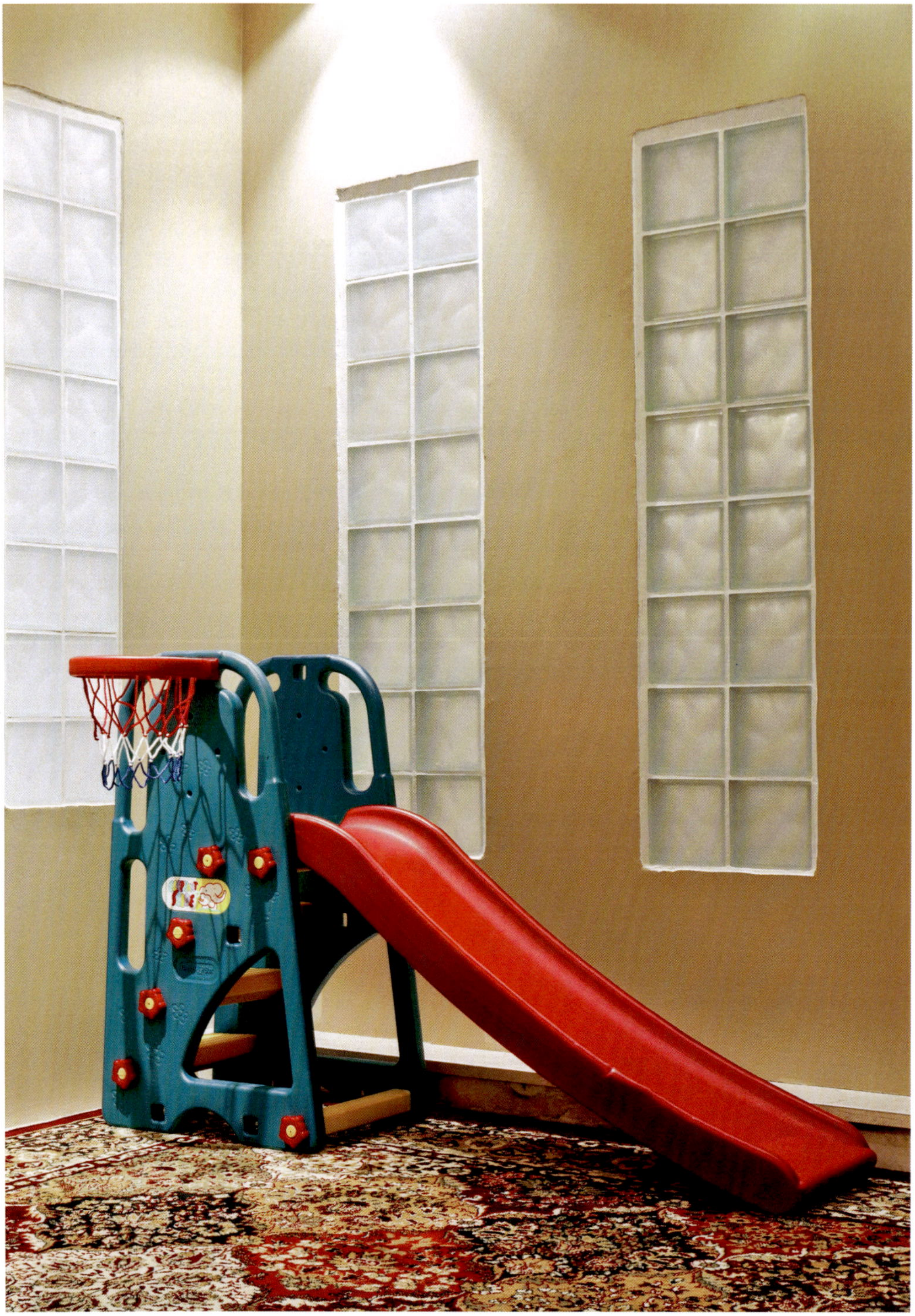

Research and practice

Research and practice are intrinsically linked and form a continuous working process, sparking new ideas and innovative ways of working. This chapter explores the connection between research and practice; it considers how all aspects of thinking, researching and producing are parts of the process. It explores taking time to reflect on your research, explaining how revisiting past research and modifying existing plans can benefit your projects. Context and audience are discussed, and the importance of research ethics is highlighted.

0.2

Title: From the series *Guantanamo: If the light goes out*

Source/Artist: Edmund Clark

Edmund Clark made this work over several years visiting the American prison at Guantanamo Bay that has housed numerous political prisoners since the attacks of 9/11 in the US. The work combines images of interiors in the camp with images of the homes that inmates returned to after their release. This combining of images from different places is disconcerting and emphasizes the extreme sense of disorientation felt by those who are trying to rebuild their homes.

The impact of research

Research is meaningful: methods of evaluating and reflecting on your research allow you to improve your future work. This final chapter looks at the value that has been placed on research in the contemporary world, in archives as well as in the display of photographers' research in exhibitions. Today's curators are keen to make us aware of the work that goes on behind the making of photographs and to emphasize that a single great image has not been made in a vacuum.

How to use this book

This book has been written to unravel some of the mysteries that lie behind the making of images and bodies of photographic work. Research is a process that is always happening when one is an artist or photographer; it is invaluable to investigate how best to do your research and then allow it to inform your practice. The best way to use this book is to start from the beginning and read the chapters in the order they were written. Our explanation and discussion about the research process unfolds gradually through the chapters, each chapter building on the previous one. Each case study gives you more specific information on a particular photographer, revealing the research process for one of their projects. Each activity gives you an exercise to do that illustrates some of the points we are making in a practical way. When you undertake these activities, you will reach a new level of understanding about research.

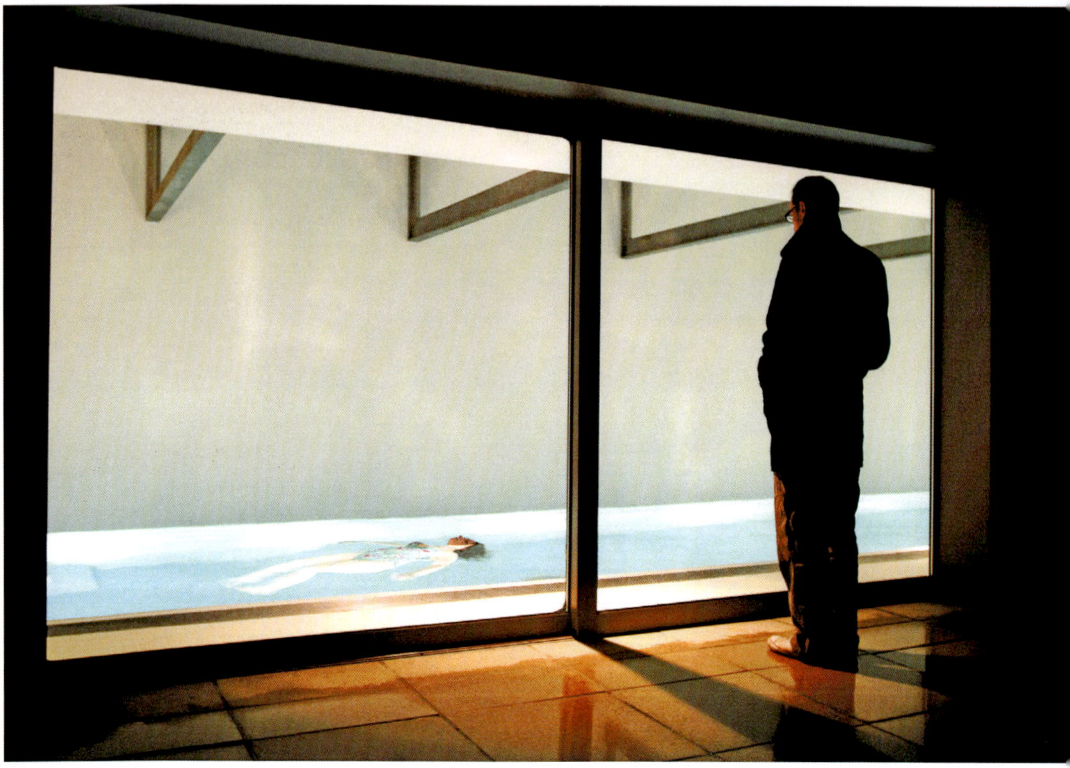

1.1

Title: The Vantage Point 1

Photographer: Ellie Davies

This image, set in a private home, is part of a series that explores the psychological relationship between individuals and the spaces they occupy. Ellie Davies creates a dream-like sense of menace derived from childhood memory. Although staged, the photograph clearly relates to a possible reality: there is a sense of a story pending, and as viewers we do not know how the narrative will unfold.

1 Planning

All photographic series are harvested from research, which may begin with a scholarly investigation or with an overheard conversation on the bus. Researching a project is as challenging and exciting as taking the photographs – sometimes more so. It frames, informs and focuses the final photographic images. As a photographer, you need the skills and knowledge to be able to nurture the seed of an idea.

Ideas do not exist in a void; nothing is completely original. You bring your own unique vision to any body of work and that vision has been informed and influenced by everything you have researched along the way. Embarking on research can feel daunting and overwhelming. Take a step back and draw up a plan or map to help you navigate the options you have ahead of you. The first stages of this plan will involve looking back and uncovering what brought you to the project in the first place. Where did the initial idea come from? Trace back the idea to your possible sources and use these as your first key areas to research. Do not self-censor or dismiss unexpected sources; include all minute details.

Did your influences derive from your own personal history – your memory? Travelling to a new place? Reading a comment on social media? You may have gained an understanding of contemporary life by reading fiction or poetry, or listening to music lyrics, or reading an article online. Everything has the potential to contribute to your research.

Once you have a draft research plan, you are ready to direct the vision for your work. Look for visual references and explore the medium of photography to help you translate your idea into photographs. The plan is simply an initial guide to use as a starting point; new knowledge always opens up possible new directions. Regularly update your plan to reflect what you discover on the way.

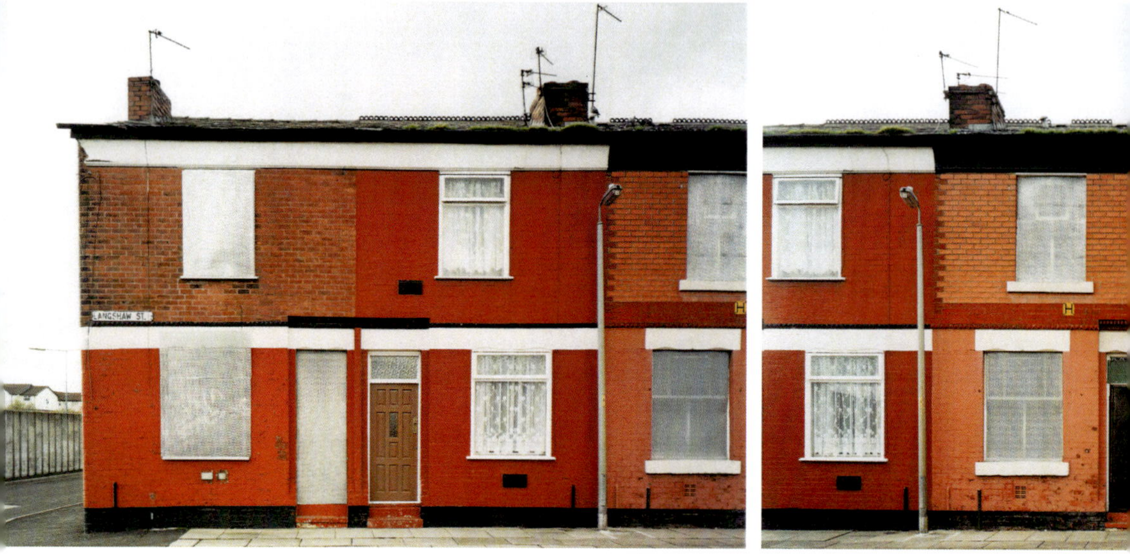

1.2

A research proposal

Research proposals are a key part of the research process, for students and professional photographers alike. Developing a basic research proposal will benefit the structure of any project and the way you go about making it happen.

More advanced proposals (discussed in chapter 2) can be used to apply for funding for particular projects, so being able to produce a successful proposal is a key skill for all photographers. By breaking a proposal down into the following sections, you can write clearly and make appropriate points in relevant places. You can refer back to your proposal during the working process and amend it when necessary; a proposal is a plan and needs to be updated regularly as things change.

The title

Simple as it may seem, a title is vital and reveals more about a project than you may imagine. You could include a subtitle to give a little more information about the project, and you may also write a short summary of the work to be undertaken.

Start with a working title. It could be quite simple, and then continue beneath your title with a straightforward subtitle that clarifies what you are doing. You may change your title three or four times during the research process as you search for the most appropriate one.

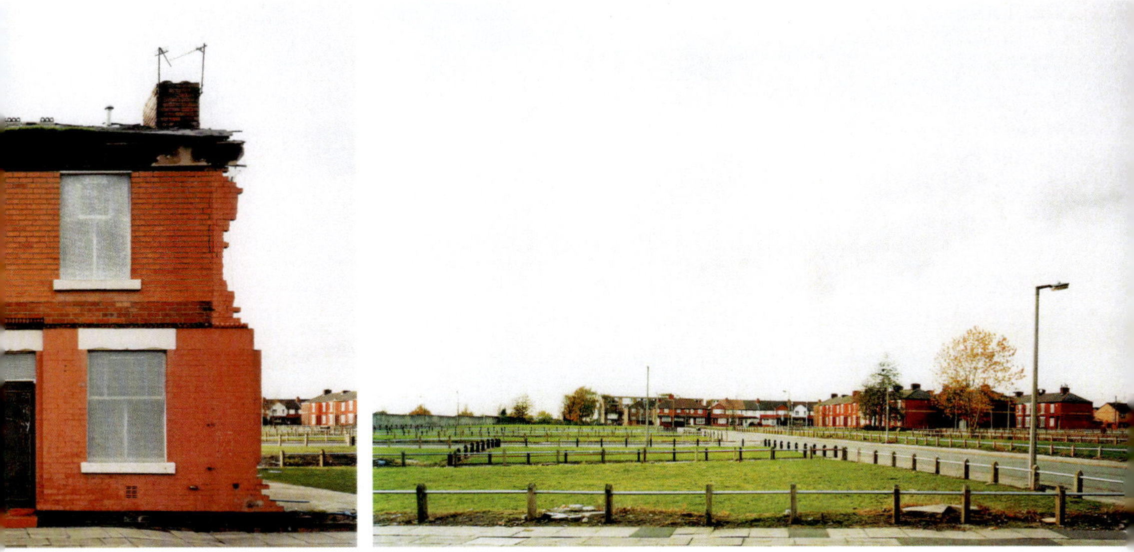

1.2

Title: from *Nummianus*

Photographer: Steffi Klenz

Nummianus is a body of work that looks critically at the displacement of people through the decline in the housing market. Steffi Klenz photographed boarded-up, terraced houses in order to comment on the plight of people experiencing severe economic change. The title of the series is from a Latin inscription found in the remains of a house in the destroyed city of Pompeii. Klenz uses this title deliberately to emphasize the sense of loss and disaster experienced by the community.

Developing a basic research proposal will benefit the structure of any project and the way you go about making it happen.

The topic or theme

The subject, topic, or theme is the most significant part of your proposal; it will contain all the key details of the project. You do not need to write a long, essay-like piece; rather, you should try to get as much information as possible in two to three paragraphs. The writing should be positive and convey your sense of interest and enthusiasm about the idea. Most importantly, you need to clearly explain what it is you intend to do, giving as much relevant information as possible about the subject, how you will approach making the photographs, and how you expect the project to develop.

Who is your audience?

Your proposal should discuss the context and audience of your proposed work; consider where you would like your finished work to exist in the world. Is it an exhibition? A publication? A public artwork? A picture essay to be published in a magazine? Or something else entirely? To do this effectively, you need to consider how each context might give the work a different meaning.

Thinking and reading about how photographs are read and consumed in the world will help you make decisions about the context for your own work. Next time you see a body of photographic work in a public arena, try imagining it transferred to a different context. How would it fit in? Would the meaning of the work be altered if it existed in a new context?

1.3

Title: Emergency Briefing Room (digitally censored photograph) from *The Last Things*

Photographer: David Moore

David Moore's series, *The Last Things*, documents a top-secret secure military location below ground in central London. It is the space that will be used as the first port of call in any situation where the safety of the country is under threat. The Ministry of Defence allowed David Moore an unprecedented level of access, enabling him to observe a live working space that is continuously on standby and fully prepared for the most extreme national emergency. Moore was able to make this work by negotiating access and having a strong proposal.

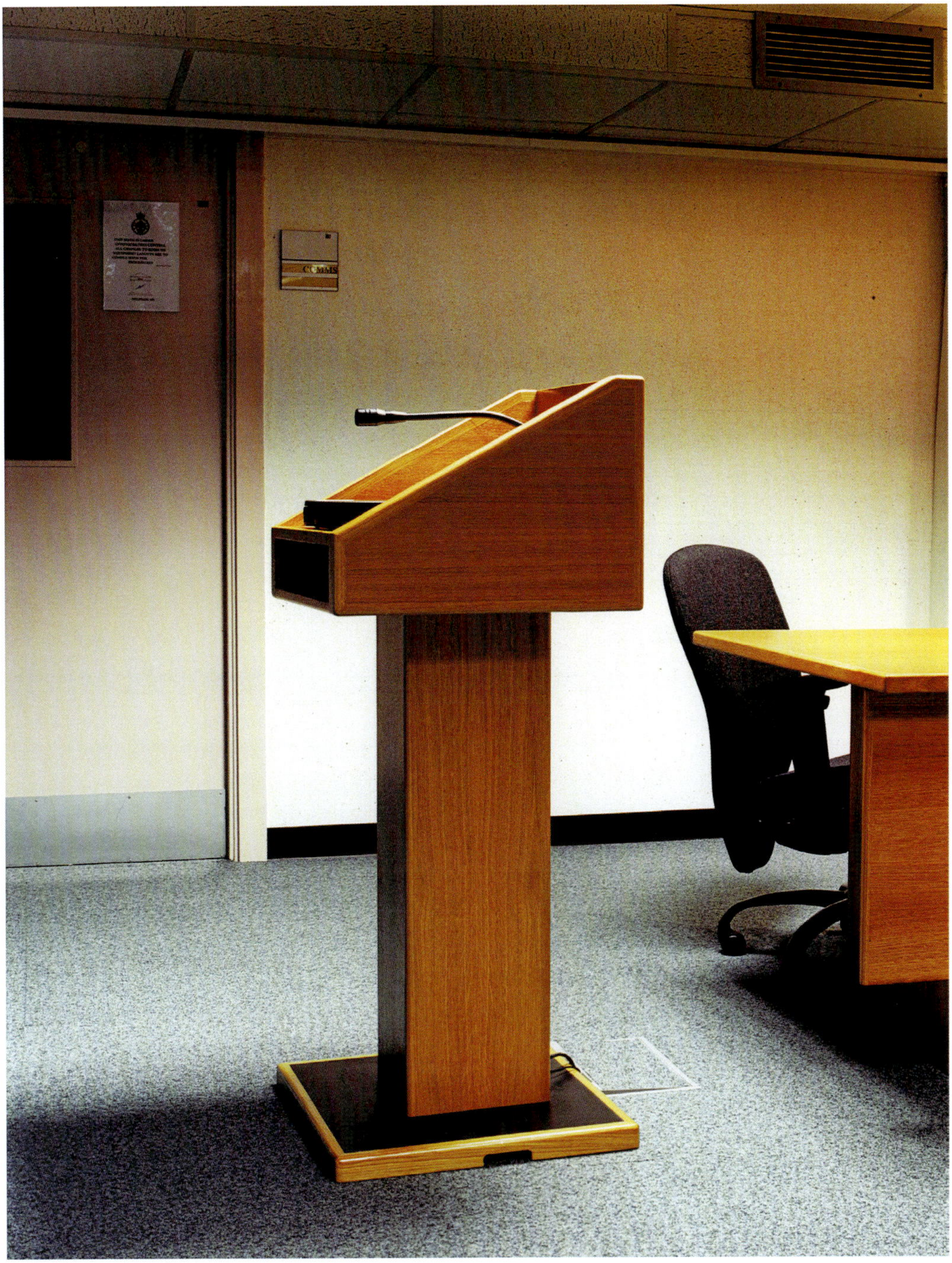

1.3

Approach and methods

A proposal should detail your approach to making the work and the different practical methods you will explore during the project. This can simply be a list of the types of film, camera, lighting and processing that you might use. It could also be more of a discussion around technical issues and how they relate to the meaning of the project, as well as how you might produce the final work. These predominantly technical aspects of the project should be appropriate and show that you are interested in the medium and the possibilities for experimentation. How you choose to finish the work should reflect an understanding of the context it will go into or appear in.

This section of your proposal must also detail the ways in which you intend to conduct your related research. You may also want to explore the possibility of a collaboration and explain this as part of your methodology for practice. Explain why you intend to collaborate, what collaborations you have researched, and the impact this way of working would have on your project.

Photography can be a vehicle to help you step into new environments and new fields. When drawing from an unfamiliar arena, you could decide to collaborate with someone from the field of interest in order to gain vital support and specialist knowledge. Making work with someone from another area of expertise can aid the creative process, making it a fruitful and enriching experience. When working with another person, issues of time management and division of tasks need to be well planned. Co-writing a proposal with a collaborator can help to crystallize your idea; it enables both partners to be clear about the aims of the project from the start.

Getting in

You may want to gain access to a location or organization as part of your project, and your written proposal will be key in doing this. Seeking permission to photograph is one aspect of both documentary and location photography that needs to be considered in the proposal. Laws governing who and when you can photograph differ from country to country and you should always be sure that you understand the law before attempting to take photographs in public or private spaces. The parts of your proposal that describe your subject, and also the context you are placing the work into, will be the most relevant to an organization or individual that you need to gain permission from. It is also essential to be able to clearly communicate these aspects of the proposal in emails, telephone conversations and at meetings.

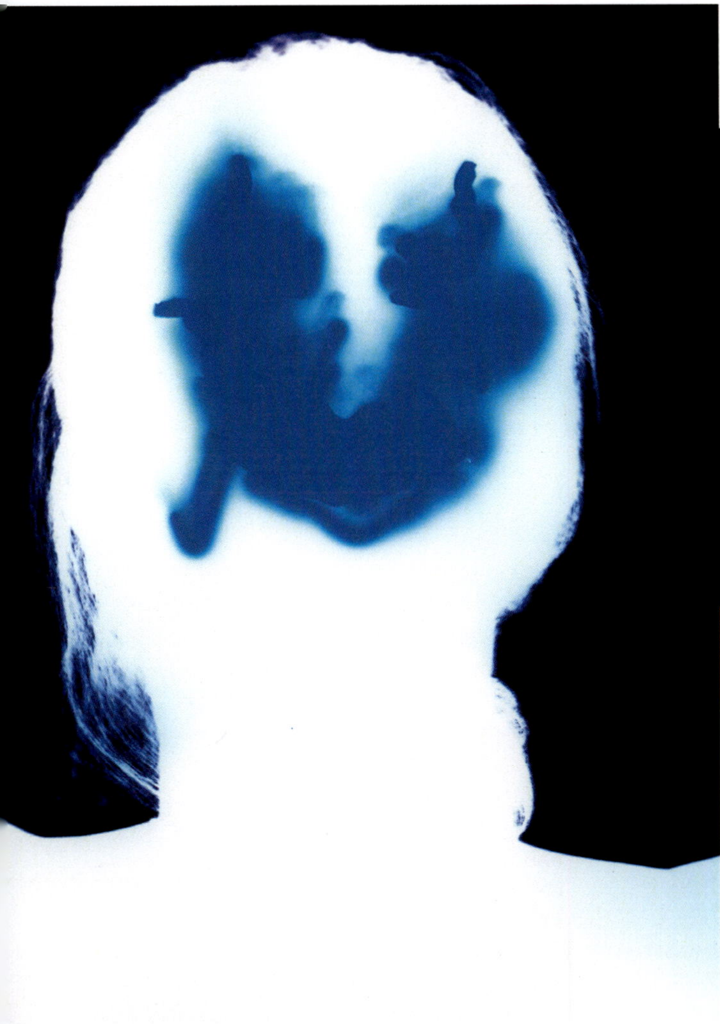

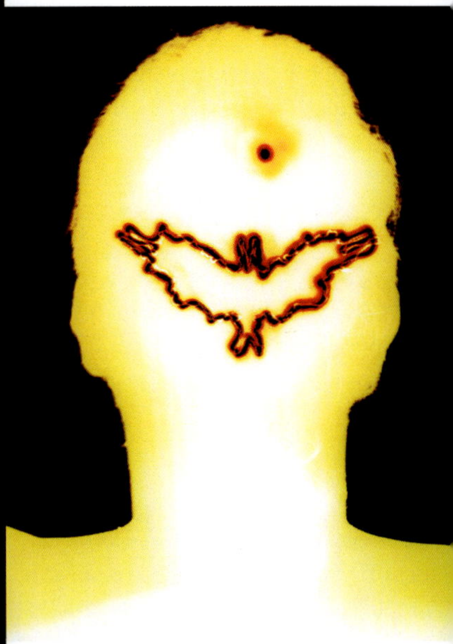

1.4

Title: from *A Suicide Constellation*

Artist: Pedro Vicente

Pedro Vicente made these photograms in a darkroom by flashing an enlarger light over his head and adding patterns to each image before it was developed. He collaborated with psychology student Carol Davies to interpret the photograms using the Rorschach psychodiagnostic test, which analyses how people respond to certain patterns, and wrote down his responses to each image. Vicente then brought the work together as an artist's book, with the images shown alongside the writing they inspired.

Making work with someone from another area of expertise can aid the creative process, making it a fruitful and enriching experience.

Proposals for funding

When creating a more advanced research proposal to apply for funding for a body of work, there are additional considerations to take into account. Potential sources of funding include government art bodies, private funders, grant-giving bodies and trusts, awards and commercial sponsors or partners. Each one will have a different application form and you must think carefully about the specific headings or questions on it. You must take your idea and your initial research findings and tailor them into a proposal for the funding organization in question.

Some funders ask for a written proposal only, others may request visual examples of your work. Think carefully and objectively when selecting images to submit with a proposal for funding. Do the chosen images portray a coherent vision, a clear story, as well as aesthetic and technical competency? Remember that 'less is more'. Keep the edit strong and concise.

If you are asked to write a project summary, it is likely that the text could be used in some form of publicity for the project. With this in mind, it is worth considering how your summary would work across multiple platforms such as social media and blogs. A summary needs to be upbeat in tone and make the reader want to know more about the project. It is often possible to find other project summaries on websites or by calling the funding body to see if they can direct you to successful past examples.

Timetable and budget

These two elements of a proposal for funding are straightforward and vital: whoever the proposal is directed at will need to know if the project is feasible. A timetable and a budget are a basic version of a business plan. They may seem almost too obvious to write down, but remember that the person or people who will read the proposal are unlikely to know much about you. They need evidence that you have the ability to sensibly plan a project, both in terms of the time and money that is available. A project has to be achievable within its budget and its timeline.

Proposed research references

A list of potential references (and where you might go to investigate them) helps the proposal reader to understand the scope or ambition of the proposed project. The list should include references to photographers and artists whose work relates to the project, research sources relating to the subject or theme, links to where you might research working methods and any other related information. It may include references to fiction, music and film, as well as theoretical debate.

1.5

Title: Budget example for 'Timely Tale'

Photographer: Natasha Caruana

'Timely Tale' was commissioned by Photoworks and House Biennial in Brighton. It was a mixed media project which involved new technology never used before by the artist. The budget outlines estimated costs of the project and has been created through doing research into these costs. The commission gave the artist £5000, and this had to include all aspects of the making of the work and production of the exhibition. The budget can change as you go along, though it should be as close as possible to the real cost from the start.

	Item	Amount	Description	Notes
FEES	Artist Fee	£1,000	Directing	1000
	Jon	£1,000	Shoot and edit	500
	Sven	£400	Sound recording and final mix	Plus find extra £100
	Emilie	£250	Composer	250
	Simon A	£160	Consultation on Edit	100
	Sarah	£300	Production Assistance	342
	Medical Researcher	£200	NHS Statistics	-
	Designer	£400	Screen/Poster Graphics	-
	Ab Rogers	£500	Consulation on Installation	-
	Tech	£200	Brighton Install	-
	Data Film	£50	Phil	50
TECH				
	Headset tests x 2	£33.98		
	Headset and phone hire x12	£1,992	Elevated Cost - for 10 x £1,722	1896
	Headphones			
	Phones	£360 s6 x10 - £200 / £250 used		
	Screen 32"	In kind		
	Screen 12"	In kind		
	LED Scrolling Message	£100		
MATERIALS	Stud Frame	£120	Wall one	167
	Sheet MDF	£57.25	Wall one	
	Door Frame	In kind		-
	Skirting Board			15
	Door	In kind		-
	Reception Hatch	In kind		-
	Flooring	52 paid		52
	Paint (Magnolia)	£118		23
	Tape / Underlay			63.91
PHOTOGRAPHIC	Metro SS (press image)	£23.00	Film Process	
	Snappy Snaps SH (press)	£25.48	Film Process	
	Disposable Camera	£7.99		
PROPS	Felt Notice Board	In kind		
	Trunking	In kind		
	Plants	In kind		
	Chairs	In kind		
	Table	In kind		
	Water Cooler	In kind		
	Water Cooler Refills	In kind		
	Leaflet stands	In kind		
	Fire Extinguisher	In kind		
	Magazines	In kind		
	Toy Box / Table	In kind		
	Fire Alarm	In kind		
	Hand Sanitizer	In kind		
TRAVEL	Parking SS (volunteer day)	£15.60 paid		
	Brighton (HOUSE Meeting 1)	£31.60 paid		
	Travel (Sven)	£25.80 paid		
	Brighton (HOUSE Meeting 2)	£31.60 paid		
	Brighton (HOUSE install 1)	£31.60 paid		
	Brighton (HOUSE install 2)	£31.60 paid		
CONSUMABLES	Sainsburys SS (volunteer day)	£11.60 paid		
	Lidl (Shoot food)	£48 paid		
	Coffee (brighton) Wed	20 paid		
	Food Friday	15 Paid		
INSURANCE	Liability	50 paid		
	Headset	75 paid		
ACCOMADATION	Air bnb x 8 people	372 paid		
TOTAL	7220		21/9 Total 6,266.48 (incl 272 Air Bnb) (does not include petrol)	Total project budget 7050.00
Tape 35.96				
Posters (amazon)				
Mirrors (amazon)				

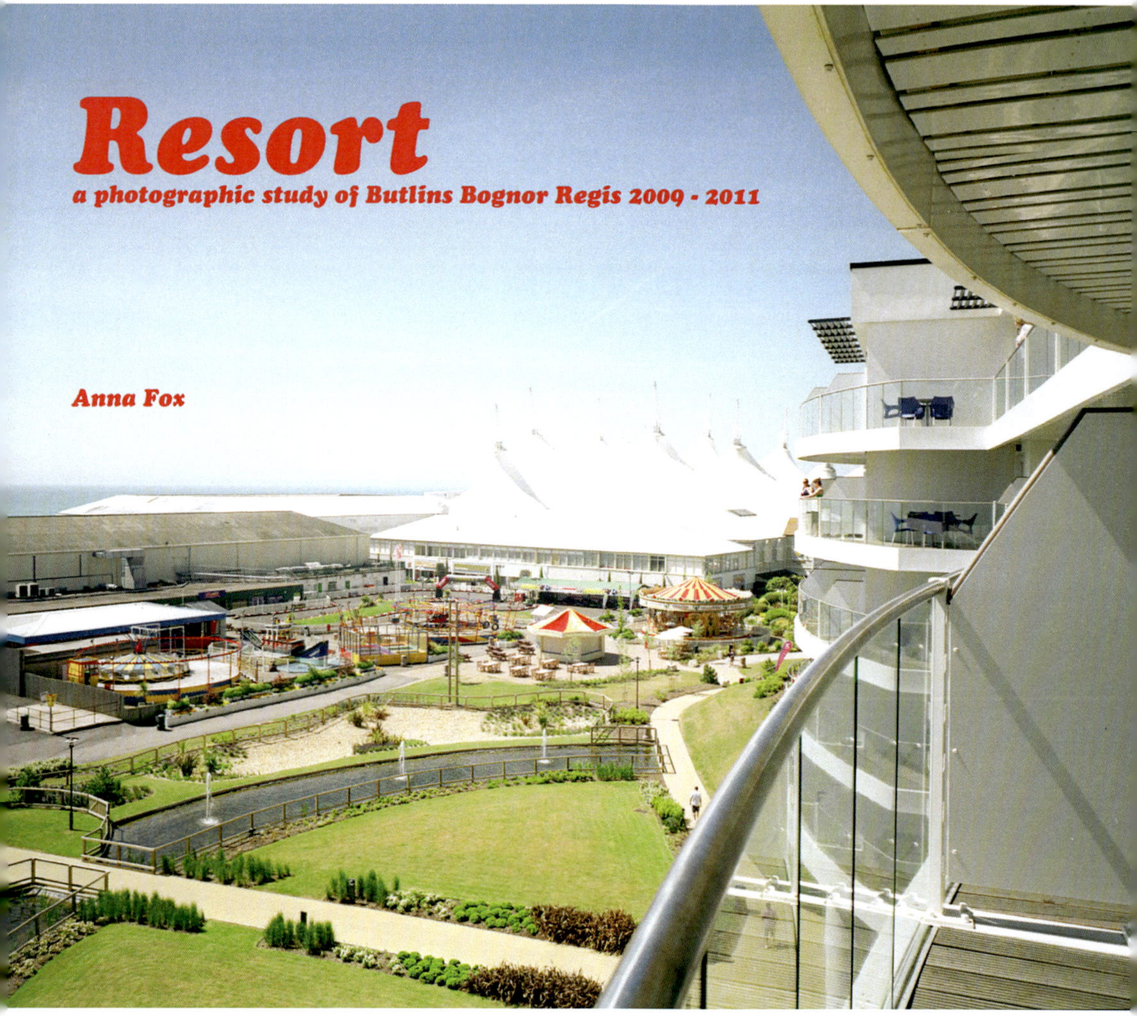
Resort
a photographic study of Butlins Bognor Regis 2009 - 2011
Anna Fox

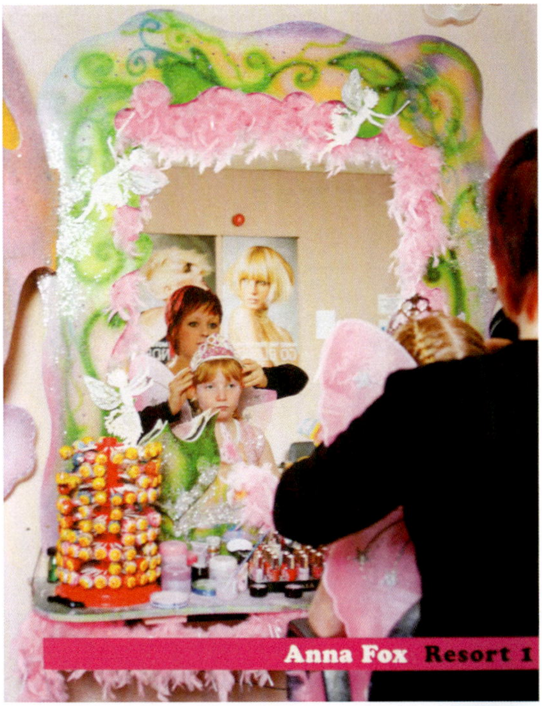

1.6

Title: Cover designs for project 'RESORT 1'

Photographer: Anna Fox

On the left is the first working title page for a commissioned project documenting the contemporary face of the holiday camp Butlins in Bognor Regis, UK. It is a simple overview of the place. This image with its title was used in a proposal applying for funding for the publication of the work. The typeface style and colour were used deliberately to reflect the Butlins style and to bring out the red in the photograph. On the right is the actual cover, which has been redesigned far more effectively by the designer Victor Levie in collaboration with Fox. This collaboration was only possible once funding had been raised for the project. The book was published by Schilt in Amsterdam. The third image shows the design of the inside cover (under the dust jacket).

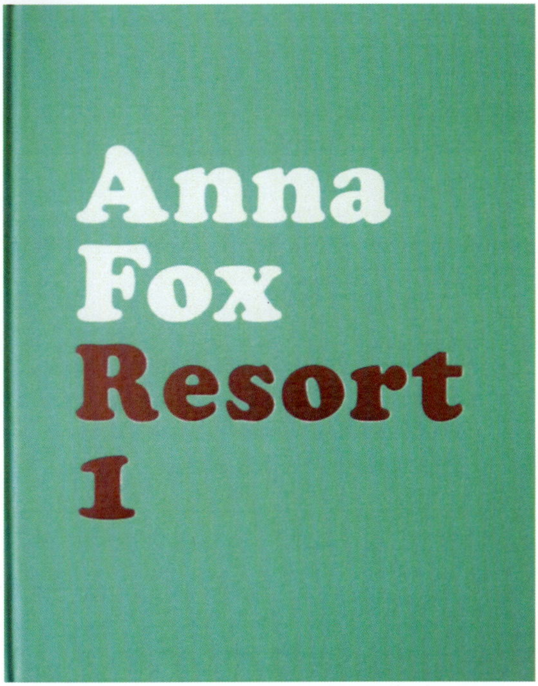

There are numerous debates and arguments about the way history is recorded and retold. Inevitably, important elements get left out and, in the case of photographic history, whole countries have been neglected. It can be a challenging and exciting part of any research project when new historical material is discovered, perhaps in an archive or in a personal interview previously unseen or unheard. Histories of photography are frequently divided by country or continent and, undoubtedly, the histories of North American and northern European photography tend to dominate the field. North America was fast to embrace and promote photography as an art form, and northern Europe was not too far behind.

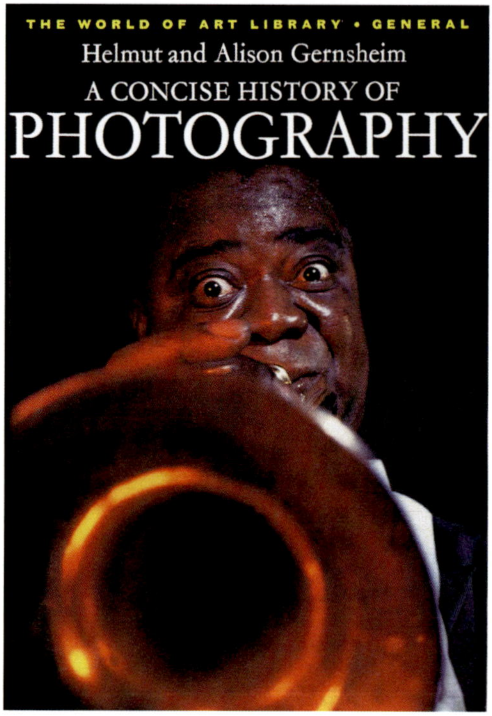

Understanding histories

Today, writers, editors and curators are expanding their research parameters. Through the growth of various diasporas, knowledge about photography and its histories is becoming a global subject. Histories of photography link photographers together and frequently propose ideas about how things are connected within a particular narrative. As a researcher, it is your job to first read, understand, and then interrogate the histories presented to you. Try reading different books that examine photography from the same continent; this is particularly interesting as you will start to gain a sense of how the personalities of the authors have shaped their stories.

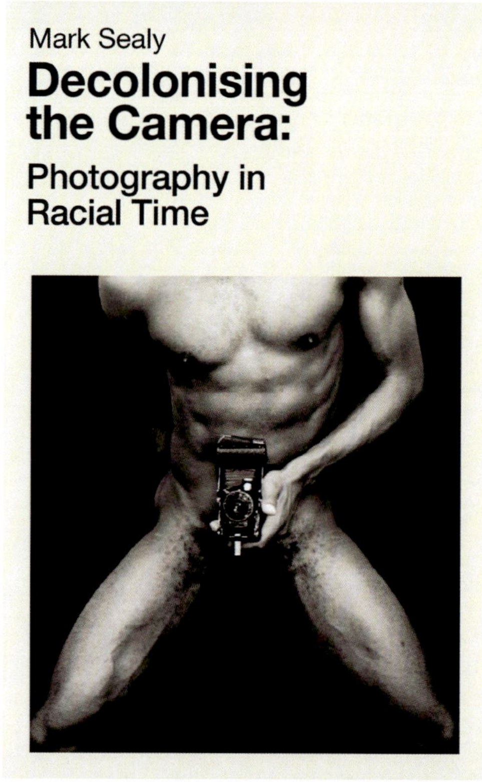

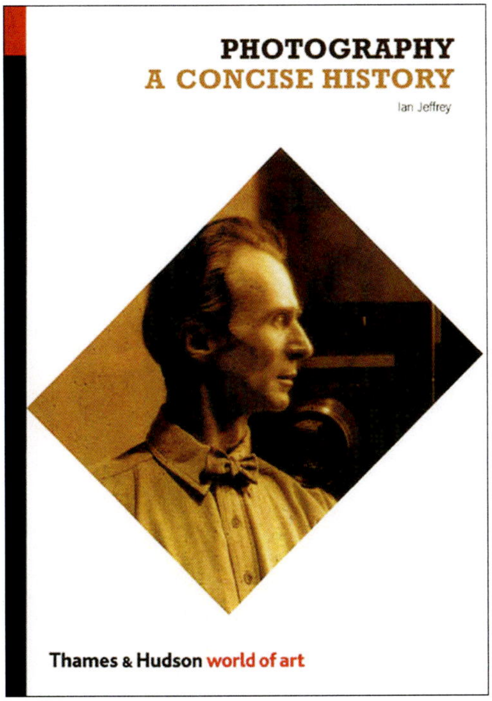

1.7

Title: Photography history books

Publishers: facing page above, Thames & Hudson; facing page below, Mark Sealy and Lawrence & Wishart; above, Thames & Hudson

There are numerous histories of photography. It is always interesting, as part of the research process, to research the authors of the books you are reading and discover their histories. Learning about an author's history can reveal much about the way a book has been written and edited.

Further information

Once you have found photographers that interest you, or a period of photographic history that is intriguing, make a note of the details and search other publications and the Internet for further leads and information. If the photographer is living, research their own website and social media platforms. Their résumé, albeit a list with no commentary, will tell you more about their history. Obituaries are also interesting and will give you a short overview of a photographer's life and work; you may need to visit a newspaper archive to find past examples.

Looking at historical examples and research enables you to think about why a body of work was made and the relevance of its context from a distance – time providing the distance. Histories inform you of how things happened and why. It is often revealing to investigate the political and social histories of the period alongside that of the photographers; this will give you more understanding of why things happened when they did.

Research into the practice of other photographers, a particular subject, or a theme can reveal a huge volume of material, particularly if carried out on the Internet. When undertaking this type of research, you will need to refine your results by looking at information about the photographers and subjects in closer detail. You can do this by researching a photographer's history via their own website; looking at their projects and résumé; and by searching websites, such as Wikipedia. From this you will gain a basic overview of the status of the photographer and can gauge whether they are still relevant to your research list.

Refining your results

Once you have narrowed down your initial search results, you can look in more detail at relevant photography exhibitions, magazines and agencies. You should check the history of each organization and find out who they are, what they do, how recognized they are, and in what context they operate. Amazon, Abe Books and other Internet booksellers that sell second-hand material can be a useful source of information about museum and gallery publications.

You need to keep in mind that the Internet is not always the most reliable resource for research. Ultimately, you need to attend talks and lectures, listen to radio and television programmes and go to exhibitions to find out about photographers and their work. Always carry a way to record information: taking images on your mobile phone is often useful to record book covers you might see in shops or markets.

Magazines

Photography magazines are a rich source of photographers' work. There are numerous magazines published around the world that might help you with your research. If your local library does not stock a particular magazine, you could put in a request for them to do so. Magazines such as *Photoworks* (UK), *Aperture* (US), *EXIT* (Spain), *PHOTOWORLD* (China) and *FK* (Latvia) will all give you the opportunity to look at the work of emerging photographers alongside more established practitioners.

Read widely

Refresh your thinking about photography by engaging with a broad range of written materials. If you find a piece of writing difficult, move on to the next essay or book; you can go back to the more complex pieces later. Re-reading texts at different points in time encourages new ways of seeing the world and of seeing photography. A broad-minded approach to selecting your reading material will keep you informed and inspired.

1.8

1.8

Title: *Dream Villa*

Source/Photographer:
Dyanita Singh/Steidl

Photographers often aim to have their work published in monographs.

In her monograph *Dream Villa*, Singh explores the ways in which the night transforms what seems ordinary by day into something disquieting and enigmatic; the series of color photographs illustrated in this book presents a landscape that exists as much in the artist's imagination as it does in the real world. In search of these mysterious nocturnal effects, Singh travels to many cities across India, never knowing where her 'Dream Villa' or its shadowy inhabitants will present themselves. The book is designed and edited in a way to emphasize the inherent meaning of the narrative of the work.

1.9

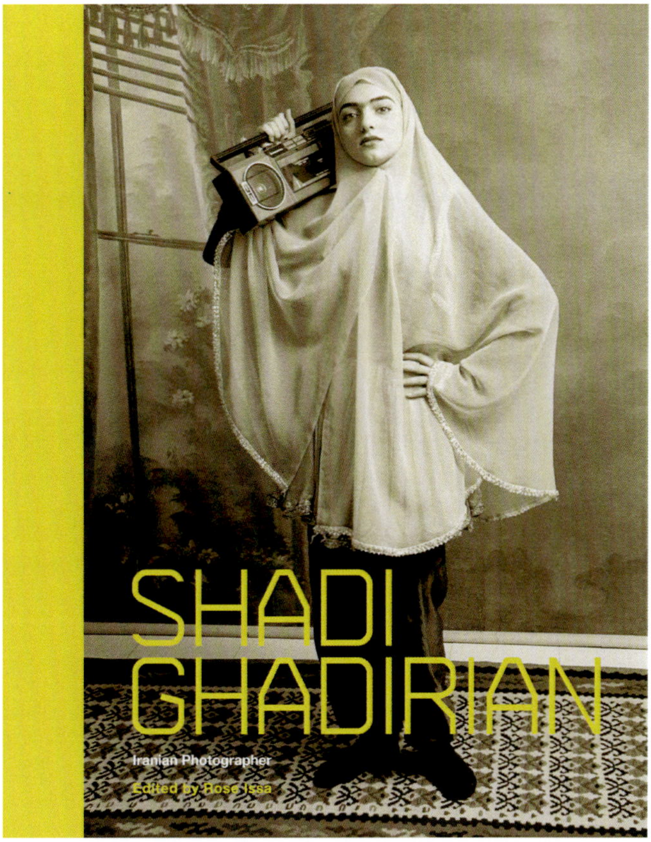

1.9

Title: Shadi Ghadirian: Iranian Photographer

Source: Rose Issa Projects/Saqi Books

Shadi Ghadirian is a female Iranian photographer whose work looks at the paradoxes faced by Iranian women. The *Qajar* series, shot in the late 1990s and featured in this monograph, juxtaposes historical backgrounds and clothes with elements of the modern day.

The development and writing of theory, like history, grows out of a research process. Theorists bring ideas and concepts together in a way that is often surprising; they look at the world from various perspectives, sometimes based on theoretical thinking from different disciplines. A theorist can shed new light on familiar aspects of daily life and question conventional or traditional ways of thinking. Reading theory can be more challenging than reading history; some of the ideas are unfamiliar and complex, so you need time to make sense of them. Try breaking up theoretical reading; read a chapter that interests you, then allow yourself thinking time to reflect on what has been said. Keeping notes, discussing the text with a peer, or sharing key facts on your social media platforms will help you digest the information.

Photographic theory

Certain theoretical models established in fields outside photography, such as linguistics or psychoanalysis, have been applied to photography by theorists. As with the history of photography, there is a predominance of theoretical writing on photography by North American and European writers. This is an inevitable result of the academicization of photography in higher education since the 1960s in the US and Europe. As photography education continues to spread further afield internationally, perspectives are changing. It is also interesting to research cultural or media theory alongside photographic theory to gain another point of view.

Photographic journals

In the UK alone, there are several journals dedicated specifically to photography. A journal publishes essays and papers that have usually been peer reviewed. This means that a panel of experts has commented on the text and the writer or editor then edits it accordingly, before publication. Journals are published frequently and so promote the most contemporary views of theorists around the world. Your local library may subscribe to an online or paper copy of a journal, and it is a resource well worth exploring. Journals and magazines are increasingly available to be read via apps.

Books

Theory books discuss photography from a critical perspective, often analysing its construction and content from radical positions. This kind of writing often turns familiar concepts upside down and may challenge your vision as a photographer. This is useful in terms of refreshing your thinking and questioning accepted attitudes to the world you are recording or representing.

A photographer has a certain responsibility in terms of how they choose to represent the world, so being informed by theoretical opinion can enable fresh thinking on this. Theoretical concepts can be applied to practice; theoretical ideas can be explored as part of the practical research process.

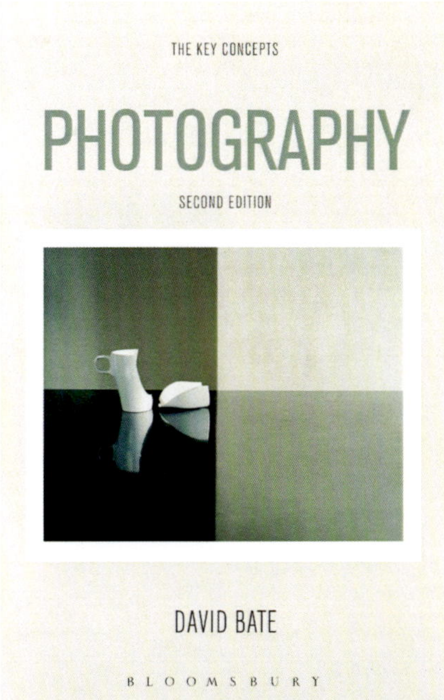

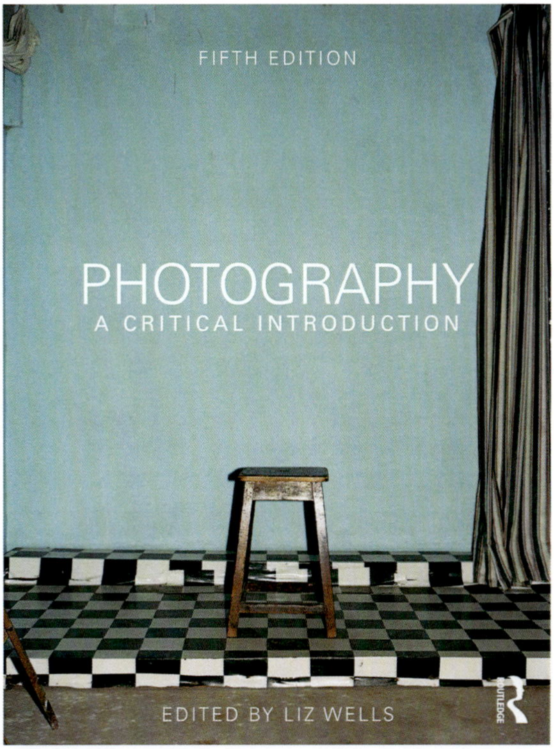

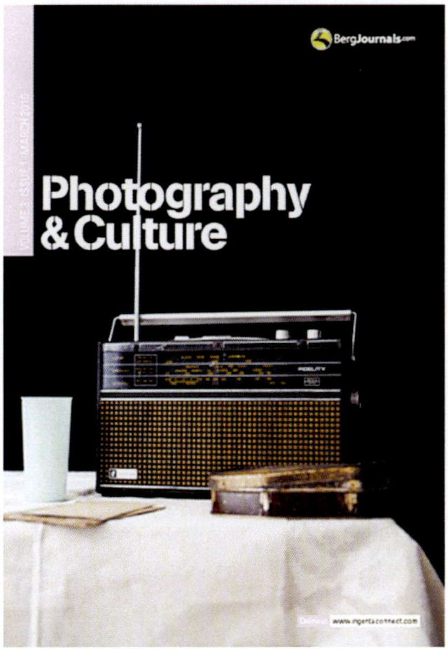

1.10

Title: Photography journals and theory books

Source: Bloomsbury/Bloomsbury/ Routledge

Journals predominantly publish theoretical texts with some images as reference. *Photography & Culture* is one such journal, releasing three issues per year since it was set up in 2008.

David Bate's book *Photography: The Key Concepts* is an invaluable text on the most important ideas underlying the development of photography as a medium.

Photography: A Critical Introduction is a theory book that looks at key debates in photographic theory and practice.

Case study 1
Shot at dawn

Chloe Dewe Mathews' project *Shot at Dawn* bears witness to acts that happened over one hundred years ago in World War I. The project consists of twenty-three final images which are the outcome of an intense research investigation into desertion; it questions our traditional ideas about cowardice. In military terminology, desertion is the abandonment of a duty or post without permission. During the First World War, if a soldier was found guilty of this crime they would be sentenced to death by a firing squad, often made up of members of their own regiment. An extended and methodical research process enabled the photographer to uncover and work out a way of representing a part of this little-known (often intentionally hidden) history.

At first the photographer knew little about WWI, but bit by bit, through the process of investigating and collecting information from different sources, Mathews developed new knowledge about these gruesome execution sites, and with this new knowledge she was able to develop her photographic approach. The two-year research period involved making several trips to France and Belgium at different times of the year and included the reading of personal stories of individuals' psychological suffering discovered in military medical records.

By meeting with a network of individuals, including war historians, academics, museum curators, local historians and battlefield guides, Mathews slowly identified the places where the executions took place. The use of military records and aerial photographs allowed her to painstakingly fulfil her ambition to not only locate the sites but also identify the exact time, position and time of year of the executions.

On one occasion, a military record listed that an execution had taken place in an abbey, but little detail was included in the entry. This led her to visit the Abbey Sint-Sixtusabdij in Westvleteren to meet with the monk, Brother Johannes, who showed her the monastery diary. The diary provided the final clues, which Mathews pieced together, to take the photographs on the same day and time that most closely matched the dates of the military death of Private Herbert Chase.

For Mathews, it was conceptually important to point the camera in the same direction that the firing squad had shot; she felt this was an important echoing of what had happened – a reinforcement of the terror – and that it fortified the idea of creating a memorial to a past act that had happened within the landscape.

Mathews' images refer to the relationship between two parties: the firing squad and the victim. She used her research to work out where each person had stood during the shooting scene. She had lengthy discussions with academics on why and where people took their positions. The images offer up a powerful yet empty framework in which the audience can visualize the act, imagining the scene from the position of the soldier firing the gun, which in a very uncomfortable yet simple way seems to implicate us all.

The knowledge collected during the research journey is integral to the series right through to the final presentation of the work. The time, date and location of the deaths of the fifty-four cases across the twenty-three sites are presented alongside the final images within the gallery and in the project monograph. These landscapes, already melancholic through their muted colour palette, are rendered desperate through the inclusion of these circumstantial texts.

The photographs have allowed a contemporary audience a new kind of access to a poignant and ghastly moment in time, a new war memorial. In some way these landscapes are documents, yet the time that has passed allows them to be more open and act as metaphors for other, similar modern-day tragedies.

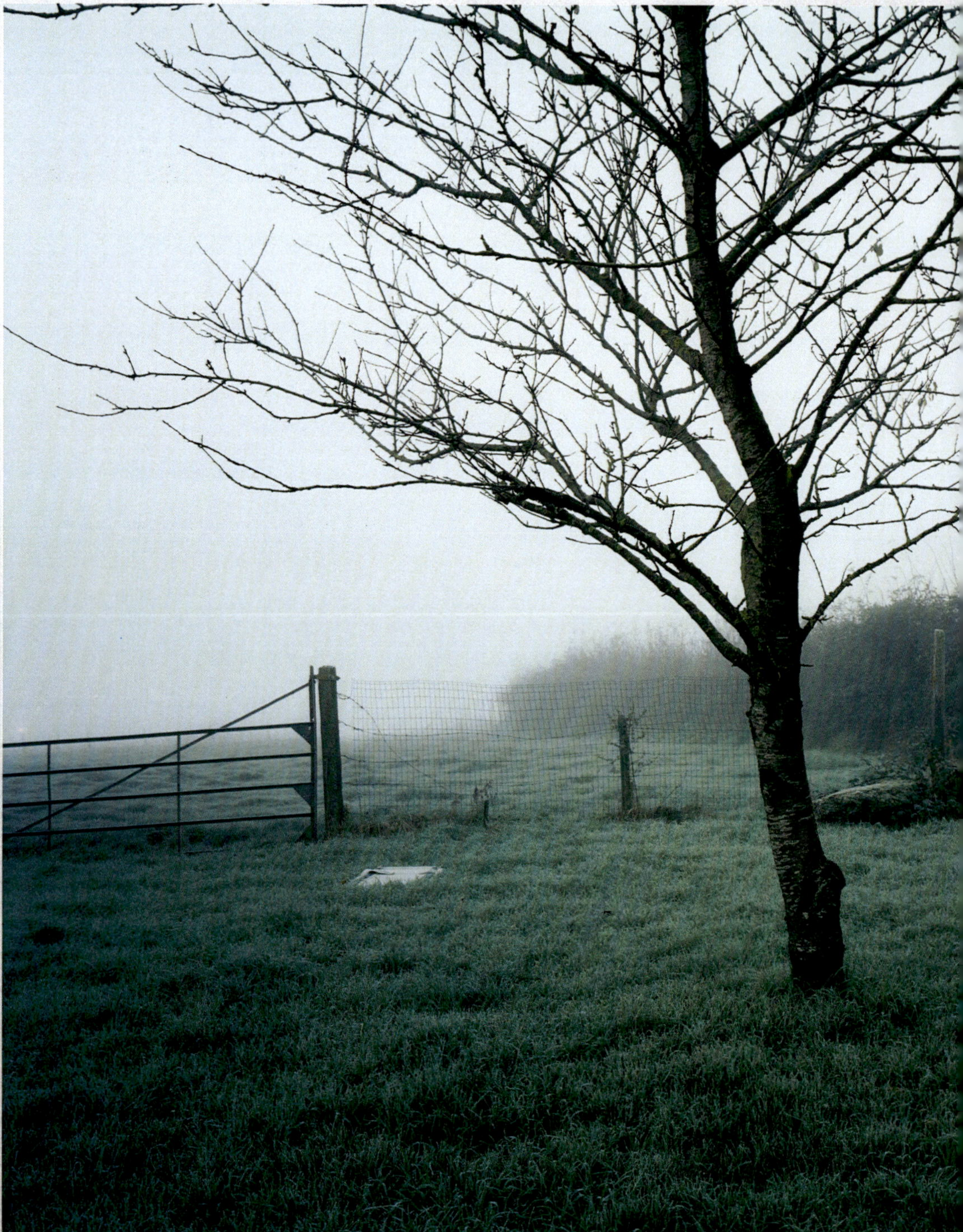

1.11

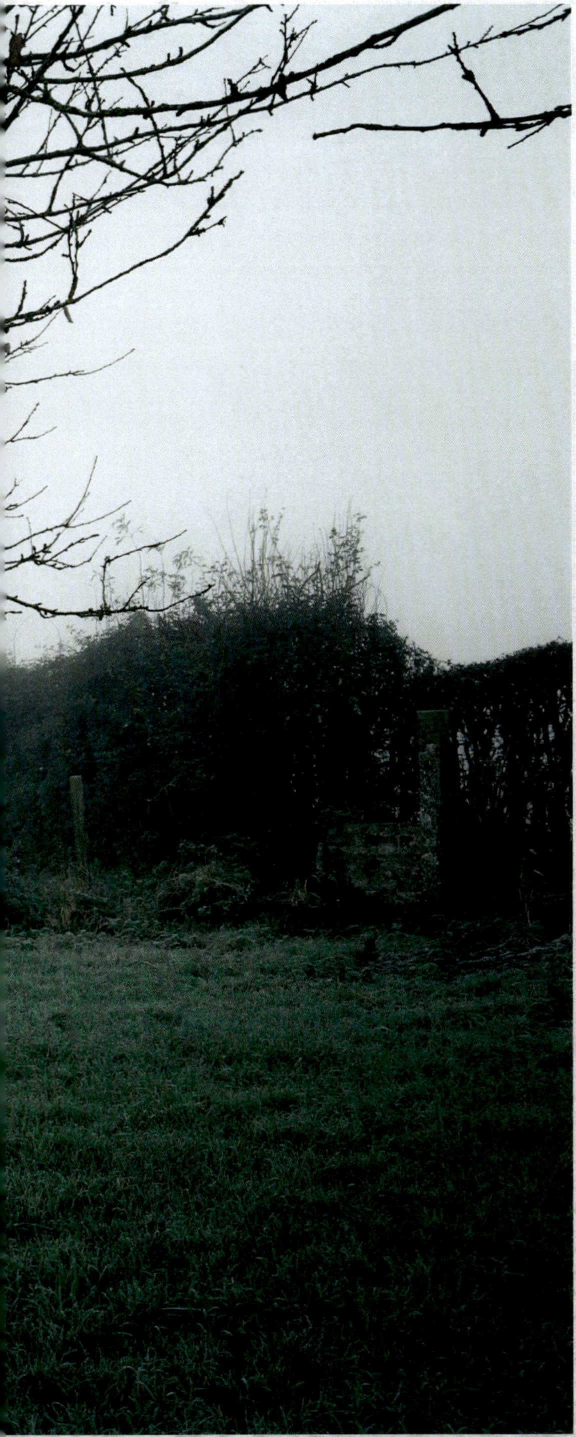

1.11

**Title: Private Joseph Byers, Private Andrew Evans, time unknown/6.2.1915.
Private George E. Collins, 07:30/15.2.1915.
Six Farm, Loker, West-Vlaanderen**

Photographer: Chloe Dewe Mathews

This is one of the images from the series *Shot at Dawn*. The project was commissioned by the Ruskin School of Art at the University of Oxford as part of 14–18 NOW, WWI Centenary Art Commissions that formed part of the commemoration of World War I.

Activity 1: Recording ideas

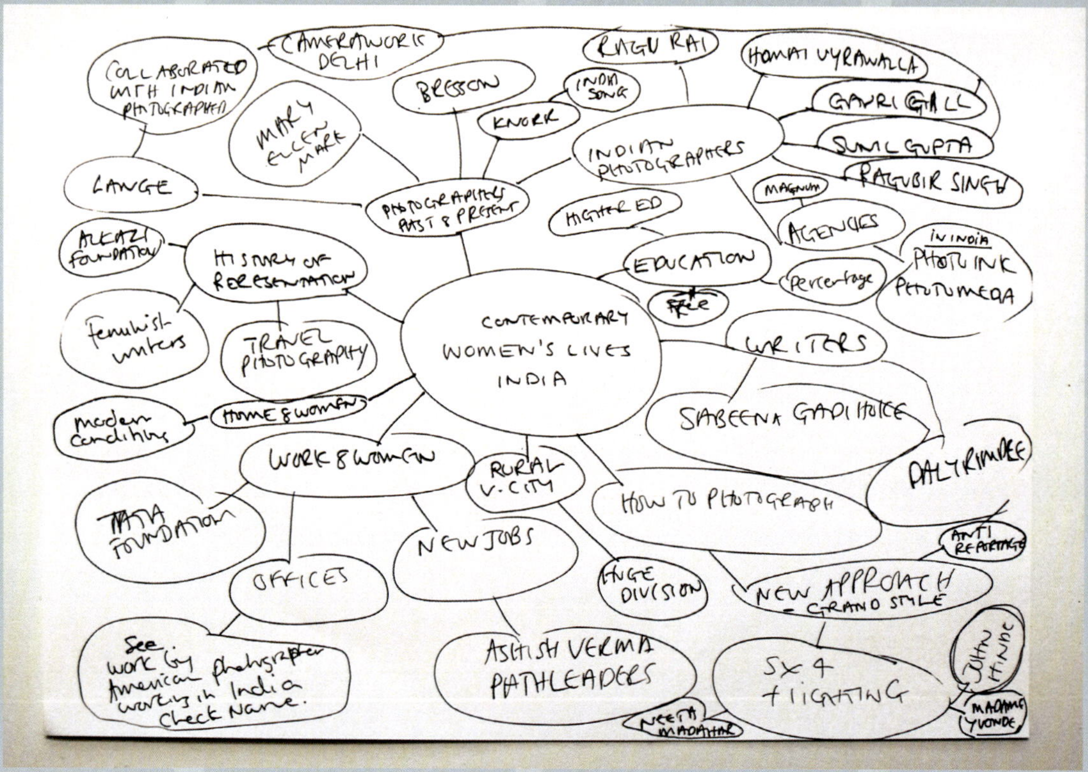

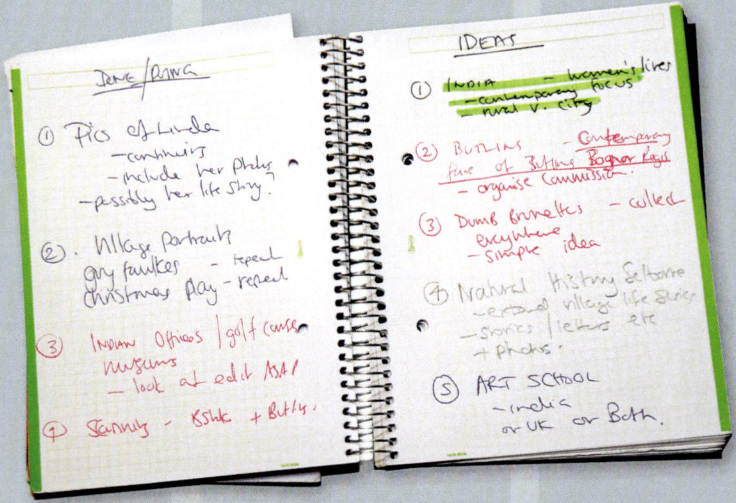

1.12

Title: Mind map and photographer's notebook

Source: Natasha Caruana

These images illustrate different ways of recording ideas. The web-like structure of the mind map contrasts with the linear nature of the list used in this photographer's notebook. Both are valid ways of recording your ideas – try each method and see what you find most useful.

Activity 1 Recording ideas

Ideas are fragile and have a habit of materializing anytime, anywhere. Without a means to record and preserve them, they are liable to vanish from the imagination as abruptly as they appeared.

It is important to find a system of documenting your ideas at the moment of conception. This could mean having a notebook or sketchbook with you at all times. Or using your mobile phone as a notebook or to record sound or voice memos on location. The camera on your phone is an important tool to photograph and video key inspirations, locations, exhibitions, characters – anything that acts as visual reminder for your idea.

Notebook project

Keep a notebook with you at all times. Populate it with every creative thought surrounding your projects and your photographic practice. This means that even though some things might sit on the back burner for a while, you still have concrete documentation of your ideas for future reference. The notebook or ideas book can also be used to trace your work back to its origins.

Mind map project

A mind map allows you to think about an idea from a number of perspectives; it is a visual diagram, branching out from a central theme or topic. It has the potential to connect research possibilities in a new way through its web-like structure. A mind map is circular rather than linear, like a list, and can shed a different light on the scope of your idea. It helps you draw on previous knowledge.

As you create mind maps, you may find that using larger sheets of paper enables a more 'helicopter' view of your project, giving more space for notes and links. You could also incorporate images, clippings and photographs.

Looking at your mind maps, which idea now seems the most interesting? Which idea is most feasible? You may need to make separate mind maps to explore the feasibility of each idea.

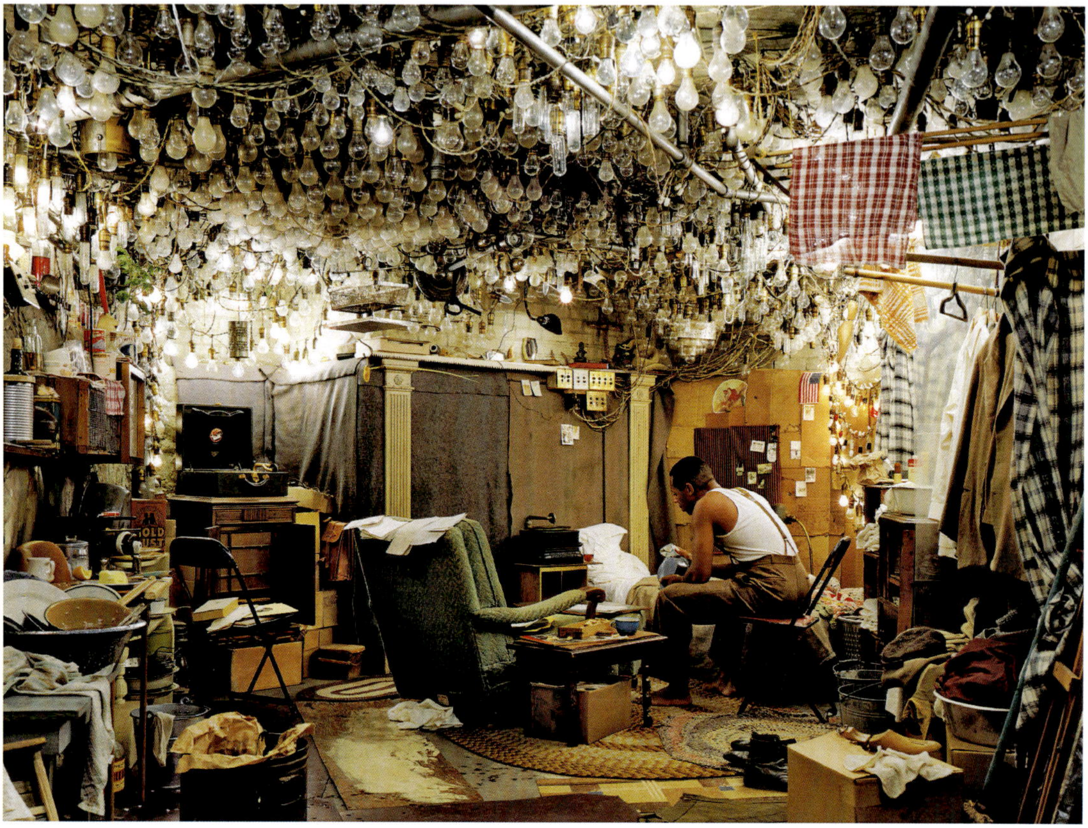

2.1

Title: After *Invisible Man* by Ralph Ellison, The Prologue

Artist: Jeff Wall

Photographic works can be inspired by researching other creative genres, such as film, literature and theatre. Ralph Ellison's 1952 novel *Invisible Man* inspired this Jeff Wall image. The novel centers on an unnamed African American man who falls into a forgotten room in the basement of a large apartment building during a riot in New York.

The man's social invisibility is symbolically highlighted by his increasing collection of illegally powered light bulbs. In a painstaking production, using exactly 1,369 light bulbs as described in the text, Jeff Wall depicts the narrative through the construction of a large-scale photograph.

2 Developing ideas through research

Artists and photographers throughout history have searched for references in libraries, museums and archives. Many contemporary photographers have huge personal archives of their own that include books, photographs, objects, magazines and more. These photographers will use their archives regularly to investigate an idea or contemplate a new direction.

Today, many emerging photographers and writers depend on gathering a large percentage of their research on the World Wide Web. The Web has democratized knowledge in a way that was previously unimaginable. However, before you dedicate yourself to days in front of your computer screen, take a moment to consider the value of getting out in the world: going into places that contain important research materials; discovering archives that you had not known before; going to talks, events and conferences that may introduce you to new ways of looking at the world. The Web provides us with a broad starting point, but you need to be aware that the material you find there may also have its limitations and, in some cases, may be far from correct.

The concept of 'truth' or what is 'real' is a difficult one; no research source is infallible. Even if you meet with an admired photographer to discuss their work, they may not be able to (or want to) give you the full picture of the story behind the scenes. You need to bring a level of your own interpretation and critical reflection to what you find.

Photography comes in a number of different forms. It is used to record our families and places we visit on holiday; to promote products, companies and clothing; to report on news stories; and to illustrate books and magazines. It is also used by artists and photographers to create stories and artworks. All aspects of photography are fascinating; as a researcher in photography it is wise to investigate all the places where photographs exist in the world.

The library

Libraries are extraordinary places; they have many different types of resources, from books to databases, slide libraries, digital archives, sound archives, special collections, journals and magazines. There are many types of library; some specialize in particular subject areas. Clearly, a library will contain books, but what may not be immediately evident are the special collections or archives that exist behind its walls. Some libraries have significant collections of photographs.

The British Library Sound Archive holds the Oral History of British Photography, in which you can find interviews and listen to a photographer's history in their own words. You can attend courses on how to be an oral historian and how to interview people. The National Gallery of Art in the US has a collection of interviews with photographers, as well as podcasts and lectures which can be viewed online.

Photography also exists in image libraries; many of these banks or libraries provide 'stock' material primarily for commercial use. An image library can also be specialized. If you want to use photographs from an image library, you have to pay for the privilege; this is one way that photographers make a living.

2.2

Title: Interior, British Library

Source/Photographer: Alamy/B. O'Kane

The British Library has a vast collection, holding around 150 million items, of which 25 million are books. It also houses journal and newspaper titles, patents and sound recordings.

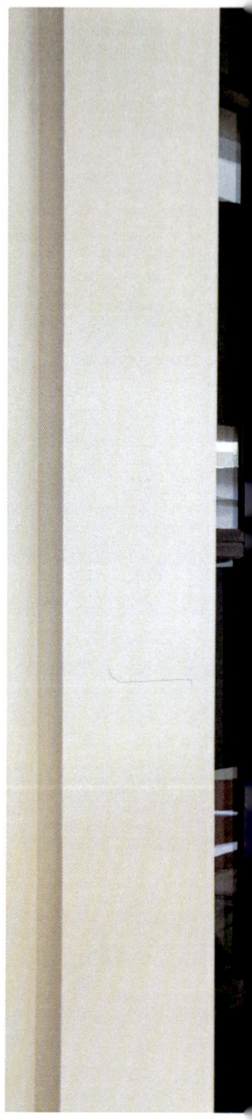

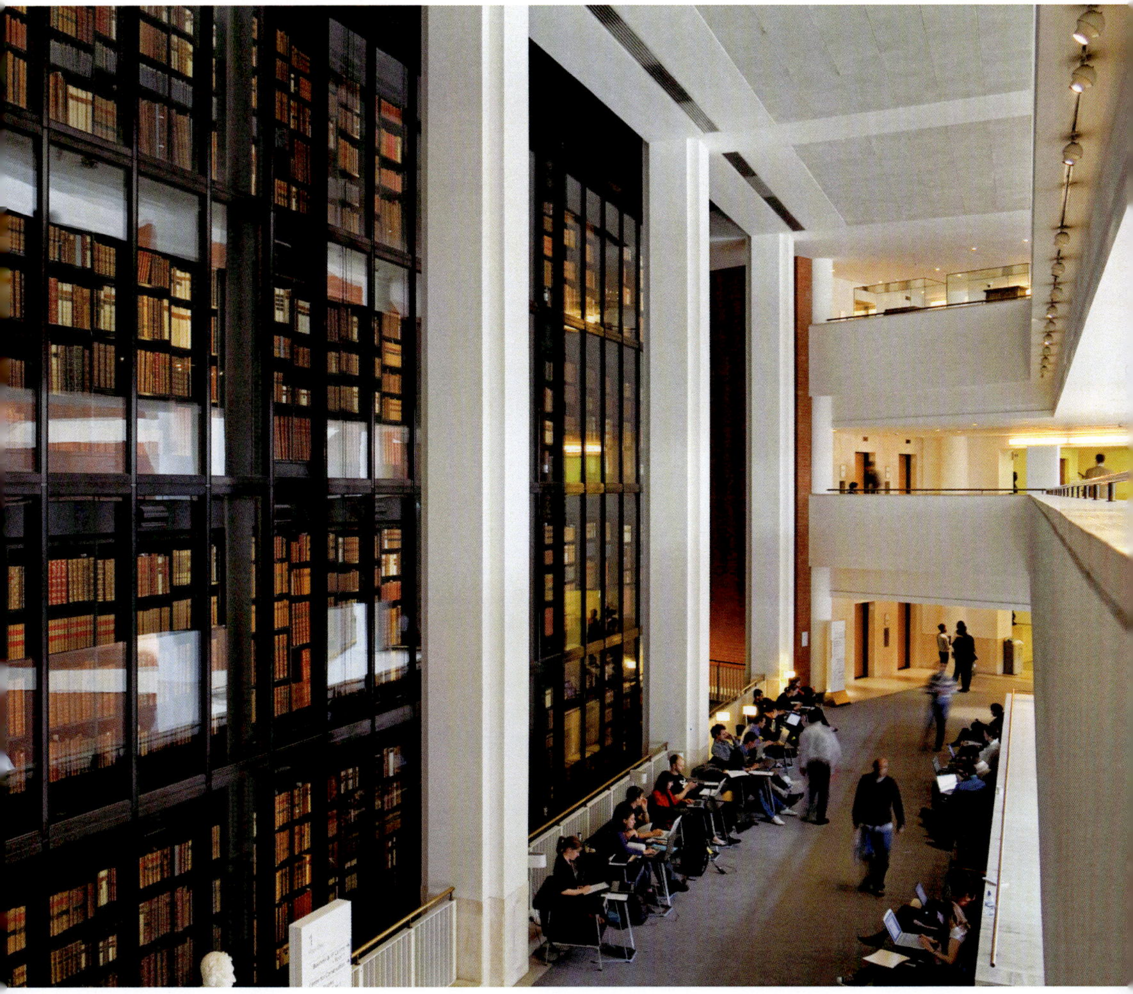

2.2

All aspects of photography are fascinating; as a researcher in photography it is wise to investigate all the places where photographs exist in the world.

Specialist libraries

A specialist library will hold books and material concerned with a particular subject. It is a good idea to search for such a library right at the start of your research journey. The Internet can provide details of specialist libraries. For instance, the Women's Library <www.londonmet.ac.uk/thewomenslibrary/aboutthecollections/> is based at the London Metropolitan University. Their website gives a clear indication of who they are, how long they have existed, what they do, and what is coming up. Simply visiting a library and going to some of their events or study days can spark new project ideas and avenues to research.

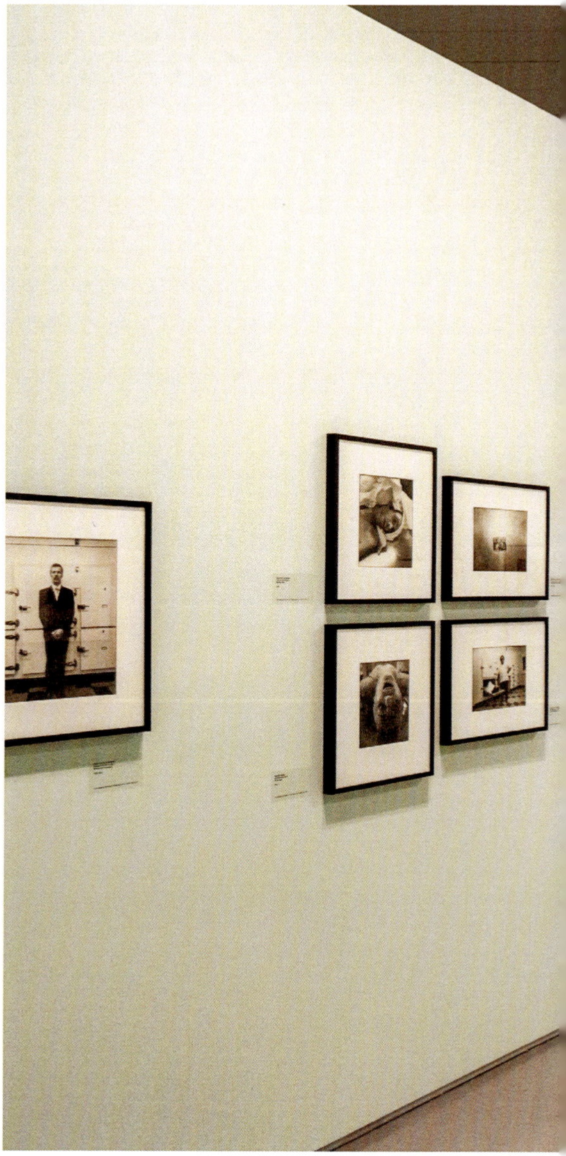

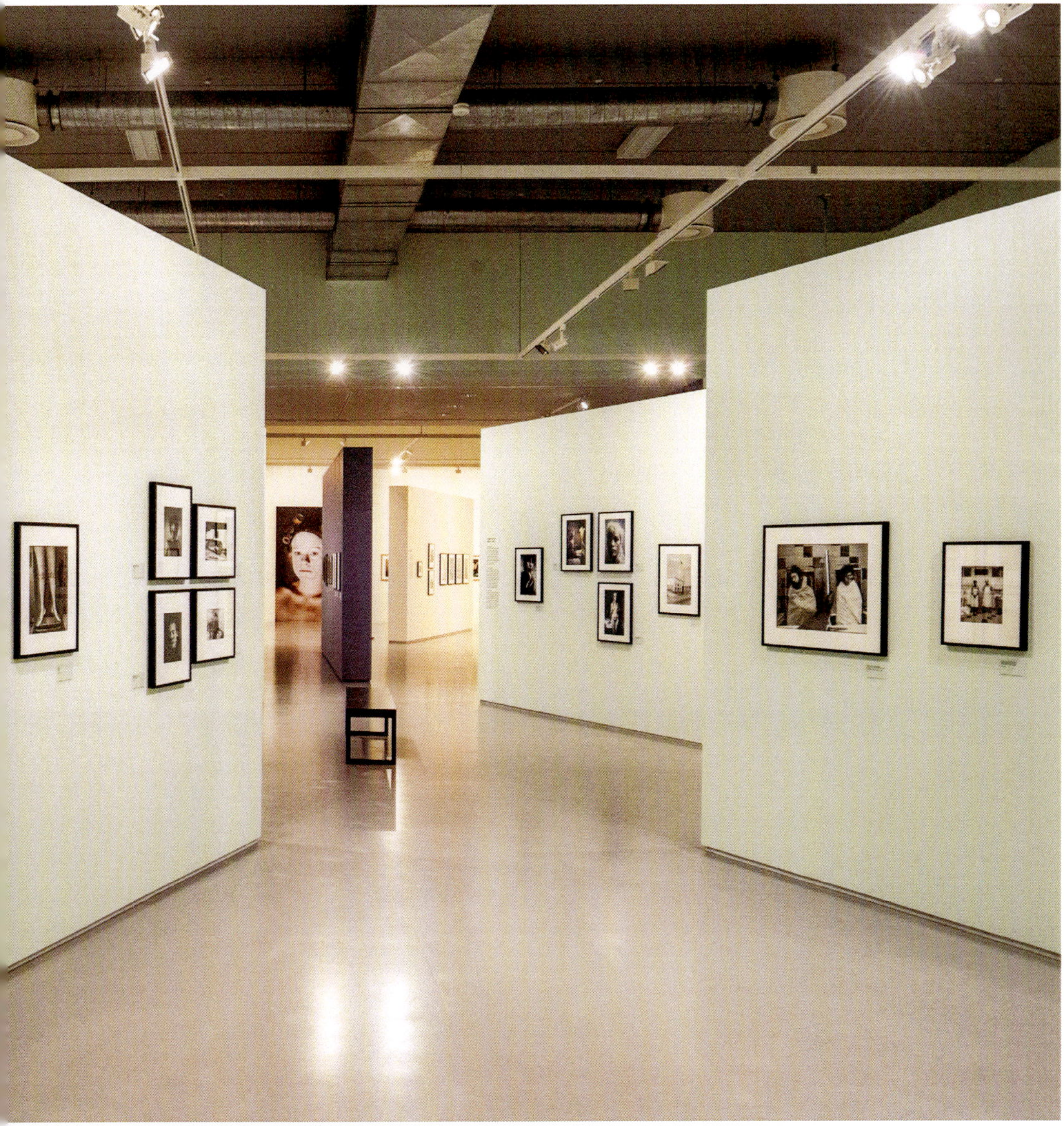

2.3

Title: Fotomuseum Winterthur

Source: Michael Jacobs/Art in All of Us/Corbis via Getty Images

The Fotomuseum in Winterthur is one of the few European museums dedicated solely to photography. The Fotomuseum houses an archive of its own collection of contemporary photography which can be accessed by researchers, curators and writers. It was founded in 1993, and presents exhibitions of both contemporary and historical photographs as well as hosting talks and seminars on a regular basis.

Museums

Many museums, like libraries, house collections of photographs. For example, the Pitt Rivers Museum—a fascinating museum of anthropology at the University of Oxford—has collected photographs since it was founded in 1884. The collection contains important fieldwork archives, such as those of anthropologist E. E. Evans-Pritchard, as well as the photographs of travellers such as Sir Wilfred Thesiger, whose collection alone numbers some 38,000 images. The museum still collects photography and has a number of interesting online research projects that use photographs.

Some art museums boast wonderful photography collections, such as the Museum of Modern Art (MoMA) in New York, which has been collecting photography since 1930. Museums dedicated to photography, such as the Winterthur Museum of Photography in Switzerland, are committed to education and collecting significant work. They also exhibit and publish the work of contemporary photographers, re-evaluate photographers from the past, and put on historical exhibitions. The Winterthur Museum has an extensive collection of both Swiss and international photography, which it regularly includes in its exhibition schedule. An archive provides a mine of information about the past. Museums, newspapers and companies all over the world also have their own archives, and these are well worth exploring.

Museums are committed to education and continuously run events, talks and conferences that are of great value to both the student and the professional researcher. You can often subscribe to regular email newsletters to keep you informed about particular museums. You will also find different types of experts in museums, from archivists to curators and directors. Investigate the different roles and responsibilities these people have as part of your research process.

Museums are committed to education and continuously run events, talks and conferences that are of great value to both the student and the professional researcher.

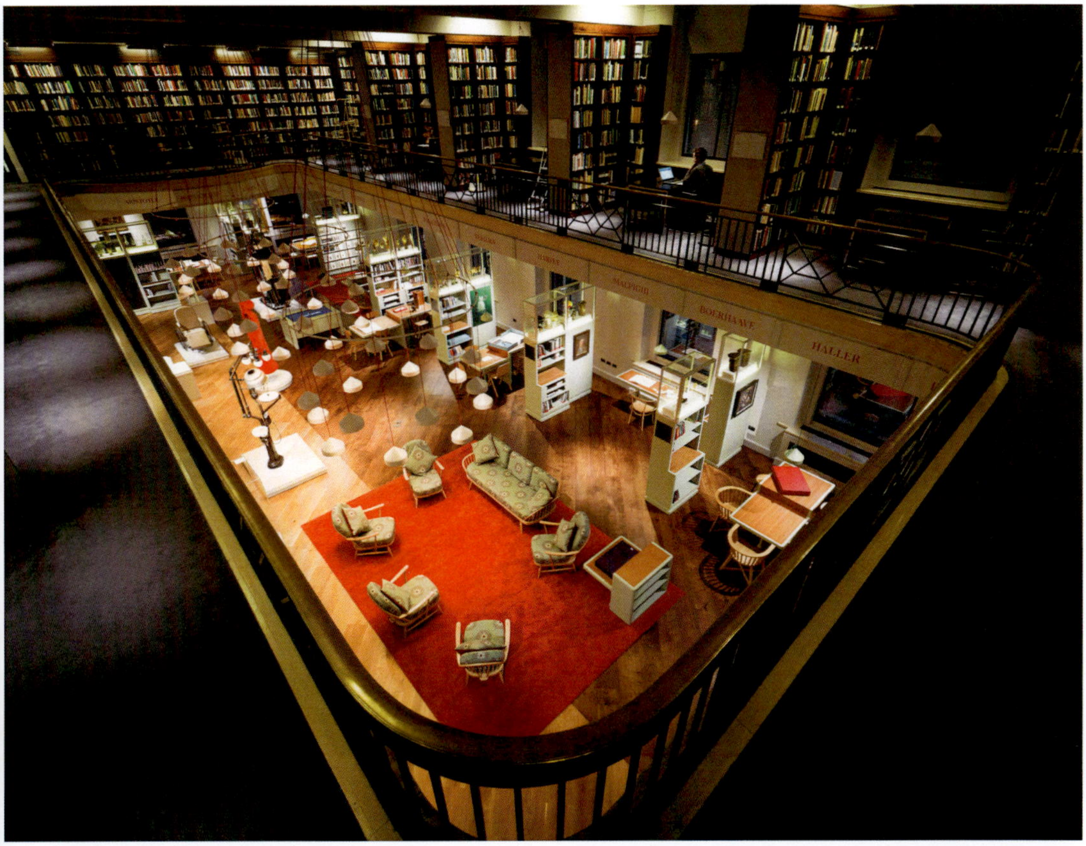

2.4

Title: Interior, Wellcome Collection, London, UK

Source: Courtesy of Wellcome Collection

Founded in 1936, the Wellcome Collection is a museum and library that hold more than 750,000 books and journals and an extensive range of manuscripts, archives and films. The Wellcome Collection explores health, life and our place in the world and is part of the Wellcome Trust. The Trust has a history of fostering collaboration between science and art (as well as other disciplines) through a range of projects, including exhibitions and publications.

Galleries

Galleries exhibit photographic work that is considered to have artistic and/or historical merit and, in the case of commercial galleries, commercial value as well.

It is rare for a gallery to have its own collection; rather, they often exhibit a particular show or collection that has been loaned to them for a given period of time. Some gallery owners and staff may be collectors themselves and have interesting private collections that, on occasion, you may be able to access. Museum curators may borrow items from galleries when they put together major exhibitions.

In the UK, there is a history of independent photography galleries, which grew in number in the 1970s and 1980s. Independent galleries help new, emerging photographers to exhibit their work alongside more established photographers. Most had, and those that still exist still have, a degree of state funding to aid them to do this and part of their mission is to provide educational material through events and exhibitions aimed at the general public, photography researchers and students. Outside of the UK there are many independent galleries, including the Centre for Contemporary Photography in Australia, Shanghai Centre for Photography, and SF Camerawork in the US.

Viewing exhibitions is an important part of the research process: going to gallery talks and events expands knowledge and understanding of the practice and processes behind the work on the wall, frequently giving insight into the life of the photographer. Gallery talks are a valuable opportunity to hear views and opinions from contemporary writers, critics and curators.

2.5

Title: Exhibition installation from *Lost Languages and other voices*, Joy Gregory

Photographer: Colin Davison

Lost Languages and other voices is an exhibition of artist Joy Gregory's work curated by Anne McNeill (Director of Impressions Gallery) in collaboration with the artist for Impressions Gallery in 2010. The exhibition was a mid-career retrospective highlighting Gregory's most significant work from the 1990s to 2010. The installation was designed in a way that contributed to the meaning of the work and informed the way that the audience moved around and interpreted the exhibition. The Impressions team used cabinets, shelves and screens to display the work in order that the audience could experience it in different ways appropriate to the meaning of the work. Installation is an important part of making work for exhibition.

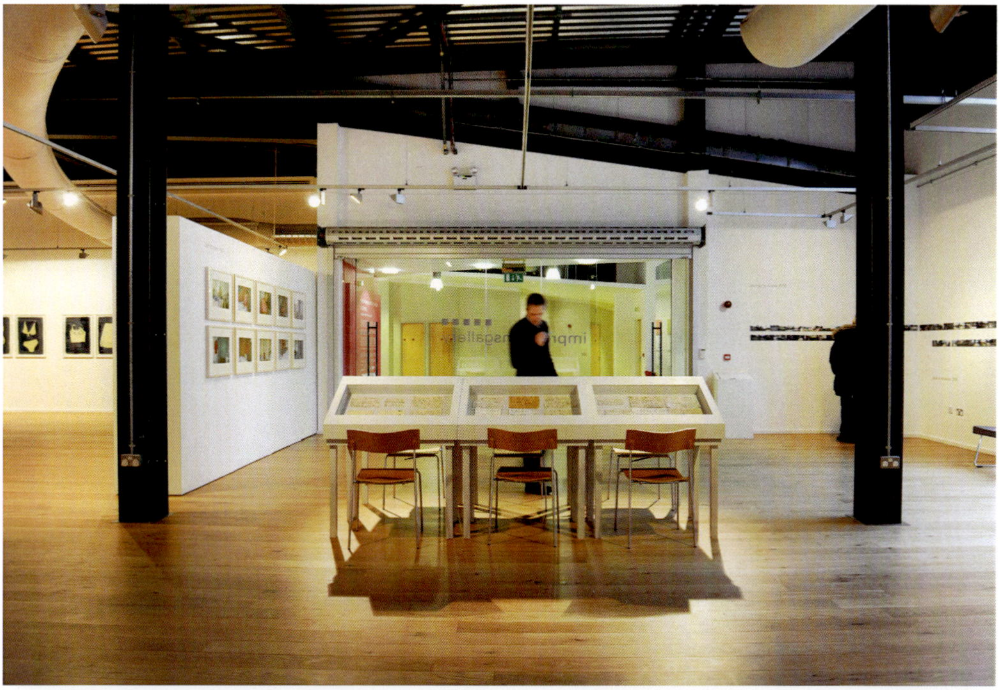

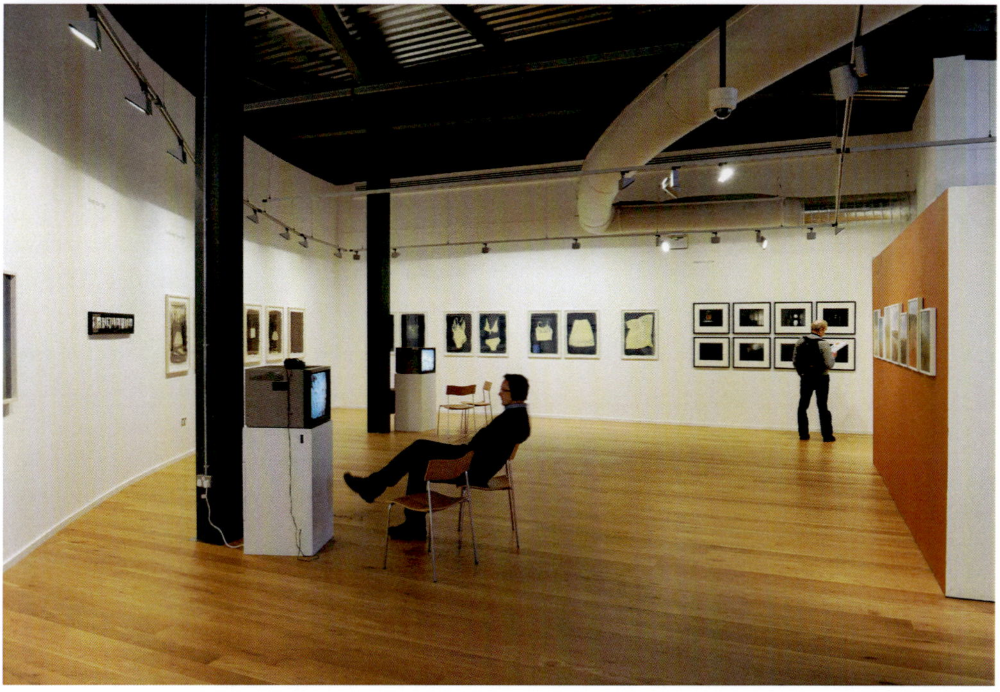

2.5

Collections and collectors

There are all sorts of different collections and collectors: some are private, some public, and some are a kind of hybrid mix. Many collections allow you to view prints and research materials, usually through making an appointment. Collections are important research sources; it is often interesting to find out more about why a collection is being built.

The Hyman Collection consists of artworks in all media, with a particular emphasis on photography; it holds vintage prints of many of the most famous and iconic photographs in British Photographic history. Claire and James Hyman began collecting together in 1996 and are the most active British photography collectors. In 2015, they launched the website www.britishphotography.org to provide online access to British photographs in the collection and as an educational resource to increase international awareness of British photography. They regularly lend work from their collection to museum exhibitions.

2.6

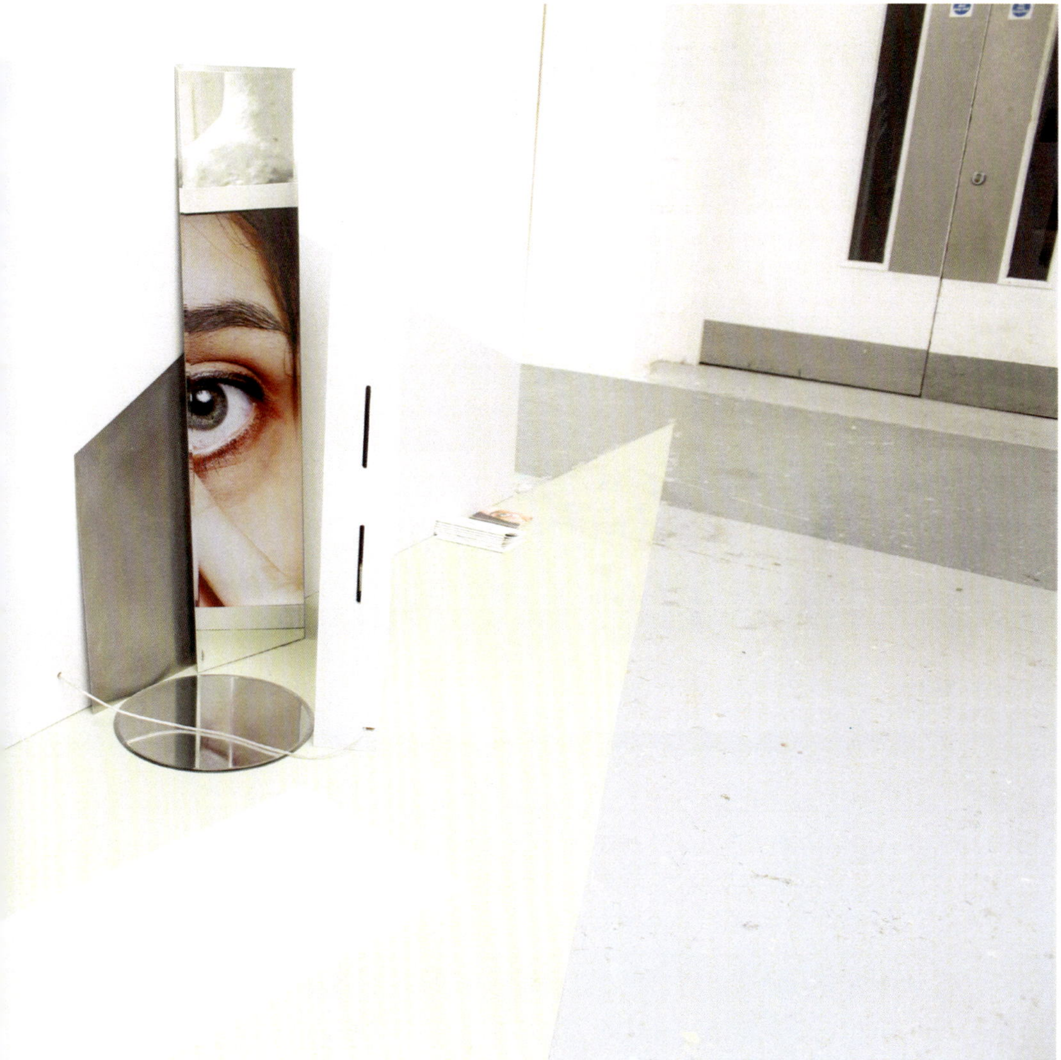

2.6

Title: Consider Falling

Artist: Sarah Howe

This installation shot shows the way that Sarah Howe used installation as the basis for the making of her work 'Consider Falling'. The work is concerned with contemporary experiences of depression and uses primary research in the form of interviews with depression sufferers as a basis for the sound track, which the audience experience as ambient sound when they enter the display. Howe uses moving images, mirrors and three-dimensional objects to create a set that fragments her picturing of gestures and expressions. The viewer walks into the installation and literally experiences the work as a set of broken bodies.

The Internet has revolutionized the distribution and access of information and services to varying degrees across the globe. For a photographer, the Internet can provide vital information in the initial stages of formulating and developing an idea. As your idea evolves from planning and preparation through to production, the Internet can play a critical part as you source photographic equipment, master new photographic techniques and watch online tutorials; it also facilitates practical and logistical tasks, such as checking opening times of libraries and making travel arrangements. Internet resources can also be used in direct relation to the photographic project. For instance, a landscape or street photographer could use Google Maps and Google Street View to determine possible locations.

Bookmarking and search engines

If you find a useful website and want to revisit it at a later date, add it to your browser's bookmarks or favorites directory. Creating bookmarks of frequently visited websites saves you time and prevents you from forgetting potentially useful sources. Organizing your bookmarks will make your time on the Web more efficient and, over time, will create a digitized personal research directory. It is vital to be as organized as possible and to make sure that you have archived the material you need in a way that makes it easy to retrieve.

A search engine such as Google will enable you to find research locations as well as images. Web links are also useful; each site you visit may have a list of links to other related sites.

The Internet has revolutionized the distribution and access of information and services to varying degrees across the globe. For a photographer, the Internet provides vital information in the initial stages of formulating and developing an idea.

Internet research

Organization is the key to keeping your Internet based research in order.

Compile lists of websites that interest you and add them to your Internet browser's bookmarks or favorites directory.

Alternatively, you could use an online bookmark manager. These have the benefit of being accessible from more than one computer and may allow you to share your bookmarks directly with friends and peers. There are many online bookmark managers to choose from, each with different features.

Once you have decided how you would like to manage your bookmarks and have started compiling them, refresh your memory by returning to bookmarked pages regularly and keeping notes on important points you want to remember.

Share information about interesting pages through your blog or social networking sites: the perspectives of your friends and peers are valuable. They may also be able to share links to sites that could be of interest to you.

Apps provide another important new way of doing research. Apps like Evernote help you make notes of all your ideas, organize them and share them across all your devices as well as with friends and colleagues.

Blogging

Blogging is a useful tool for documenting research and, for that reason, it is inspiring and insightful to read other practitioners' blogs. It is an accessible way of gaining further information that can be harnessed to nurture your own ideas.

Magazines, galleries, agents and individual photographers are all increasingly keeping blogs. By accessing these blogs, you can gain insight into a particular photographer's creative process, get updates from behind the scenes of an exhibition or read about forthcoming features that will be in the next edition of a magazine.

A convenient method of keeping abreast of a multitude of blogs is by using an 'RSS' (Really Simple Syndication) reader such as Google Reader. RSS readers allow you to access all of your blogs from one page. The blog entries will be posted in the form of a list, making it easy to see the latest updates quickly.

As a photographer, you can blog throughout your project using text, images, videos, audio and Web links to relevant and inspiring sites. This will drive online traffic to your own website, as well as evolve to become an accessible, online, multimedia archive of your project. Blogging will also allow you to publish content that may otherwise not be possible within the limitations of an exhibition, book, or press article. In chapter 3, we look in more detail at blogs as a valuable means of compiling your research.

Social media

Social media networking is a relatively new and increasingly widely used way of communicating and sharing information. Sites such as Facebook, We Chat and Twitter provide users with simple tools to create a custom profile using text and pictures, and newer social media options include Steller Stories, Vero and Youpic; they can all be valuable tools for photographers. They are all quite different, so consider the advantages of each platform and use each to its best advantage. Snapchat, Instagram and Pinterest provide varied methods of picture storytelling or mood board creation which will be discussed further in chapter 4.

A photographer can use social media in a number of ways: as a basic self-promotion tool or as a more advanced and interactive platform to engage in online dialogue with followers and the wider photographic online community. This powerful, direct dialogue between image creator and audience allows both parties to bypass the traditional media outlets of print journalism, TV and radio. As such, social media can present students and photographers with a new avenue for researching the work of other practitioners. You can use social networking sites to ask questions and help find answers to otherwise difficult research questions. You can also share your research and findings.

The use of social media can raise issues with privacy. If you decide to use social media to start creating a fan base, it's worth setting up separate Facebook or Twitter accounts for your professional and personal profiles. This way you can keep your photographic and project material separate from personal exchanges and information.

It is inspiring and insightful to read other practitioners' blogs. It is an accessible way of gaining further information that can be harnessed to nurture your own ideas.

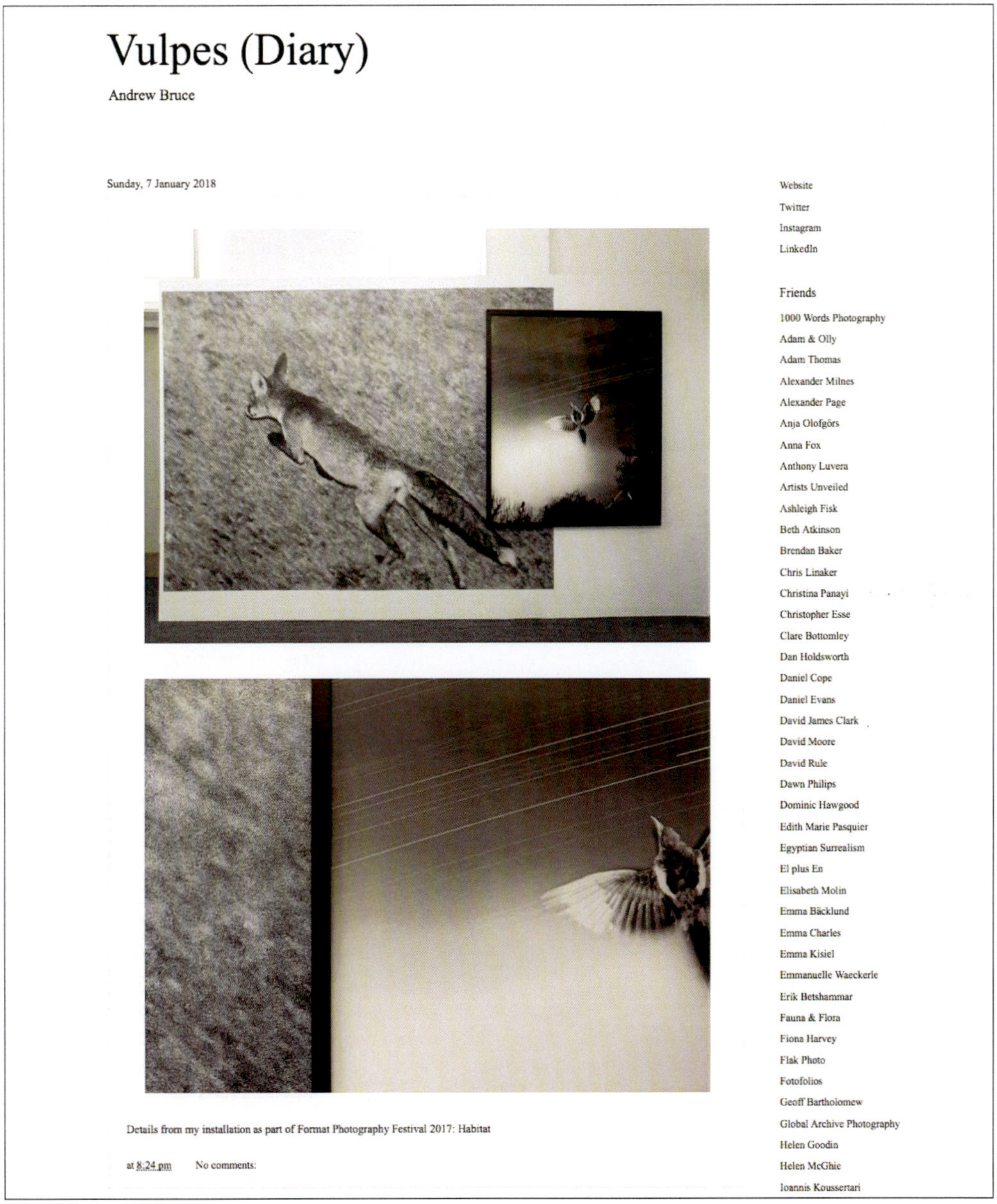

2.7

Title: Diary by Andrew Bruce

Source: <www.abruce-images.blogspot.com>

This screengrab shows an example of a blog becoming a digital research page. Bruce uploads information found on the Internet for others to have access to references and also for him to keep a record of his own research.

Archives are everywhere and vary hugely in scale and content. They can be any of the following: a small-scale personal archive that we keep ourselves; a large, historically significant museum archive; the archive of a company, institution, or newspaper; or the archive of an individual photographer. Photographic archives may contain more than just prints. For example, the Victoria & Albert Museum in the UK also holds photographers' diaries and letters and the Getty Research Institute in the US has collections of letters, sketchbooks and albums.

Some organizations and museums keep quite general archives, while others are far more specialized: some may be dedicated to a particular subject, period, or place; and others to the work of an individual photographer. The history of how an archive has been collected is often as interesting as the material it contains; if there is no published material about this history, you may want to interview the curator.

Archives can move; an archive that was started by one person or organization can be moved to a bigger institution. For example, the archive of photographs of London collected by Erik Franck (a well-known London photography dealer and collector) has recently moved to the archives of Tate Modern. It is important to research the history of any archive you investigate as this is part of its heritage and can give an insight into the context of when and why the material was originally collected.

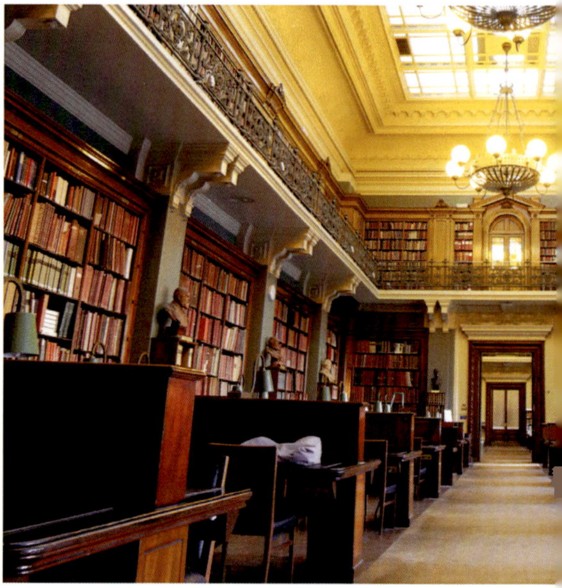

2.8

Title: Inside the V&A Print Room

Source: © Victoria and Albert Museum, London

The Victoria and Albert Museum in London has a fantastic archive of art-based photography. You can visit as a student group or as an individual and book in advance the material you are interested in viewing. Great care has to be taken when handling precious original materials: gloves may need to be worn and notes can only be written in pencil.

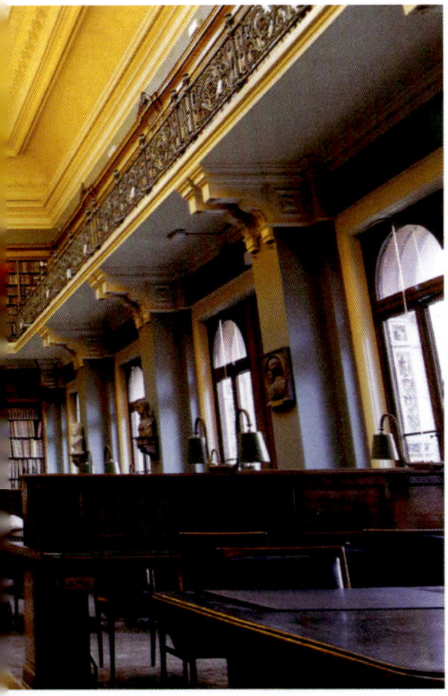

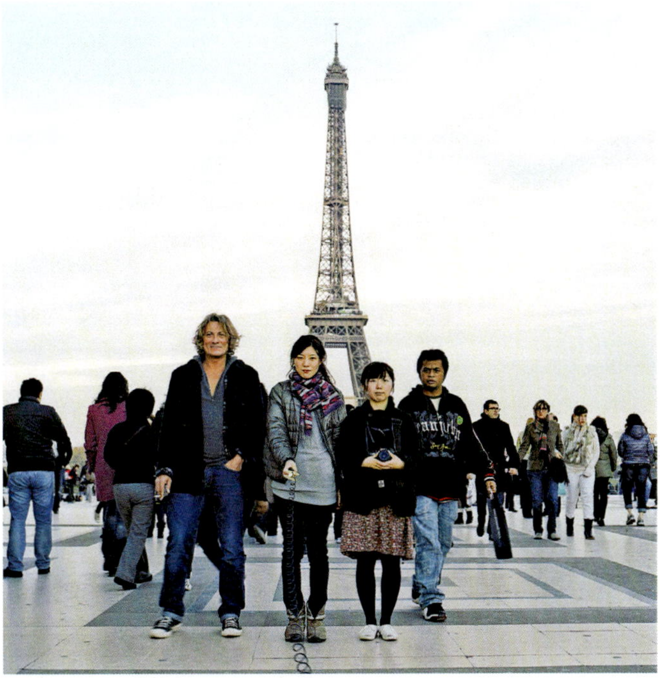

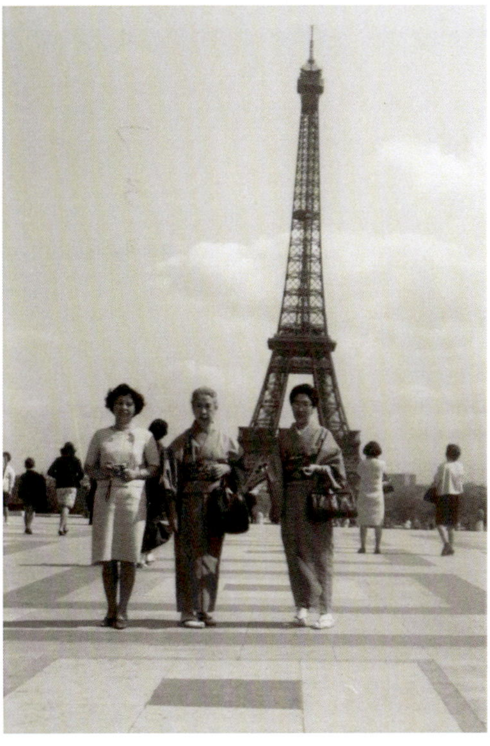

2.9

Title: Landmark—European Tour

Photographer: Anonymous/Yuri Gomi

Yuri Gomi, a Japanese photographer, made this project to reinterpret her own family photographs. Her great grandmother and a friend made a European tour in 1966 and asked passers-by to record them outside various significant monuments as a document of their trip. Gomi re-visited the same monuments and created self-portraits at these locations. This work reflects on the differences and similarities between past and present in relation to social and cultural behavior. The juxtaposition of the two images gives the work a humorous tone.

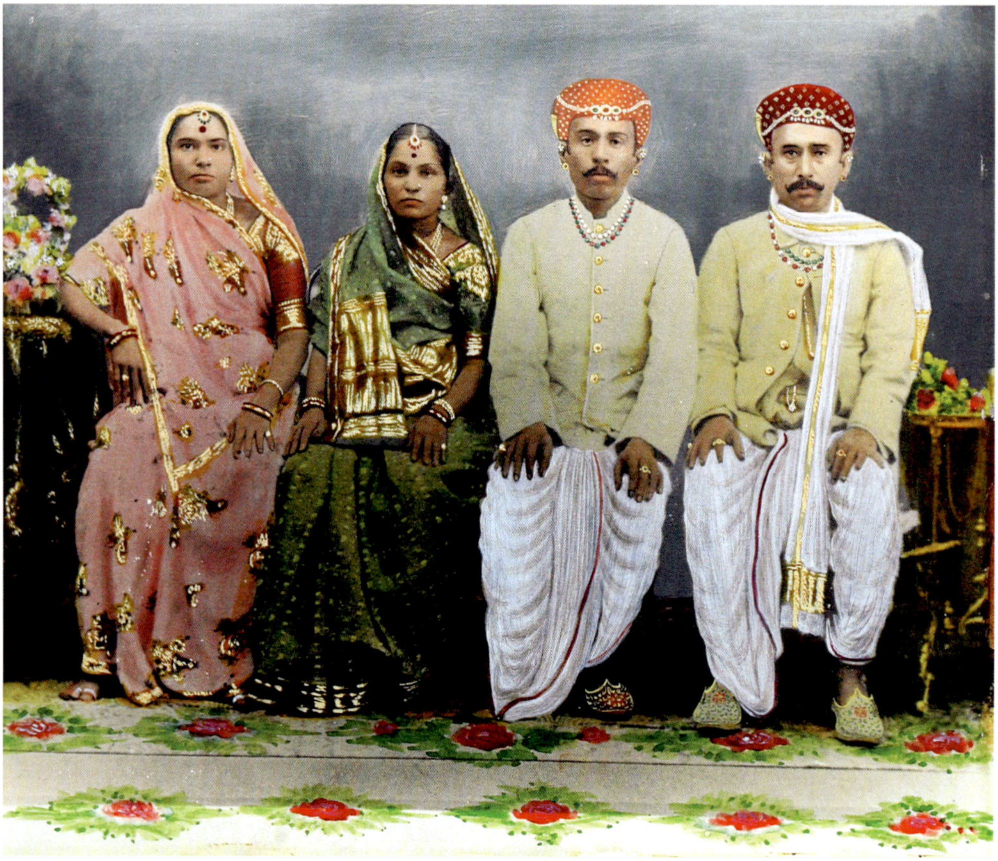

Accessing archives

To gain access to an archive, you will need to book an appointment in advance. Many archives are busy places where researchers go on a regular basis to look closely at photographs and other related materials. Seeing a physical print, often made by the photographer themselves, is a very different experience to seeing the image reproduced on the page of a book or on the Web. Detail, focus, color and tone in a photographic print can often be quite different to the reproduced versions, and it is always interesting to see the scale that the photographer chose to make the print. You may get the opportunity to talk to one of the specialists in the archive you visit, which is also an enlightening experience.

2.10

Title: Family portrait, gelatin silver print and oil painting, c.1920–1940

Source: The Alkazi Collection of Photography

The Alkazi Foundation for the Arts has been collecting 19th- and 20th-century photography of South and Southeast Asia for over 30 years. Painted photographs such as this are one part of the archived collection. The foundation encourages scholarly research in its archives that also include architectural, anthropological, topological and archaeological photographs. They have published a number of important books from this research.

History

An archive can give you an insight into past and present, both in relation to the history of photography and the social and economic history of a given time or place. Discovering a collection that has been hidden is an exciting business. It takes time to order and archive such a find, and the process reveals new knowledge. Photography and the Archive Research Centre, based at the London College of Communication, employs researchers who explore the idea of archives both through the creation of new work and through the investigation of the past. Many archives have now been digitized, and links to them can be found on the Internet. The Internet has become a valuable and accessible way to connect researchers to archives around the globe – some well-known and some only recently uncovered.

2.11

Title: Painted Cow, World War II

Source: Alpha Press

Many museums have historical photographic collections specific to their subject of interest. This image shows a cow being painted to make it more visible to pedestrians and motorists during the blackouts of World War II.

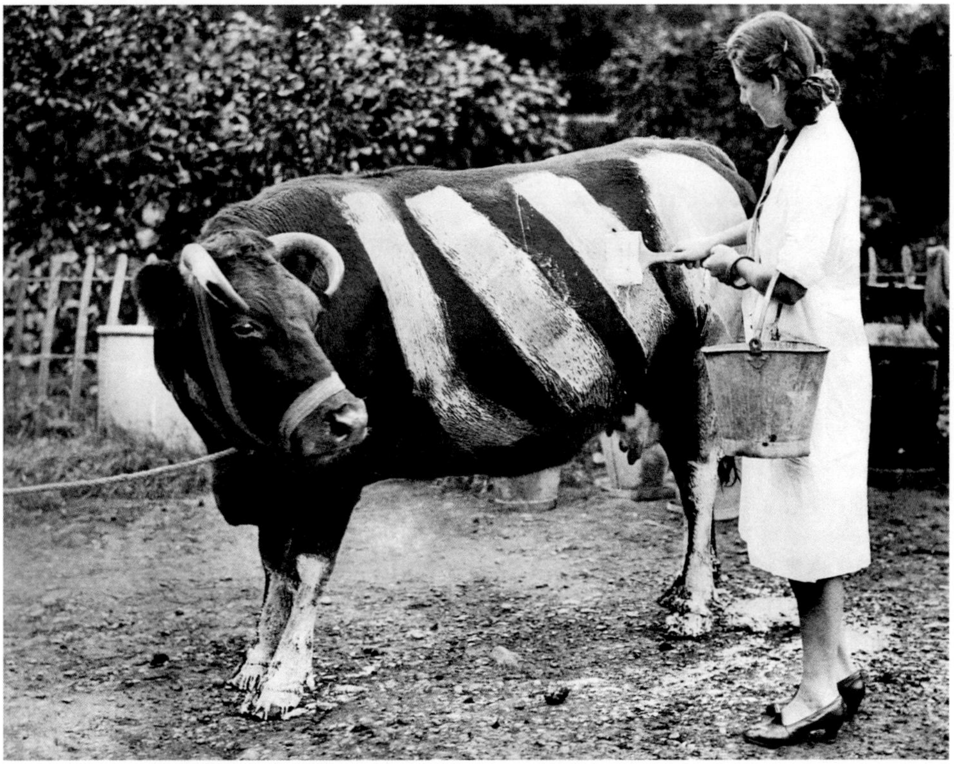

Vernacular photography

There are various interpretations of what is or isn't vernacular photography. The most common perception is that vernacular photography is photography of the everyday: snapshots, wedding photography, industrial photography, high-street studio photography, train and plane spotters' photographs and so on. One of the wonderful things about photography is that you can find it in so many different places: it is the most democratic medium, in the sense that it is everywhere and almost everyone has access to use it. This is what makes vernacular photography such a fascinating and valuable research area and tool.

Artists and photographers use vernacular photography in different ways. Some will use it simply as part of the research process, as a reference, to inform a way of working or as part of investigating a subject area. Others may use vernacular images as part of their finished work.

Looking at vernacular photography from the past is a vital part of historical research: curators and photographers may use this type of photography as part of the narrative of a historical exhibition. Curators Val Williams and Susan Bright used vernacular photography from cookery books, picture postcards and family albums alongside the work of well-known photographers, such as Martin Parr and Paul Graham, in the exhibition *How We Are: Photographing Britain, from 1840s to the Present* at the Tate Britain in 2007. It created an extraordinary picture of how Britain has been represented in photographs.

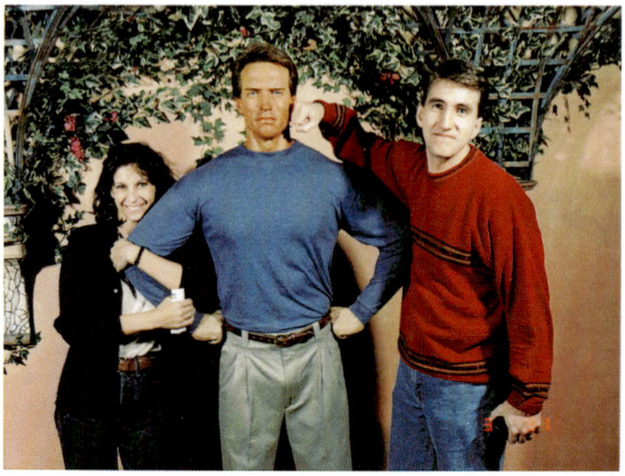

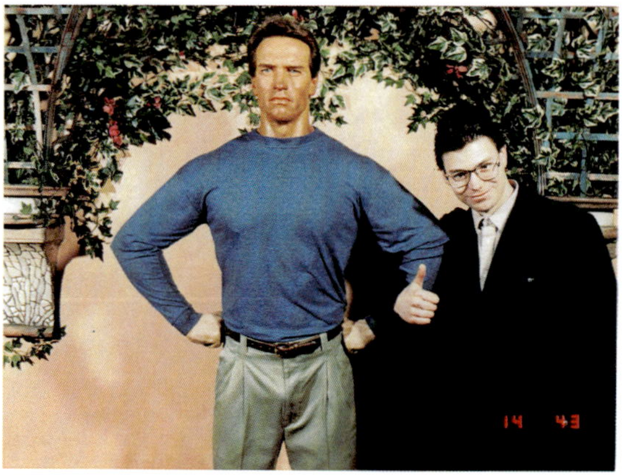

2.12

Title: from *Waxworks*

Artist: Stephen Bull

Stephen Bull has been working with found photographs since the early 1990s. He is fascinated by how photography is used in popular culture. *Waxworks* is compiled from hundreds of unsold photographs from the photography shop at the tourist attraction Madame Tussauds in London. The series, usually exhibited in a largescale grid, reveals the different reactions to the model of Arnold Schwarzenegger and to the camera, and perhaps represents what is and what is not meant to be shown in such souvenir photographs.

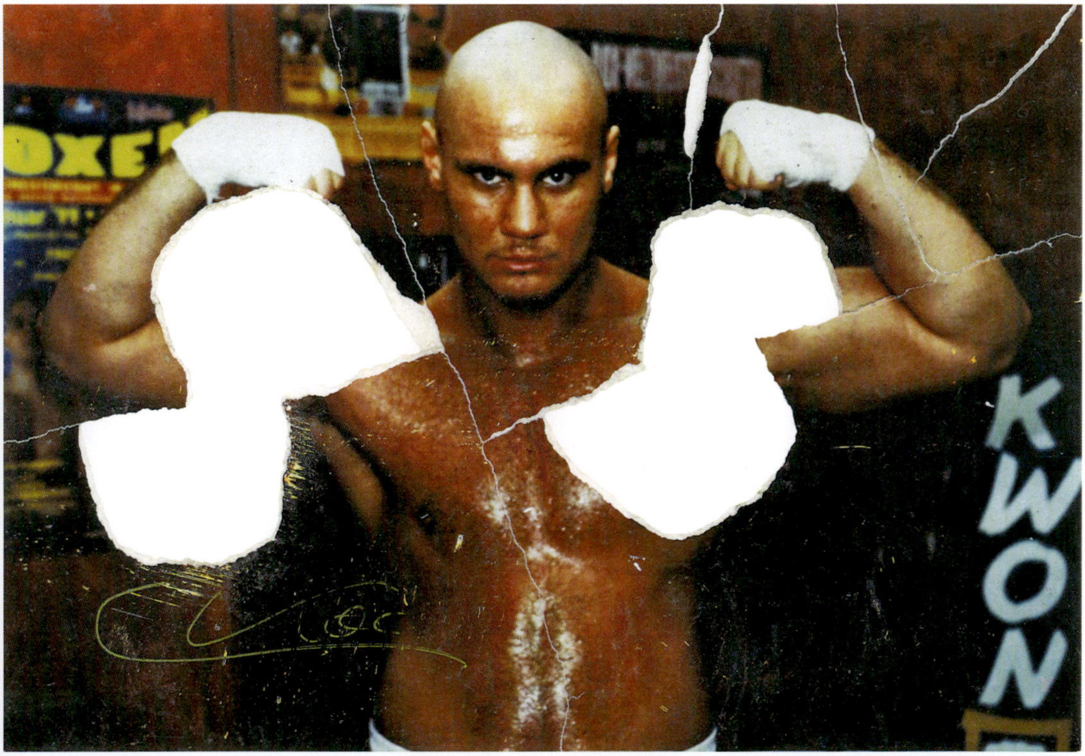

2.13

Title: Bilder von der Straße No. 832, Berlin, April 2004

Artist: Joachim Schmid

Artist Joachim Schmid has been collecting waste photographs for over 15 years. The work has evolved into several different series, including *Pictures from the Street* and *The Photographic Garbage Survey Project*. Schmid collects and preserves thrown away or waste photographs, systematically archiving them for future use.

The result of his collections and travels is a report for each city consisting of the found photographs, a list of discovery sites, maps with the inspected streets marked, and a statistical evaluation. Altogether these reports form an international compendium of photographic pollution in modern cities.

Being an active researcher means doing more than simply sitting in front of a computer: you need to find out what is happening around you and get involved with different activities that could have research potential. A starting point might be to investigate local galleries and museums to find out if they host lectures, artists' talks and workshops, or have an interesting archive. You may also decide that you want to take your research a step further and conduct your own interviews.

Lectures

Attending a lecture, whether in an educational institution or another venue, is a great way to research a topic: they offer a concise and self-contained means to gather knowledge. The manner in which information is delivered—in a lecture, by a live speaker—cannot be replicated by any other means, and you get to put a face to the expert's name.

Within educational institutions, lectures take the form of a series of presentations given by a professor or lecturer on a particular topic. Lectures are not normally interrupted for questions, but will often be followed by either panel discussions or question-and-answer sessions. Within these forums, the audience is in the privileged position of being able to question the experts directly.

If you cannot attend a lecture in person, enquire whether the lecture is streamed online or made available later for podcast or download.

Take note of how professional interviewers work; you need to allow your subject ample time to speak. To be a good interviewer, you need to be a good listener.

Interviews

Interviews are an invaluable way of gaining primary research material. Meeting photographers, editors, curators and any other professionals involved with photography is an excellent way of finding out what they have done, when, and why. Interviewing people is a huge privilege and often quite difficult to arrange. If you do get an opportunity like this, you need to prepare well; make sure your questions are designed around your area of interest, but also allow space for your interviewee to tell you other things that they may feel are relevant. Take note of how professional interviewers work; you need to allow your subject ample time to speak. To be a good interviewer, you need to be a good listener.

Reading

Reading is a solitary act and allows you to work independently to obtain background information in your own time. The effort invested in reading around your subject matter can pay dividends in a number of ways: the discovery of a pertinent quote, historical fact, or statistical figure to bolster your proposal; or the finding of a potential collaborative partner in the form of an author, artist, or expert. The more you read around your idea, the more informed you will be to promote it to financiers, the press, galleries, curators, and, importantly, to discuss it in peer reviews.

Tips for interviewing

- Make sure you choose a comfortable, appropriate venue.
- Prepare your questions in advance, after conducting relevant research.
- You may want to email your questions to your interviewee in advance so they can prepare.
- Ideally you should record the interview, but check that your interviewee is happy for you to do this first.
- Ensure any recording equipment is in working order before you start, and make sure you have sufficient supplies of stationery to take notes.
- If you do record the interview, transcribe it soon afterwards while the impression of the interview is still fresh in your mind.
- Give the interviewee plenty of time to answer—don't feel tempted to fill any pauses with other questions; give them time to think.
- Be prepared to ask follow-up questions.
- Send your interviewee a copy of the interview for approval before you use or publish it anywhere.

Listening

Having gained a wealth of knowledge in the course of your investigations, you can present your ideas and thought processes to others and invite their feedback. To get the most from this, you need one key skill: being a good listener. Presenting your work, often to strangers, can make you feel vulnerable and defensive. Listening is an active, not passive, task.

Listen to how others react to your work and consider whether it speaks for itself. Learn to pick up on key words and phrases that are used to describe your work. Ask for clarification if you need to, and do not be afraid to seek further explanation. While discussing your work, do people make reference to other artists or texts? If so, take note of these references.

Be open to feedback. You may receive comments that you expect and welcome. Equally, you may receive some comments that are unexpected or that you feel are inaccurate or unwarranted. Always bear in mind that the dialogue centers around the work; try to judge the strengths and weaknesses of your own project as you would judge the work of other artists.

Your listening skills will develop and improve each time you undertake an exercise such as this. Take the time to write up the feedback you hear after an event. How much do you remember? What are the key points to follow up on?

Reviewing

You need to allow time to review your project on an ongoing basis; don't feel that a review is only done with a completed body of work. Having your progress reviewed is a rich and rewarding process.

There are many means to have progress reviews during the development of a project, such as making time with peers and taking turns reviewing each other's work. Alternatively, many institutions and independent photographic organizations offer advice-led reviews. This is a great way to test out people's reactions to the project – reactions that are not biased by knowing you or your previous work. This is also an excellent way to form new relationships in the photographic world. Building a network is vital to photographers.

Alternatively, when you feel confident enough with your progress, a more formal one-to-one review can offer you in-depth tailored feedback. There are many arts organizations that offer this service; you can search the Internet to find the organizations that are local to you. You should bear in mind that reviewing is prone to subjectivity and bias; although you may have a number of reviews that inspire you, you are not always bound to agree with a reviewer's perspective.

One major advantage of being reviewed face to face is that you learn so much about the professional world. Having your work reviewed in this way is a two-way conversation: you can follow up ideas, probe responses and investigate motives and feelings. You get a sense of how someone feels about your work in a way that would be concealed in a written response.

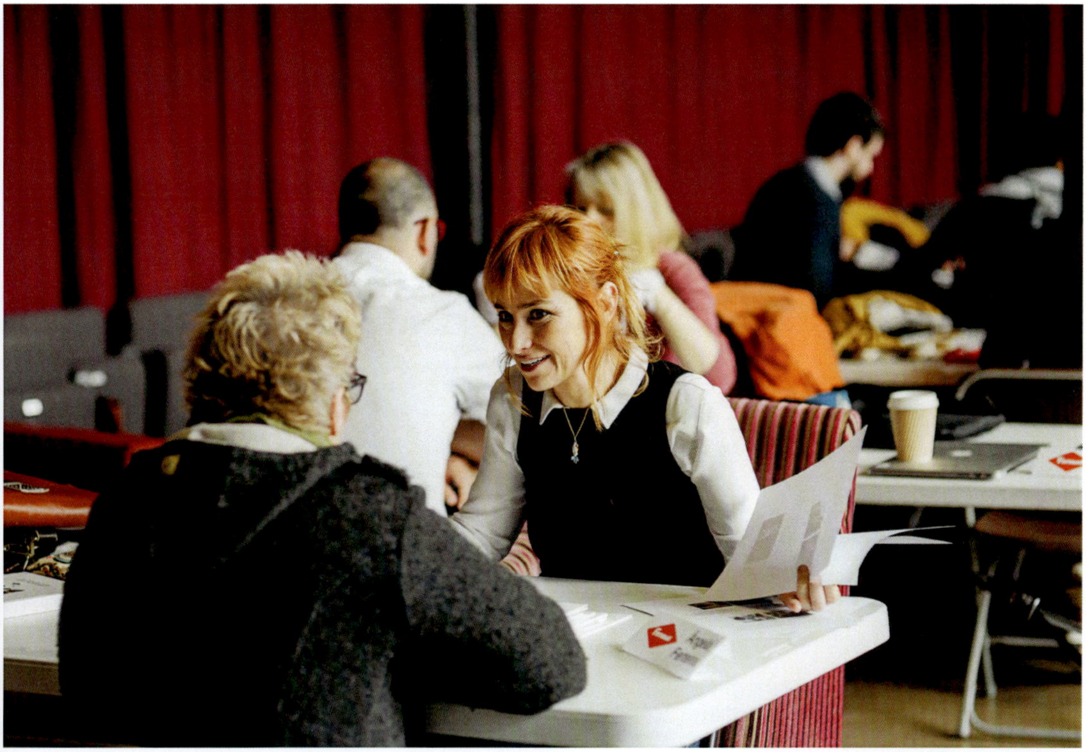

2.14

Title: Portfolio reviews, Format International Photography Festival

Source: Format

This is an image of independent curator Ângela Ferreira reviewing a photographers work at one of Format's regular review sessions in Derby. These sessions provide photographers with a forum for discussing their work with professionals and members of the public in an informal setting. Remember to research who is doing the reviewing and book as soon as you can – there are numerous portfolio review events around the world.

Having your work reviewed is a two-way conversation: you can follow up ideas, probe responses and investigate motives and feelings.

Research informs practice in many different ways. Knowledge gained through the research process will contribute to forming a photographer's approach to making work. It may be as simple as influencing a style of working or the choice of props and surroundings. It could be that background research reveals new information about a place or people. It could tell you more about a society, a way of thinking, the shape or color of something, the history of a place; almost anything that tells a story in one way or another could be part of your research.

We have been talking about background research by looking at libraries, archives, lectures and vernacular photography. All of these can aid the understanding of a subject, why it might be interesting to make photographs of it, and how to develop visual strategies for the production of photographs.

It is clear that the sources of a photographer's research will be extensive, varied and not always explicit in the final body of work. In order for this research to form a valuable and continuing resource, it should be archived. A research archive is a rich resource, both for the photographer and for future researchers trying to discover how and why a photograph worked.

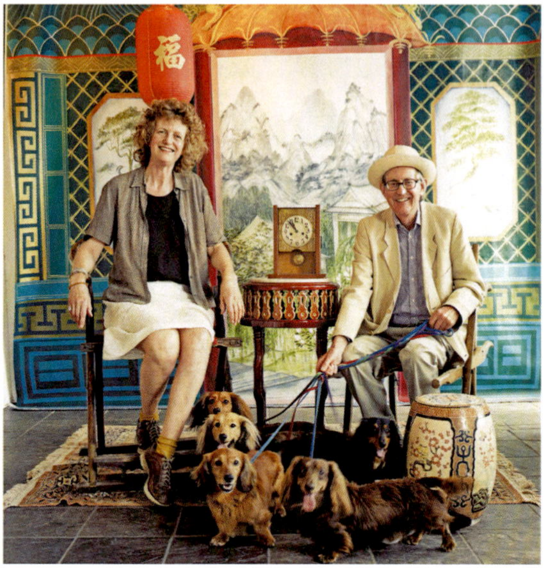

2.15

Title: from *21st Century Types*

Photographer: Grace Lau

In her book *Picturing the Chinese: Early Western Photographs and Postcards of China* (2009), Grace Lau explored photographic portraits made by Westerners in China during the turbulent years between the Opium Wars and the Boxer Rebellion. Using her 30-year-old Hasselblad camera, Lau took on the role of the 'imperialist photographer' documenting her 'exotic' types in Hastings, in the UK, in order to respond to the historic situation whereby foreign photographers recorded the 'exotic' Chinese people. As a British photographer of Chinese descent, Lau's photographs reference both cultures past and present, and raise interesting questions about the way culture is stamped onto us via the constructed set of the traditional high-street studio.

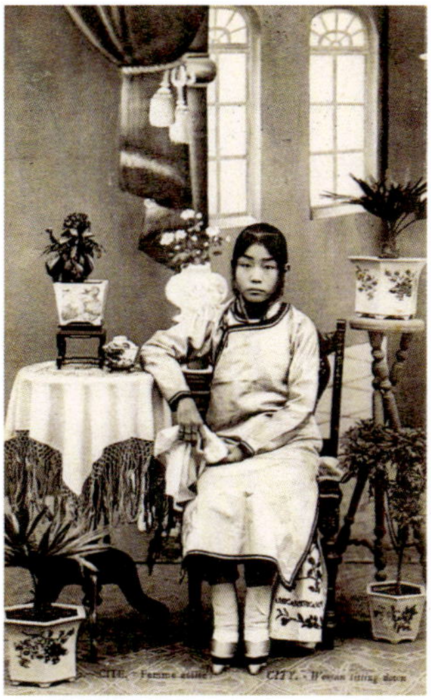

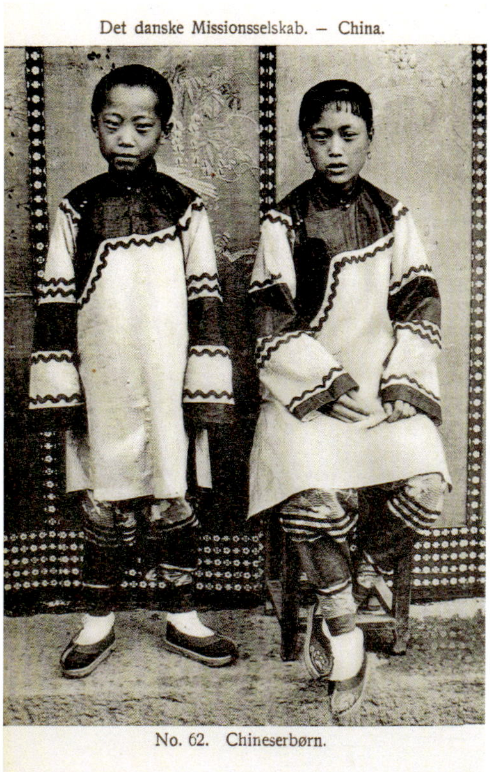

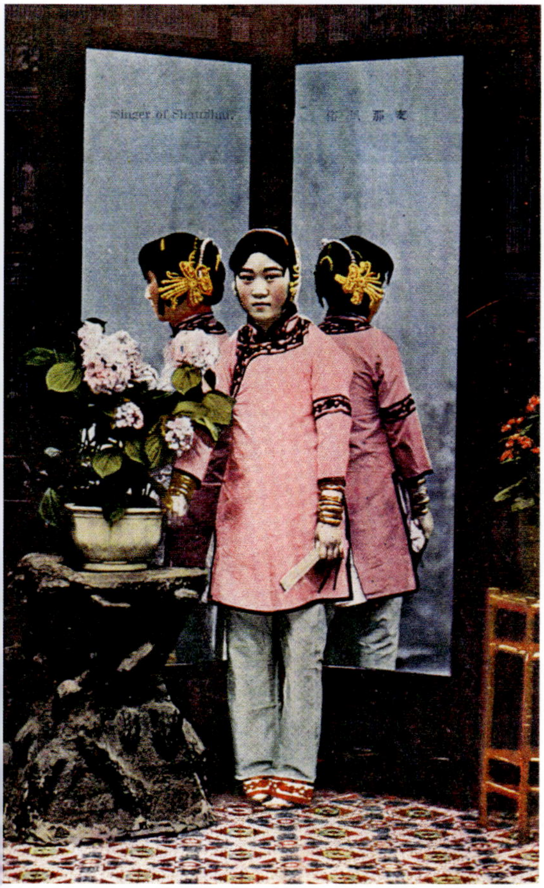

2.16

Title: *Victorian colonial photographs of China*

Source: Grace Lau

Images from Grace Lau's research archive depicting Chinese 'exotic' types. Lau bought these images as postcards at fairs. The dates and photographers are generally not specified on these postcards; they were printed to promote the work of foreign missionaries abroad.

Establishing a research framework for practice

As the ideas and research for your project evolve, you will reach a point where you realize that you have created a model way of working for future projects – this is a research framework. Using a research framework that is tried and tested will enable you to progress future projects and help you describe the research methods you intend to use when you write a proposal. You will have a research plan to follow.

A research framework in action

Sara Davidmann is an artist who has worked with both making her own photographs and using found imagery. In her latest work, *Ken. To be destroyed*, she uses vernacular photography and letters from a personal family archive that was kept secret for many years. These papers were part of her own family history and were discovered by her in two large envelopes and a brown paper bag in her mother's garage. One of the envelopes had a simple phrase scrawled on the front: 'Ken. To be destroyed'. Ken was Davidmann's uncle, who passed away in 1979. The envelope had not been destroyed, and, after inheriting the envelopes and bag of documents, Davidmann started to investigate the story behind this curious archive. Why had these images been hidden? What was the story of her uncle Ken's life that rendered it 'to be destroyed'? The archive told the story of Ken and Hazel, Davidmann's uncle and aunt, and how, very early on in their marriage (1958), it emerged that Ken was transgender.

Davidmann developed an experimental approach to working with the material, creating a unique set of images that interrogated the archive and the hidden life of Ken and foregrounded her own responses to what she had discovered. She created these artworks using a variety of methods that included analogue, alternative and digital processes.

Through a process of mark making, painting and cutting and pasting that alter the original images, Davidmann playfully explored her own feelings about the Ken and Hazel story, redeeming it from its previous dusty state and bringing it back to life. The final images veer between being decorative and full of color to being quite dark and bleak.

A book of the work, published by Schilt in 2016, was a collaboration between the curator/writer/historian Professor Val Williams from University for the Arts London and Sara Davidmann. The book brought together texts written by Williams and Davidmann, material from the archive, and Davidmann's unique images. Together Williams and Davidmann explored different ways of combining the material and how to structure it as a narrative within the pages of the book.

By keeping a record of the processes she undertook to make the work, Davidmann can use this record as a framework for her future research projects.

> As the ideas and research for your project evolve, you will reach a point where you realize that you have created a model way of working for future projects – this is a research framework. You can allow the model to evolve and change with new projects.

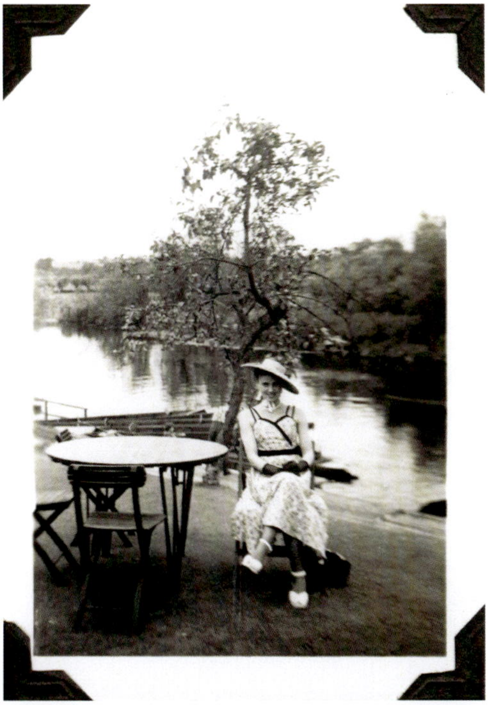

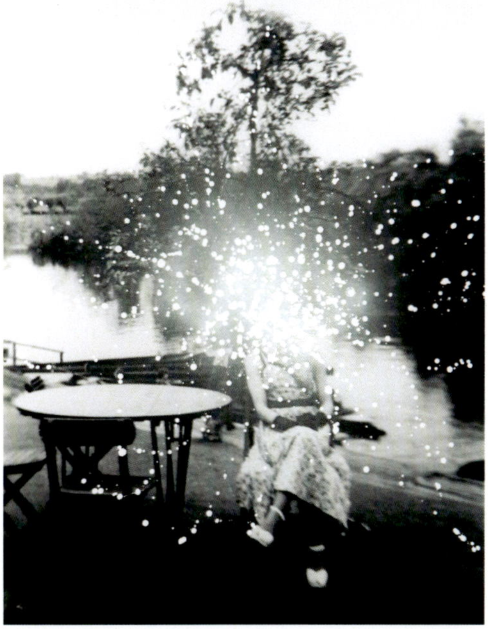

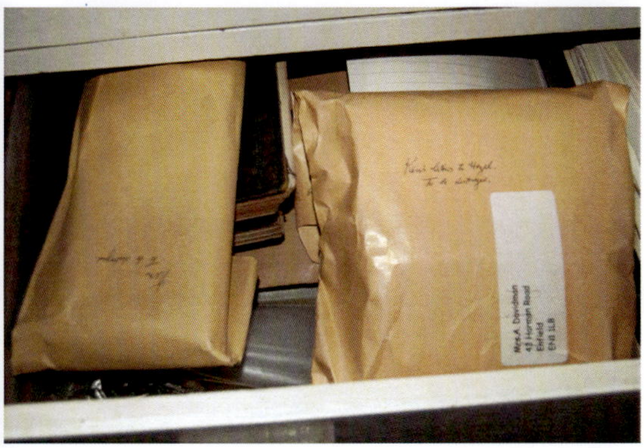

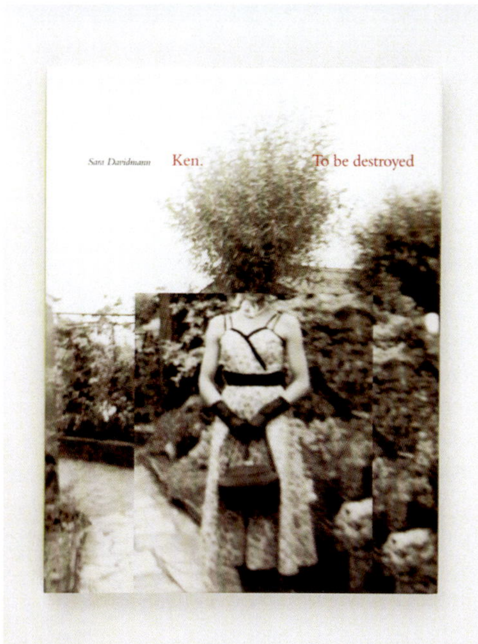

2.17

Title: *Ken. To be Destroyed*

Artist: Sara Davidmann

Top left is one of the vintage photographs c.1950 discovered inside the envelope, beside it the image created by Davidmann. Below is a photograph of the original envelopes, and bottom right is the cover of the book of the work edited by Professor Val Williams at University of the Arts London.

Writing for research

Writing for research might include developing a research proposal for an MA/MFA, a PhD, or for one of the organizations and councils that fund research. Writing is also an integral part of many research projects. If you are planning to do a PhD you will need to write a thesis. On many Masters-level courses you need to write proposals and sometimes dissertations or contextualizing documents (a document about your work and where it fits in the world of photography).

Masters photography

A Masters-level photography programme can be called either a Master of Arts (MA) or a Master of Fine Arts (MFA). These two courses are both at the same educational level, although an MFA in the UK will usually have more credits than an MA and take longer. In the US, the MFA is considered to be the exit award for arts-based subjects and it qualifies you to teach. In most parts of the world, there are very few opportunities to study what are called (in the UK) practice-based PhDs. The UK, Australia and India have developed practice routes for PhD-level research projects.

Practice-based PhDs

A practice-based PhD is a PhD which includes a major body of practical work as well as a written thesis. The written thesis is usually much shorter than one written for a science or humanities PhD; the practical work is made alongside the theoretical investigation and responds to what the author is discovering. The PhD student will have written a proposal in order to apply for the course of study, and during the first few months of the course they will develop this proposal into a full and distinctive piece of writing about their subject, raising pertinent questions and suggesting innovative ways of dealing with the subject through photographic practice.

A full-time PhD, in the UK, normally takes three years (if no breaks are taken) and can be done over five or six years part time. In order to do a PhD, you need a field of enquiry, a subject to study, and a suggested contribution to knowledge – that is, the assertion that your proposed course of investigation and research will lead to new knowledge or understanding in the field. A PhD proposal differs depending on where you are studying. It will generally require:

- a title
- a description of your project and why it is important/relevant/interesting right now
- your aims and objectives
- your contribution to knowledge
- your proposed methods of working
- potential research questions (in some programmes)

During the first weeks of a PhD, you will also have to fill in an ethics checklist and see if your project needs to be approved by an ethics committee (which all universities have). It is important that the university where you are studying complies with government research policy which ensures that research is ethically correct and that no damage is being caused to anyone through your process or work. If you are photographing, interviewing, or collaborating with anyone as part of your PhD project, you need to apply to the ethics committee to approve the project before commencing with these activities. No one can start their PhD until they have approval from an ethics committee.

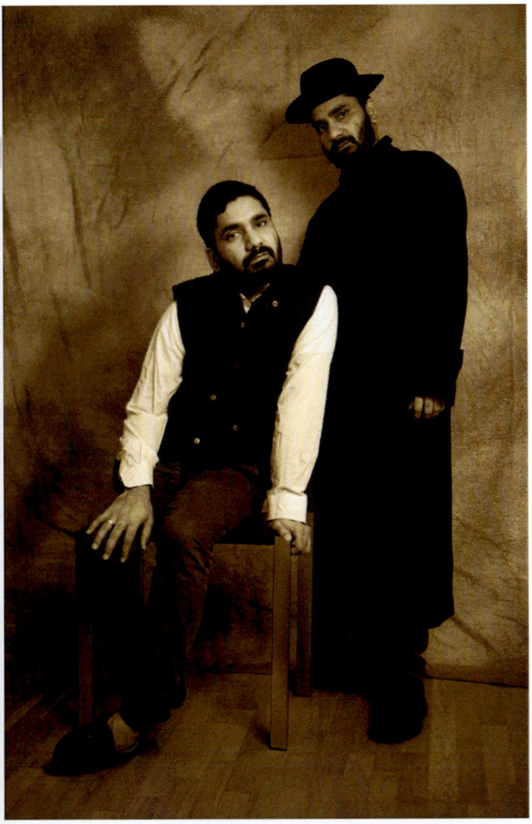

2.18

Untitled #1, What Would My Father Think?

Photographer: Charan Singh – self-portraits

Charan Singh worked in an NGO (non-government organisation) in India and used photography to document his work. He had a keen interest in politics and activism and wanted to develop his own photography in order to use it to question popular perceptions on LGBTQ identity. After a year exploring the possibilities of self-portraiture, he made this series of double portraits, where he appears twice in each image, dressed as different and quite particular characters. The series explores the difficulties of performing one's identity between the social/cultural expectations of two totally different value systems.

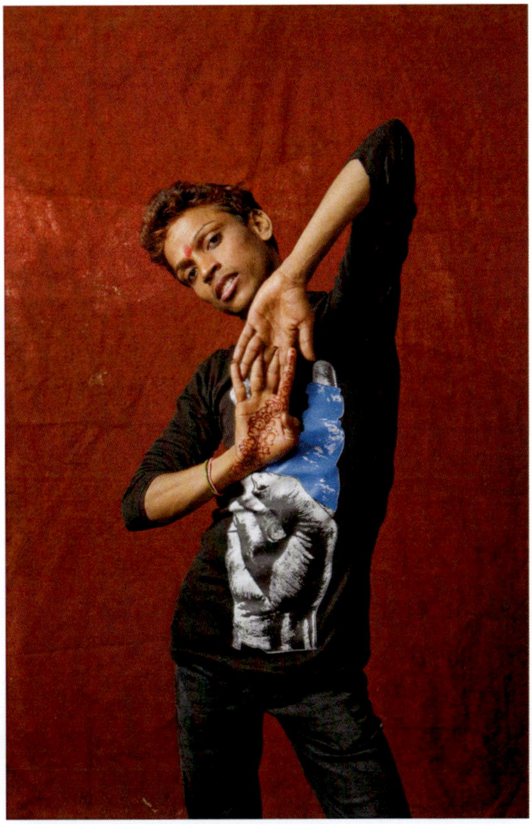

2.19

Untitled #6, Kothis, Hijra, Giriyas and Others

Photographer: Charan Singh – trans portraits

For the fourth and final semester of his MFA, Singh decided to return to India to the NGOs where he used to work and make collaborative portraits with the Kothi and transgender community that he had worked with before his MFA. The portraits were made in a way to celebrate difference and promote equality. There is no shame in these portraits and no looking down upon his subjects – they are playful and positive and at times enticing. Singh has gone on to do a practice-based PhD, which he will complete in 2020.

A PhD will include:

- regular tutorials with your supervisors (usually you have two supervisors)
- forums or reviews where you present work to others and answer questions on your research
- a research methods course
- progress reviews
- vivas: normally there are three key points where you go through the viva process. The first is when you present your final proposal and it is approved. The second is 18 months into your research; at this point you will have made some work and have a full plan of your thesis and a Gantt chart (which shows what you will do and when in quite a lot of detail). Finally, the third is when you present your finished work and thesis to the thesis panel, which includes external panel members.
- public presentation of your work: you are expected to submit to exhibitions and conferences alongside your study to try to get your ideas out into a public arena in a way that is appropriate to your area of research.

At the end of a PhD, there is a final viva with an external and an internal examiner. A viva is like an interview where the examiners have questions already prepared based on what they have read in the thesis paper. A viva can last one or two hours and includes looking at the practical work (if it is a practice-based PhD) which will either be in book or exhibition form (or both).

Research councils and bodies

There are a number of organizations, research councils and research institutions that encourage and fund research and research collaboration. These include (in the UK) the Arts and Humanities Research Council (AHRC), Leverhulme, Wellcome Trust, Arts Council England (ACE), Arts Council Wales (ACW) and, in the US, the Guggenheim Foundation. There are also bodies that deal with international research, including the British Council (their remit will always include the UK in relation to or in collaboration with another country or countries). One would normally be an experienced researcher/photographer/artist to apply to any of these organizations, although the arts councils usually have a route for emerging photographers to apply to. The Leverhulme and the AHRC have special applications for early career researchers. Other organizations may well also have specific types of application that relate to a certain subject or area that they cover and are keen to support. You can look up research funding in your university library.

2.20

Title: from the series *Dead Water*

Photographer: Marilene Ribeiro

Photographer Marilene Ribeiro decided to come to the UK to study for her PhD. She selected her university carefully in order that she could be supervised by people who were relevant to her interests (i.e. the supervisors work in the methods or subject areas she wanted to investigate). Ribeiro's project was to work collaboratively with her subjects to engage in a story-telling practice, creating a revealing study of communities that have been affected by the building of dams in Brazil. In each community, Ribeiro and her subjects (people who have been affected by these ventures) create a series of posed portraits until they reach the final image, one which every subject has directed themselves. She has also been collecting their stories of loss, which detail the river and communities that have either been moved or are about to be moved. Ribeiro's method combines text, interviews, drawings and old photographs. The *Dead Water* project is of international significance both in terms of the information she is uncovering and in regard to the innovative collaboration methods she is using in her practice.

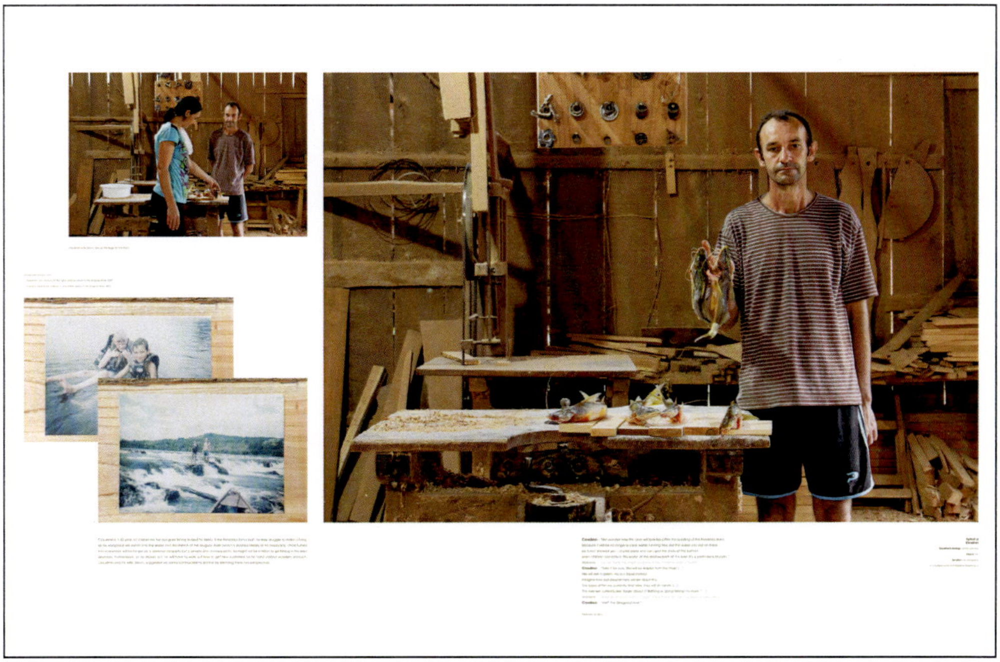

2.20a

top left: Claudinei's wife, Seloni, sets up the stage for the shoot.

middle left: Originals as photographic prints.
1. Claudinei's son, Márcio (at the right), and his cousin in the Uruguay River, 2009. 2. Claudinei and his son, Márcio, in one of the rapids of the Uruguay River, 2009.

bottom left: Claudinei is a 42-year-old carpenter. He also goes fishing to feed his family. If the Panambi dam is built, he may struggle to make a living, as his workplace will vanish into the water and this stretch of the Uruguay River (which is situated literally at his backyard), once turned into a reservoir, will no longer be a common property but a private one; consequently, he might not be entitled to go fishing in this area anymore. Furthermore, as he moves out, he will have to work out how to get new customers for his hand crafted wooden products. Claudinei and his wife, Seloni, suggested we jointly constructed his portrait by blending these two perspectives.

bottom middle:

Claudinei – "We wonder how this area will look like [after the building of the Panambi dam], because it will be no longer a clear water, running free, like the water you see on these pictures I showed you – crystal clear, one can spot the rocks at the bottom, even children can play in this water, at the shallow parts of the river. It's a pretty beautiful site."

Marilene – "Do you think this might be gone [if the Panambi dam is built]?"

Claudinei – "Take it for sure. This will be erased from the map! (. . .)

We will see a green, viscous liquid instead.

Imagine how sad people here will be about this.

The types of fish we currently find here, they will all vanish. (. . .)

This river we currently see: forget about it! Bathing or going fishing: no more." (. . .)

Marilene – "What do you not want to forget, if the Panambi dam happens to take place?"

Claudinei – "Me? The [Uruguay] river."

February 05 2016

bottom right: **Portrait of Claudinei**

Claudinei's feelings: sorrow and loss

Object: fish

Location: his workspace

© Claudinei Zuehl and Marilene Ribeiro 2016

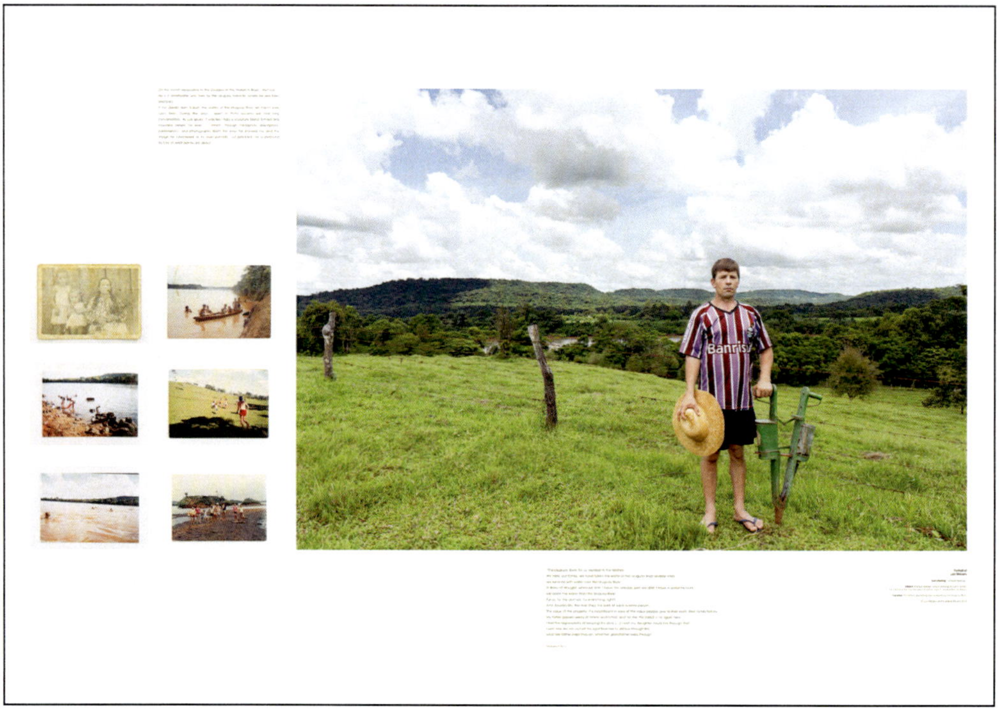

2.20b

top left: On the month dedicated to the Goddess of the Waters in Brazil, I met Luiz. He is a smallholder who lives by the Uruguay riverside, where he was born and bred.

If the Garabi dam is built, the waters of the Uruguay River will march over Luiz's land. During the days I spent in Porto Lucena we had long conversations. As Luiz spoke, it was like I had a sculpture being formed and moulded before my eyes (. . . mind?): through metaphors, descriptions, explanations, and photographs (both the ones he showed me and the image he conceived as his own portrait), Luiz provided me a profound picture of what bonds are about.

bottom middle: The Uruguay River, for us, represents the Mother!

We here, our family, we have taken the water of the Uruguay River several times;

we survived with water from the Uruguay River.

In times of drought, when we didn't have the artesian well, we didn't have a water network,

we drank the water from the Uruguay River.

For us, for the animals, for everything, right?

And, besides life, the river [has] the roots of each riverine person.

The value of the property, it is insignificant in view of the value people give to their roots, their family history.

My father passed away at ninety-and-a-half, and for me, this [land] is his figure here.

I feel the responsibility of keeping this alive (. . .) I wish my daughter could live through that.

I wish one did not cut off this right from her to still live through this:

what her father lived through, what her grandfather lived through.

February 9 2016

bottom right: **Portrait of Luiz Webery**

Luiz's feeling: "all bad feelings"

Object: manual seeder (which belongs to Luiz's family; he mentions this was the way his father used to work in the old times)

Location: his family's pasture gorge overlooking the Uruguay River

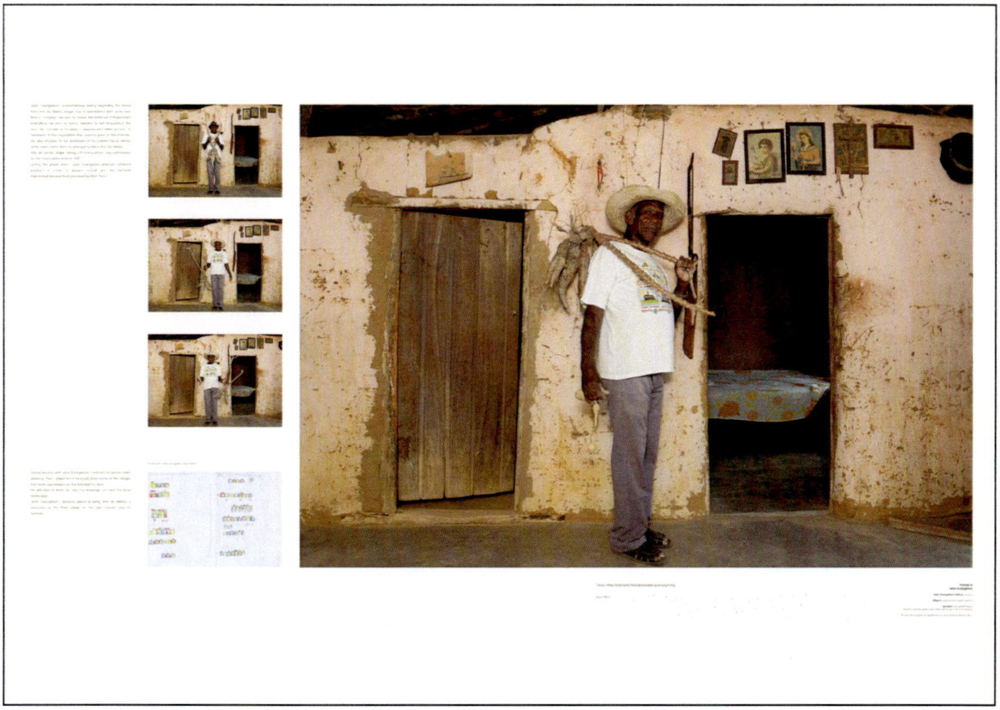

2.20c

top left: João Evangelista's overwhelming feeling regarding the move from Alto do Melão village due to Sobradinho dam works was that of "longing". He said he missed the fertile soil that provided everything he and his family needed to eat throughout the year. He chooses as his objects cassava and sweet potato, to represent all the vegetables they used to grow at the riverside. He also chooses to be portrayed at his current house whose some parts came from his previous home in Alto do Melão.

Alto do Melão village, along with many others, was submerged by the Sobradinho dam in 1978.

During the photo shoot, João Evangelista proposes different positions in which to present himself and the formerly mentioned blessed food provided by that "land".

bottom left: During my stay with João Evangelista, I noticed he appreciated drawing, then I asked him if he could draw some of the villages that were submerged by the Sobradinho dam. He decided to show not only the dwellings, but also the local landscape.

João Evangelista's previous place of living, Alto do Melão, is depicted as the third village on the right column (top to bottom).

Drawing by João Evangelista, May 12 2015.

bottom middle: "How I miss that land that provided us everything."

May 9 2015

bottom right: **Portrait of João Evangelista**

João Evangelista's feeling: longing

Object: cassava and sweet potato

Location: his current home (which contains some parts of his old house in Alto do Melão)

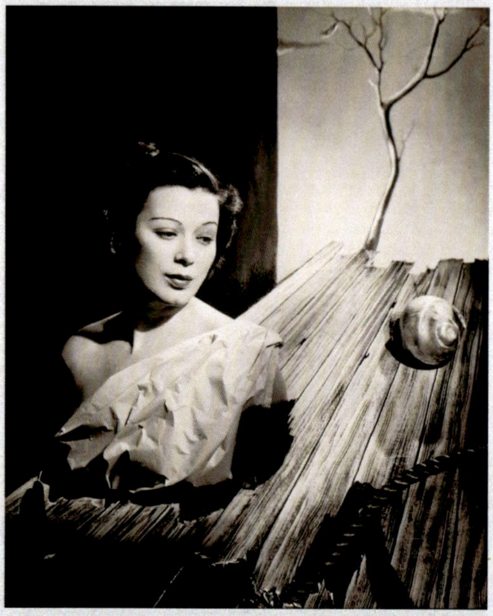

2.21

Title: *Mary Ellis*

Source: Angus McBean/National Portrait Gallery/Harvard University

The portrait 'Anna with Magnolias' from the series *Flora* was based on Angus McBean's extraordinary photograph of Mary Ellis. McBean was a studio portrait photographer working in the 1930s, an important artist working within the Surrealist movement.

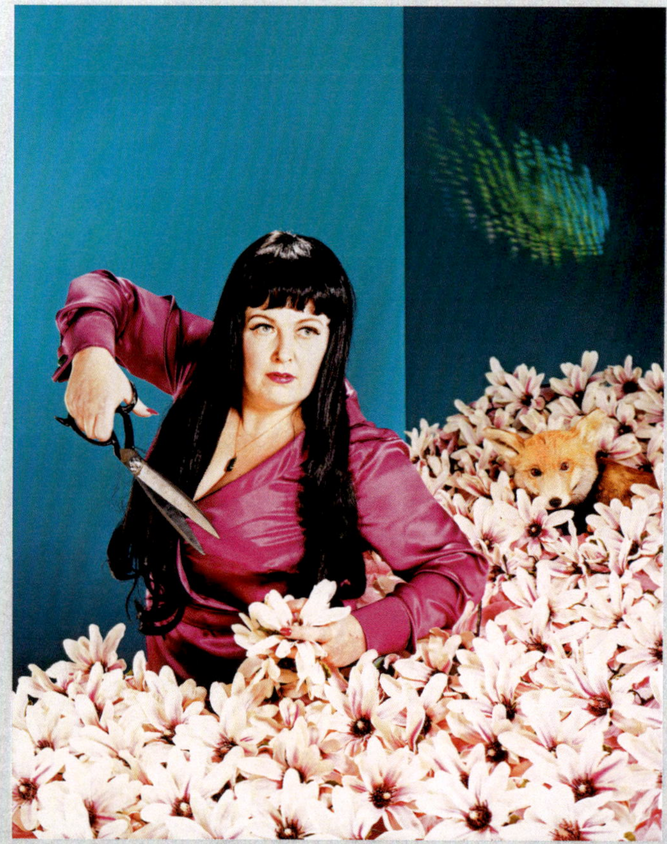

2.22

Title: 'Anna with Magnolias', from *Flora*

Artist: Neeta Madahar

After a lengthy research process, only when all the materials had been collected, did the process of set building and photography begin. Neeta worked with a lighting technician, Vicki Churchill, as well as a styling assistant, a hair and make-up artist and a photography assistant. All of her portraits for the series were shot in a large photography studio at Southampton Solent University, UK.

Case study 2
Flora

Neeta Madahar is an artist who uses photography, amongst other media, to make her work. Her portrait project, *Flora*, was exhibited at the National Media Museum in 2009–2010, and published as a book by Nazraeli Press in 2010.

In the series *Flora*, Madahar was keen to create a set of fantasy portraits working with several female friends, many of them fellow artists and photographers. Her intention was to use photography to valorize them through an exploration of glamour and desire. She wanted each portrait to be collaborative, so her subjects actively took part in the process and decision-making. For some time, Neeta had been looking into the archive of the photographer Madame Yevonde, particularly the *Goddesses* series made in 1935. In this series, Yevonde created dynamic color portraits of society women in costume for a themed ball in a way that turned on its head the conventions of women's glamour portraiture.

As she worked on the research for *Flora*, Madahar expanded her original project outline to look at further society portraiture from the 1930s to the 1950s, including the work of photographers Angus McBean, George Hurrell and Horst P. Horst. Using the imagery she was investigating and collaborating with her sitters, she built a picture of how both she and her subject wanted to be represented. Each sitter was also asked to contribute a prop or item of jewelry to their portrait so that the collaborative process had a tangible element.

The images in *Flora* explore fantasy and desire, and display a high level of stylization. All the models, friends of the artist, were over 30 and this exploration with mature women was deliberately designed to challenge the dominant glamour representations of women, which focus on young, photogenic individuals whose images have been digitally enhanced.

Activity 2: An illustrated story

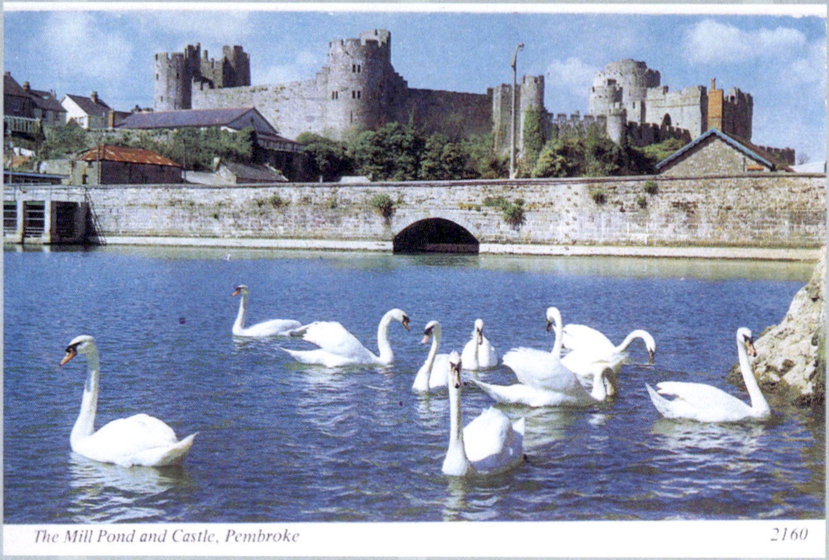

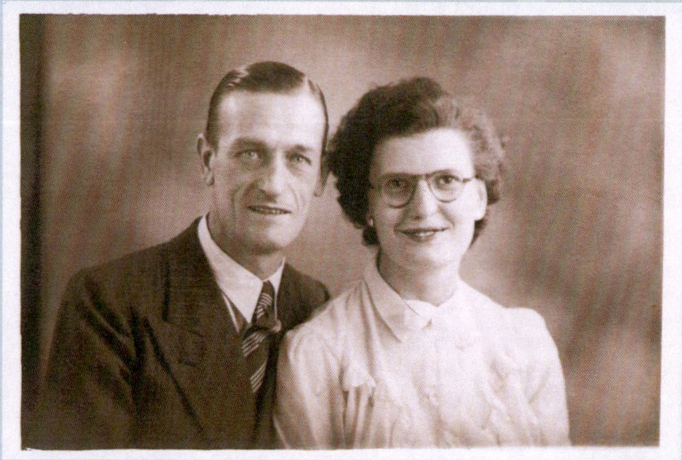

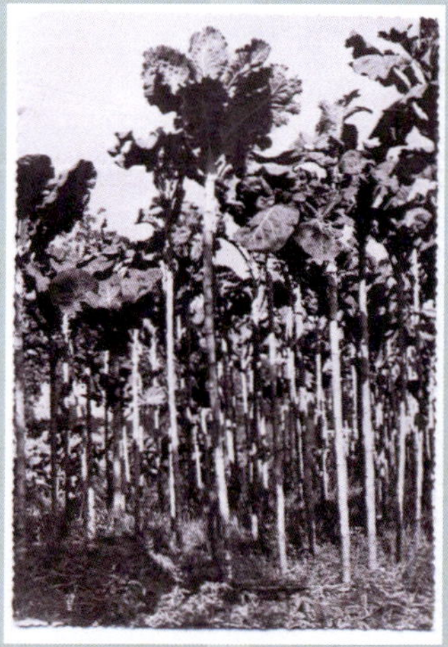

2.23

Title: found photographs and postcards

Source: Auction, Surrey

These photographs and postcards were bought at an auction in Surrey in a box with about 200 others. They are dated between 1956 and 1983. On the back of the postcards there are short inscriptions from various holidaymakers to Frank and/or Thora, who are married and live near Portsmouth. Piecing the inscriptions together one gets an idea of the relationship between these people, and also a commentary on the type of holiday making of the time. Amongst the postcards there are a series of family photographs, and one cannot help but imagine that these are of Thora and Frank and their family (though only one image has a name on it).

The image on the front of the postcard tells us where the writer is, the postmark tells us the date, and the text on the back tells us a little bit about what the holiday maker is experiencing and their relationship to whom they are writing (i.e. frequently Thora and Frank are referred to as either Aunt of Uncle, respectively). One is left to wonder what else might have been happening at the time. What would be in the text if the writer had been asked to make a detailed diaristic account of this period?

Activity 2
An illustrated story

For this activity, you need to visit a few second-hand shops, auctions, or car boot sales. Try to buy a variety of found photographs or postcards; if you are lucky, you might find a group of photographs that are from one album, or a set of postcards that appear to be linked.

Lay the photographs out on a table and think about where they could be from, who they might represent, and why. Start by giving the photographs titles, as if they all belong to the same album or archive; imagine you are recording a history. Make notes about the stories you come up with for each image. If you have some images of people, try to imagine who they are and what their lives might have been like. If you have postcards, try to imagine who is writing them and to whom. Think of why they might be writing, what would they ideally write, or how might they elaborate if they wanted to say more about what was really happening on their trip.

Once you have a reasonable amount of fictionalized writing, you can start to create an illustrated story combining the images with your text. You could do this in a notebook or digitally on your computer.

Once you have created your narrative, re-examine the photographs and try to find out as much as you can about where and when they were really made. You will need to look carefully at the architecture and costume: perhaps there is text on the back of the image that tells you the date and place the photograph was taken. Try to find a local museum or historian who can help trace the period or place. Through your research, you will start to build a more accurate story about the pictures/postcards.

You can also look at how museums use information alongside photographs and how this might narrate a history. Compare this practice with that of writers such as W.G. Sebald or Roma Tearne, who have used found photographs as part of fictional narratives.

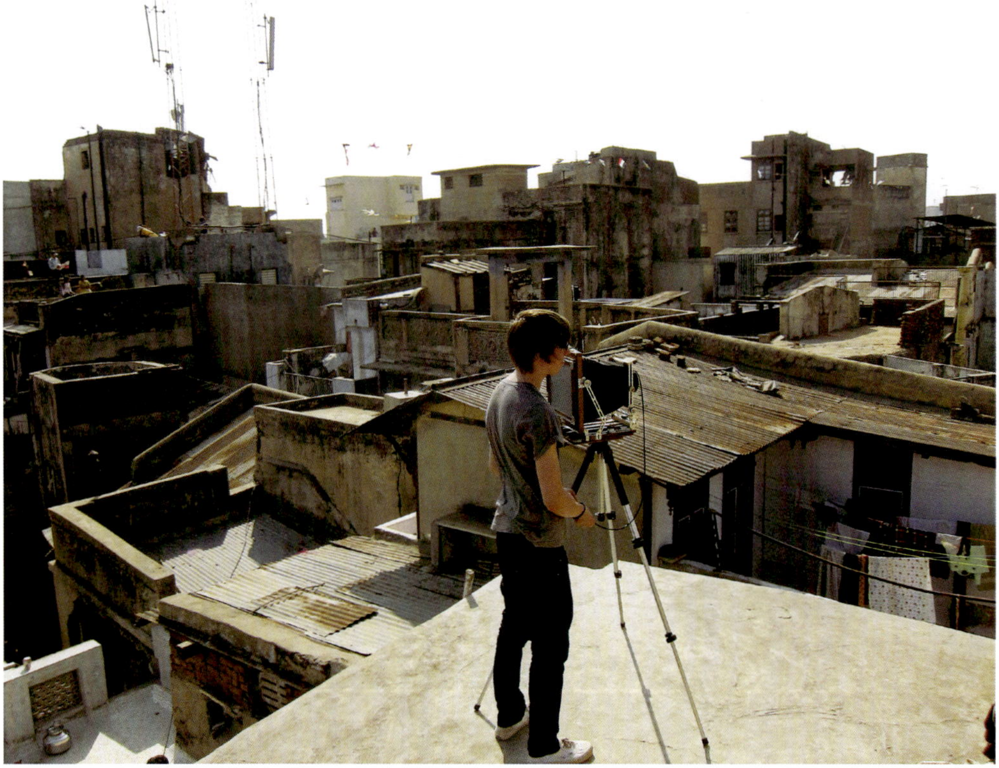

3.1

Title: Andrew Bruce at work in India

Artist: Andrew Bruce

Andrew Bruce is shown here working with his 10x8-inch camera looking at the landscape before looking through the camera. Taking landscape photographs in India pushed Bruce to work in a very different style and consider his working methods differently.

3 Practice as research – art-based photography

Practising photography, taking photographs, is a primary part of the research process. It is easy to casually shoot photographs and not record what you do, yet if you stop for a moment and consider the significance of how you are photographing – when, where, why, with which tools, and what assistance – it all starts to become part of an interesting research story.

Photographs are made through a process of exploring practical solutions. Photographers try out different cameras, lighting types, and times of day for shooting and examine how these factors affect the way the image is recorded. In the darkroom or the digital production suite, further experiments are conducted with colour, exposure, tone, joining images, changing contrast or adding special filtrations or processes that have a marked effect on the appearance of an image. Practice-based research runs through the whole process of making photographs.

Many photographers document what they do both for their own reference and for posterity. Seeing yourself working either in still photographs or on video can really make you think differently about what you are doing. Analysing results through looking back at different experiments helps you understand how you have arrived at the solution; critically reflecting on how you work contributes to the development of practice.

Ideas can come from anywhere and inspiration for new projects can strike at any time.

When photographer Jo Longhurst was looking to buy a pet whippet, she visited dog rescue centres and top breeders. She realized, through this experience, that the mysterious world of top breeders and show dogs would be fascinating to photograph, and she has spent many years producing work on this subject.

Your reasons for making a body of work will ultimately depend on what you want to achieve as a photographer and where your curiosity takes you.

Decide on a subject matter

Think about how you are going to explore your chosen subject matter. Many photographers will start with initial test images very early on in the project development. This provides a realistic visual image to work from: one that isn't coming from a preconceived assumption. Making images early on will get you in the rhythm of shooting and seeing your subject matter in a two-dimensional form. Test images can be shot on your mobile phone or a low resolution camera. At this stage, do not get distracted by feeling that the test images need to be of a high production value.

3.2

Title: Breed

Photographer: Jo Longhurst

Jo Longhurst has worked with whippets for nearly ten years. Her work explores the intimate relationship between human and dog and questions what it is to be human today.

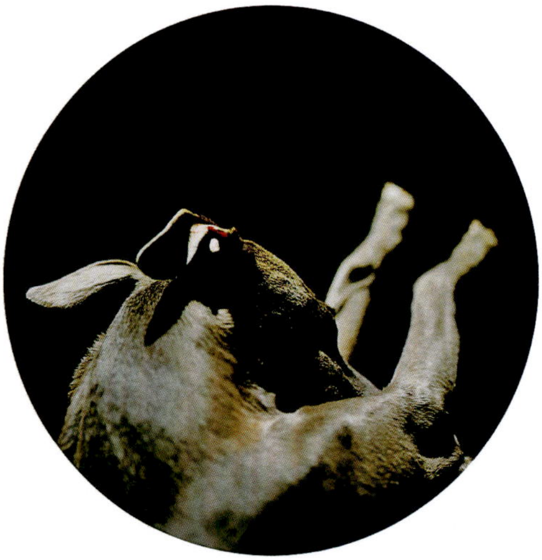

Shoot in the early stages

By shooting in the early stages of your project development, while you are still reading various texts and looking at other artists' work, you will begin to visually track your progress. As this process develops, it is possible to see how this type of practical research is informing the way you are recording your subject and constructing your image.

Making images early on will get you in the rhythm of shooting and seeing your subject matter in a two-dimensional form.

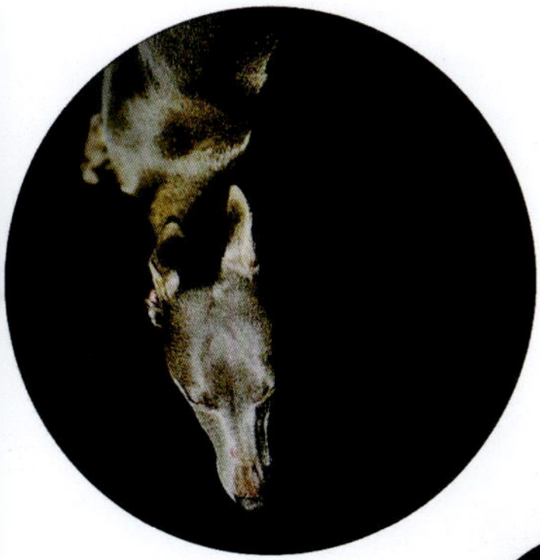

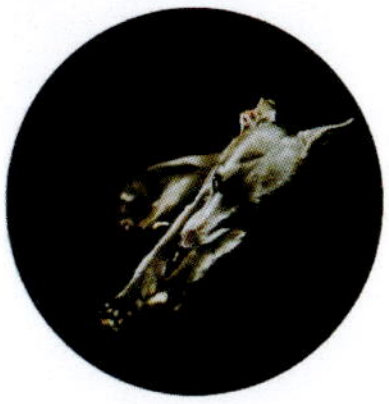

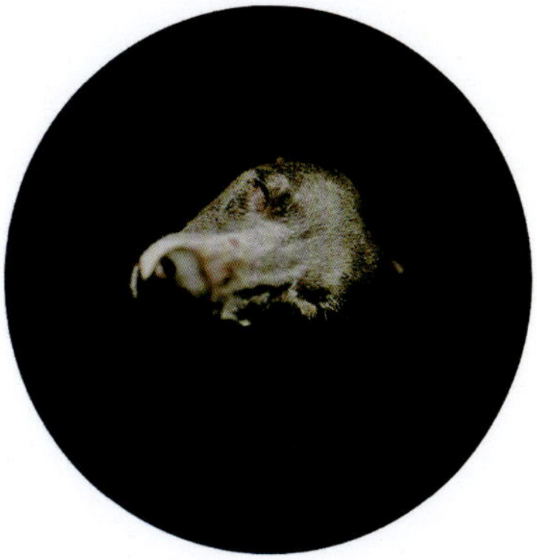

Guide the idea through

By guiding an idea through practical research processes, the photographer keeps pushing the possibilities and the boundaries of their original idea. After each shoot, a photographer will review their images and re-evaluate their approach to practice. Using fresh images as research, the photographer considers and reflects on how to improve what has been shot. As a practising photographer, things to consider include: what might happen if I shoot using a different camera format or different lighting? What would happen if images were taken from an alternative point of view?

Own images as research

By using your own images as research, you can map the practical process and use this to help decide where to go next with the project. When you write an essay, you don't start and finish with your first bullet points; photography is much the same – you need to shape and reshoot images in a similar way to drafting and then finalizing an essay.

Photographs as research

Recording the process of taking photographs provides you with lifelong documentation of your research.

You may need someone to help you document this: you and your peers can work together to record each other working.

From an outside point of view, photography may appear to be a lone profession. However, if you look into the history of how photographers work, you discover that many more people than just the photographer have been involved in making a project.

By using your own images as research, you can map the practical process and use this to help decide where to go next with the project.

3.3

Title: Evidence/Evidence Image 3

Artist: Diana Matar

This marks the entrance to an underground bunker in Gaddafi's Benghazi compound. Human rights workers found secret rooms, cells, and torture chambers within the bunker. One of Diana Matar's key artistic concerns is to photograph things that cannot be seen. The devastating forced disappearance of her father-in-law, a Libyan political dissident, impacted on Matar's thinking and approach to making work. In the series *Evidence/Evidence* Matar has photographed buildings where atrocoties have taken place under the Gaddafi regime. The buildings act as evidence for what has passed, and the act of photographing them is a metaphor for remembering not to forget. The image captions are a vital part of the work.

The studio is an important environment for the making of photographic work. Studio photographers create their photographs by adding and taking away light: they model their subjects with different types of light until they get the result they are looking for. Testing through shooting is a major part of studio practice, and the studio photographer will be totally familiar with all the different types of lighting available. Photography is 'light recorded', so being able to see light and understand how it will record is key to all photographic practices.

A studio can be any size, but the size will generally reflect the work that needs to be done. Table-top photography can be created in incredibly small spaces, such as on an ordinary flat table or an infinity table that creates an image which appears to float in space. You could even create a miniature studio with cardboard or wood. Some photographers decide to recreate the idea of a studio on location: by doing this, they make maximum use of available daylight.

A conventional indoor studio only gets daylight through its windows. Some studios have no windows and are entirely artificially lit. A photographer working in a studio with no daylight will have to think about the significance of light from the first moment of shooting.

Being able to see light and understand how it will record is key to all photographic practices.

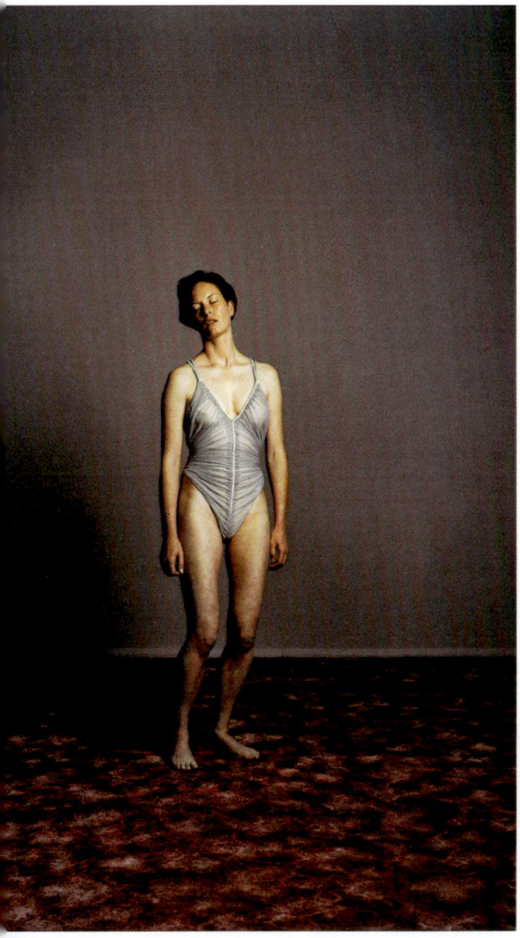

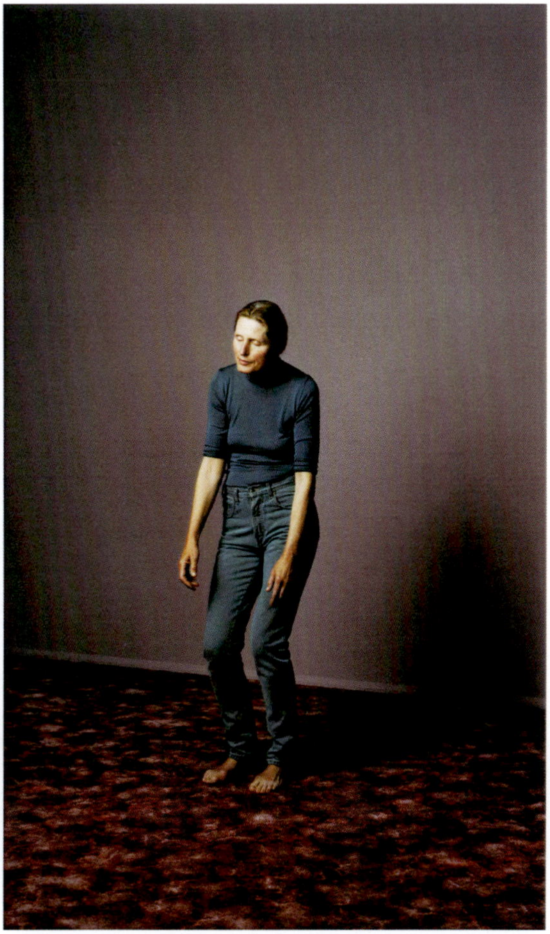

3.4

Title: Triptych: In Unheard Contradictions

Photographer: Anna Linderstam

When first looking at this triptych, it is not clear where it was taken: this ambiguity is created through Linderstam's construction of the studio space. She painted the walls of the studio and installed a large carpet. When the look was perfect, Linderstam had the models hold a single position for an extended period of time to explore the emotional, physical and psychological limits of the human body.

Studio work as part of the research process

A studio is a site of exploration: it is a space where images are constructed and built up over a period of time, while the photographer constantly reflects and tries out new approaches. There are unlimited possibilities in what can be achieved in the making of studio photography. It is overtly constructed, and a studio photographer may well spend days, or even weeks, working on the construction of images. As part of your research process, work in the studio and build in a series of experiments where you test different solutions to how the final image might look.

Lighting is crucial and there are different types of lighting that you can use, such as flashlight, tungsten light, or even a domestic light or torch light. Photographers will go through a series of tests before coming to a decision about the final construction of an image or series of images. The photographer also often applies one approach to the whole series so that there is a sense of continuity from start to finish.

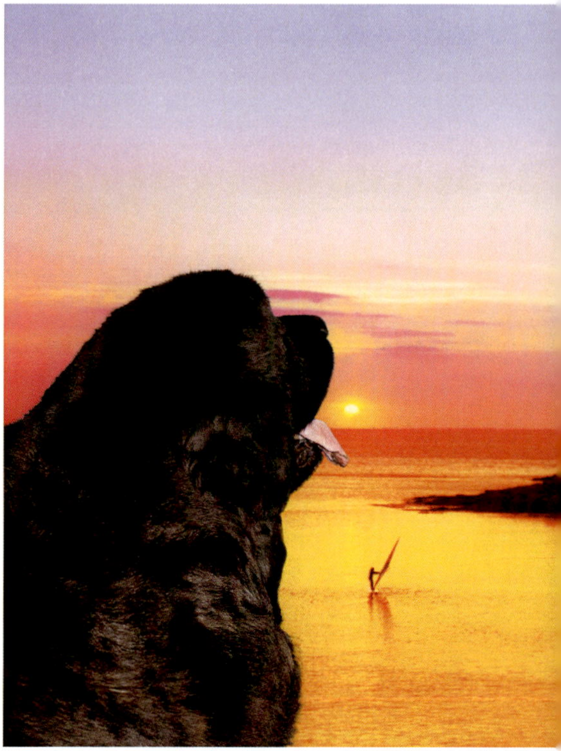

3.5

Title: Wild Style

Photographer: Mazaccio & Drowilal

These two French photographers work collaboratively making their own images as well as using found images and texts. The images in 'Wild Style' are immediately appealing and ambiguous; they are comically playful and point to the bizarre relationship we (in the western world) have to animals. The highly colourful parade of images that makes up this series allows for a merging of the real and the virtual, observing the strangeness of a modern world caught up in obsessive consumerism.

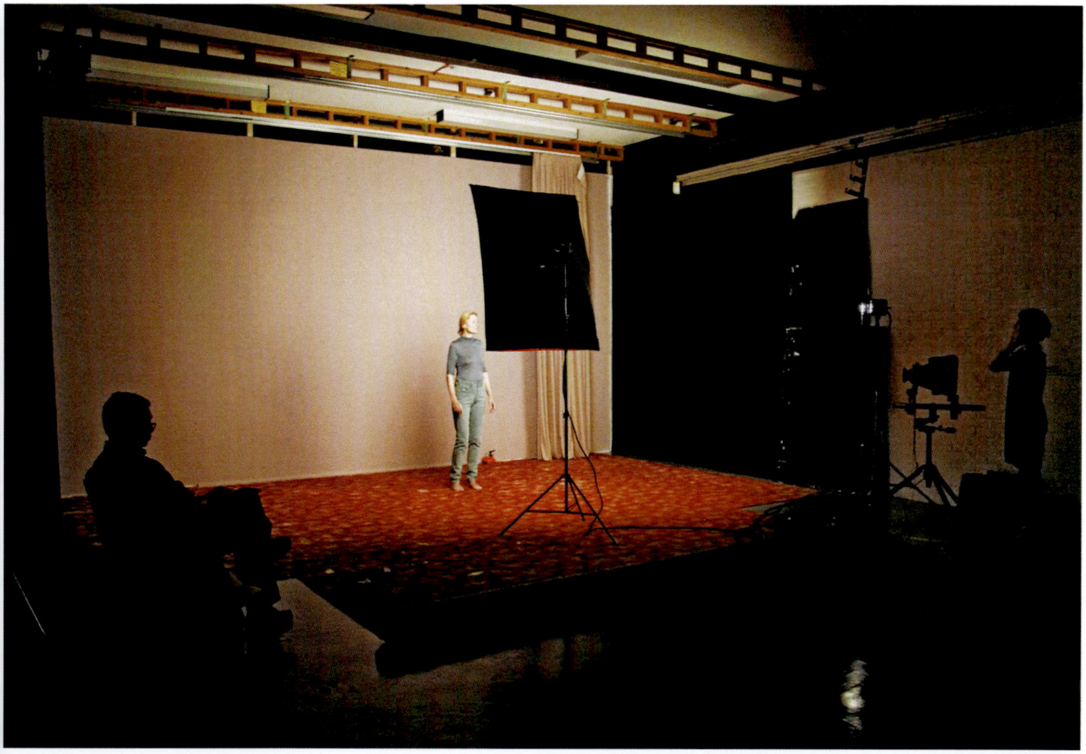

3.6

Title: The making of Anna Linderstam's *Triptych: In Unheard Contradictions*

Photographer: Anna Linderstam

This behind-the-scenes shot shows images for the triptych on the previous pages being made. The images were shot using a large format 10×8-inch camera. Powerful lighting was used and muted, using large softboxes. These create softer light and avoid harsh shadows.

As part of your research process, work in the studio and build in a series of experiments where you test different solutions to how the final image might look.

Street photographers have played a major role in the history of photography. The street is a completely different space from the studio, and compositions can emerge in an accidental manner. The photographer has to be ready to capture things that change very quickly. For instance, a cat might walk into the frame or a red car could speed past; this one extra slash of action or colour might be the making of a fantastic image. The street photographer has to be ready for moments to come out of nowhere and react quickly to capture them.

Subjects on the street

Working on the street, the photographer takes care of where they are and who they photograph. Photographing subjects you encounter on the street can be considered intrusive and raises a number of ethical, and even legal, considerations around privacy and permission. Laws relating to photographing people in public places vary across the world, so you should familiarize yourself with the laws where you are working. You may need to obtain written permission, in a model release form, to use a person's image.

Although some street photographers do not speak to their subject before taking the photograph, you may feel more comfortable working in collaboration with your subjects. This way, both the subject and photographer are involved in the creative process. There are different methods for doing this, and exploring these becomes part of your practical research.

3.7

Title: Untitled, from Basingstoke 1985/86

Photographer: Anna Fox

This image comes from a larger series about the town of Basingstoke, UK, in the mid-1980s. The photographer worked with a combination of quoted captions and photographs in order to create a strong sense of irony reflecting her concerns about the social environment.

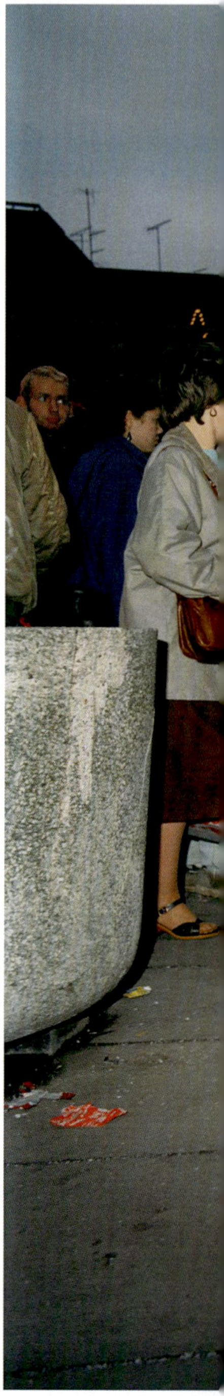

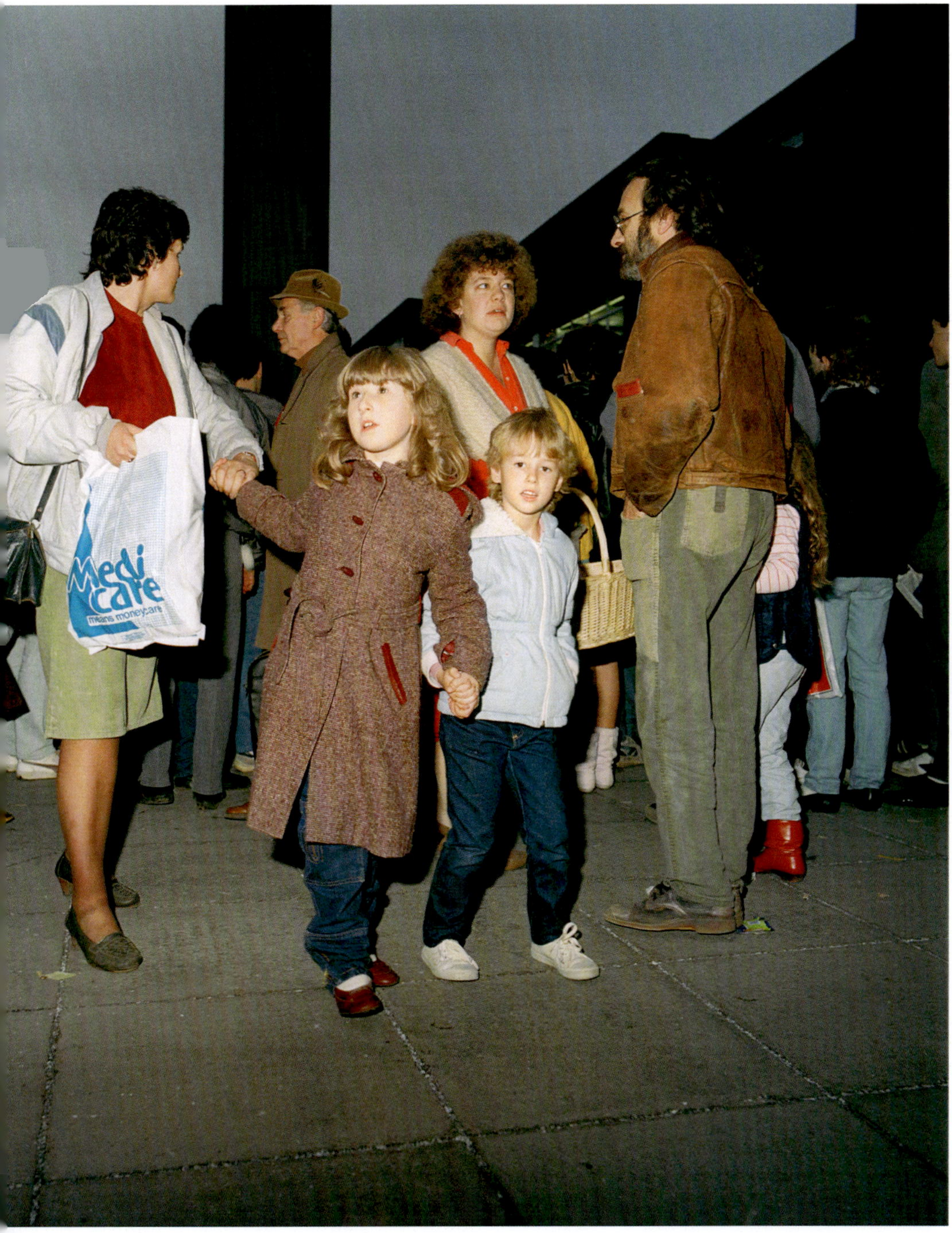
Medi care
means moneycare

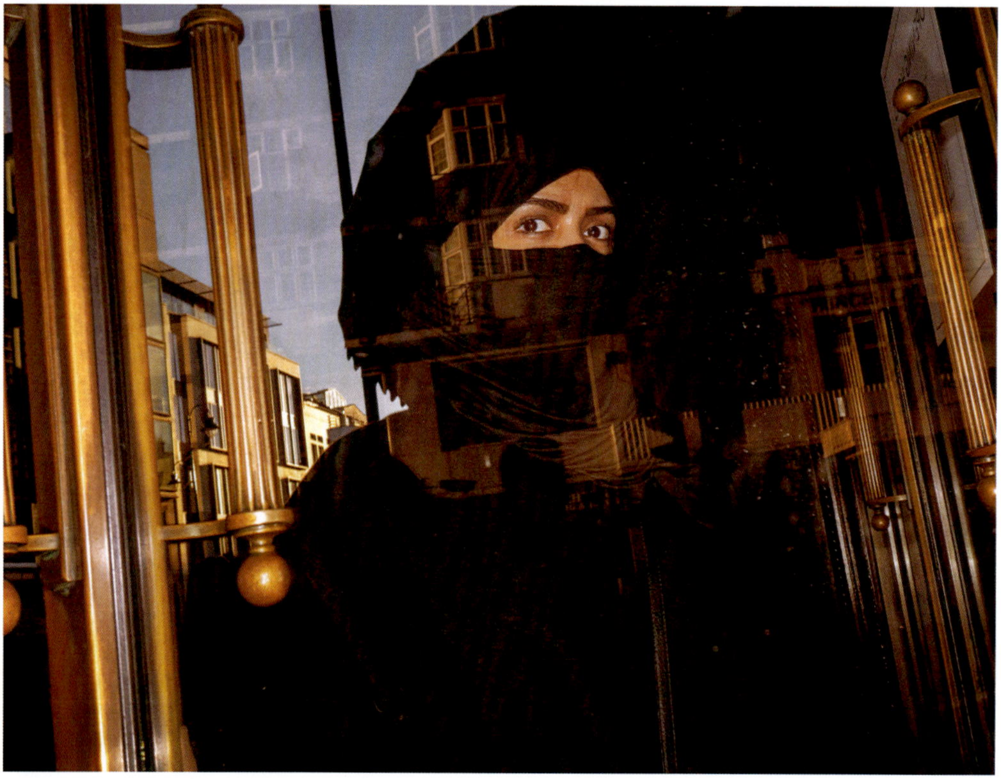

Available backgrounds

Street photography demands as much practise as any other kind of photography. It is important to learn how to observe the shapes, colours and lighting surrounding you so that the background in the photographs really works with the structure of the picture. It is worthwhile spending a set amount of time each day, at different times of day, observing changes in light and taking test shots so you start to see how the time of day affects the picture. The weather is also an important consideration: shoot all year round and don't avoid bad weather or low light; different conditions produce interesting photographs.

Visit potential locations in advance, practise what you are going to say when you approach possible subjects, and try out different points of view.

3.8

Title: from the series *Harrodsburg*

Photographer: Dougie Wallace

Windows (in this case) and mirrors are frequently used by photographers. In street photography, they add another layer to the image, like a filter, and the reflections captured create a more three-dimensional sense of the place. Sometimes, the photographer catches their own reflection in a mirror or window and the image becomes a self-portrait. Wallace's *Harrodsburg* project explores the super-rich classes of London in the regions of Knightsbridge and Chelsea.

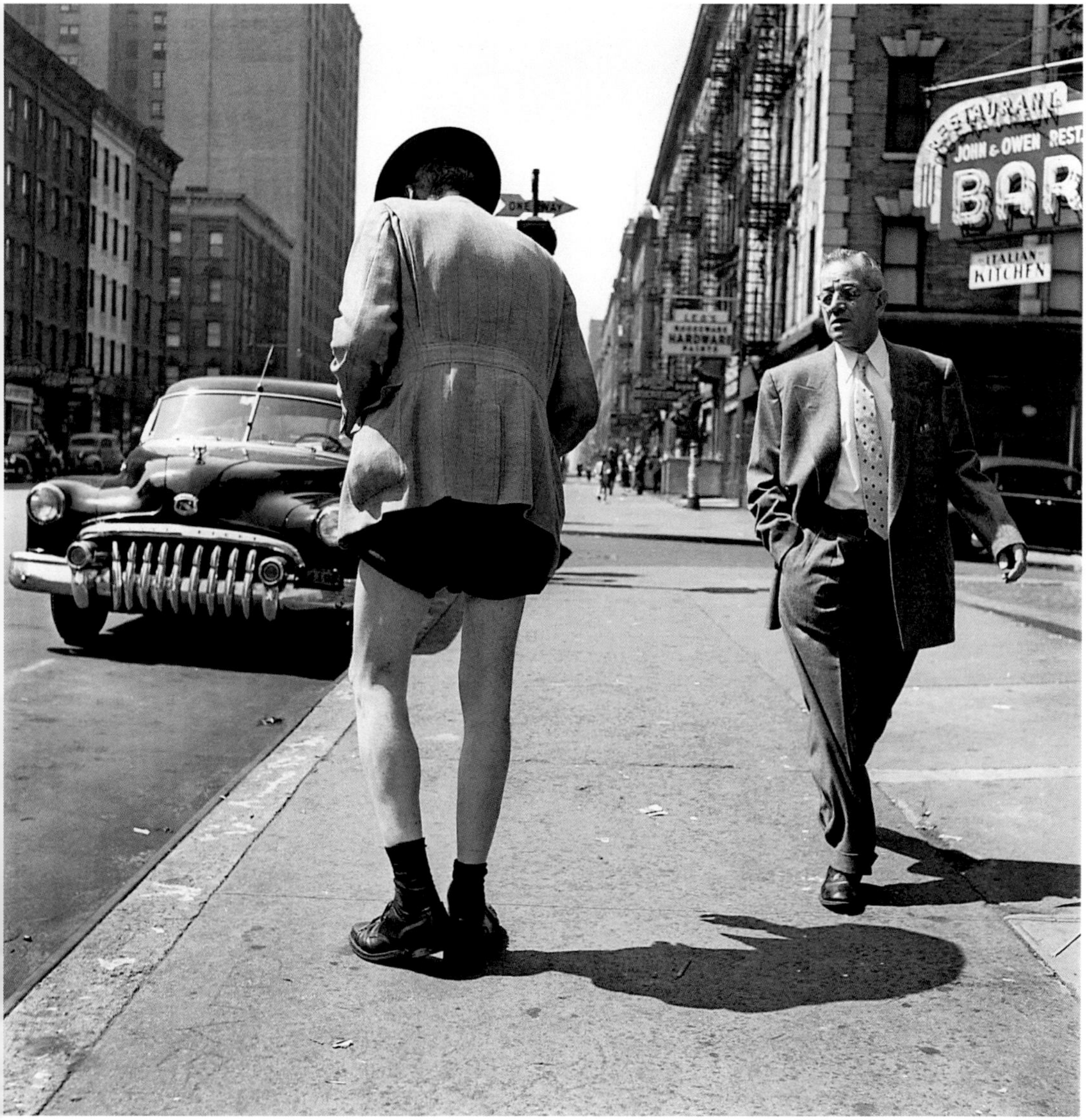

3.9

Title: Untitled, 1953

Photographer: Vivian Maier

Vivian Maier's work has only recently been discovered by an estate agent at a flea market. Maier, who for the most part of her life was a nanny, obsessively photographed in the streets of New York and Chicago. She died shortly before her work was exposed to the world.

Equipment

It is possible to use portable, small-scale flash lighting, or torch light, on the street. This can be alarming to the passer-by, so the photographer with a flashgun is likely to talk to their subjects after the shot has been taken. Some photographers relish the shock effect of the flash and the expressions this produces on the faces of their subjects. Other street photographers do not feel comfortable with this rather bold approach!

Much street photography is shot on 35mm equipment but trying out other formats can dramatically change the look of the image. Street photographers can employ assistants to help them shoot. This is most useful when heavy, large-format equipment or lighting is being used. An assistant can also be useful to help guard the photographer and their valuable equipment in a busy street.

3.10

Title: Assisted Self-Portrait of Charmian Edge

Artist: Charmian Edge/Anthony Luvera

Anthony Luvera has made a vast body of work concerned with portraying people who live predominantly on the street. He titles the work 'Assisted Self-Portrait', reflecting the way the photograph was taken. It is a collaboration between the artist and his subjects. Luvera aims to give his subjects an equal right to representation: he gets to know them; he explains why he is doing the work; they try out different poses; and then, when they are both satisfied, the subject presses the button to take the picture with a cable release.

A change of perspective

The street photographer has to learn to think in a different way from a studio photographer. In the studio you have more control, with time to make plans, to build up lighting, and to test it.

In the street there is more pressure to shoot quickly and you may need to shoot a large amount of material before you get the result you are looking for.

Try photographing your subject from different angles, changing the background as you move around. If you only shoot from one perspective, you will not be able to see the way an image changes when the point of view is altered.

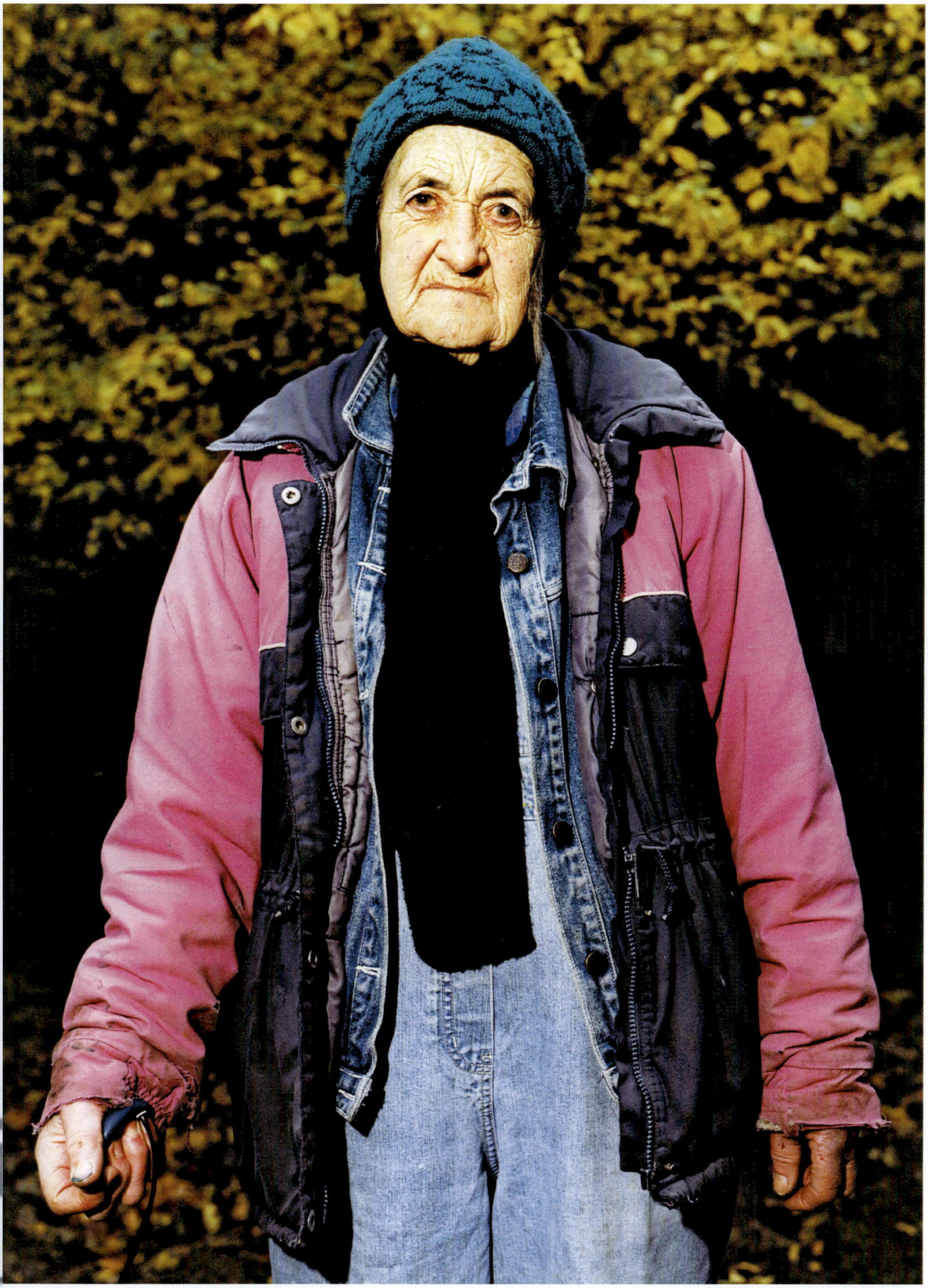

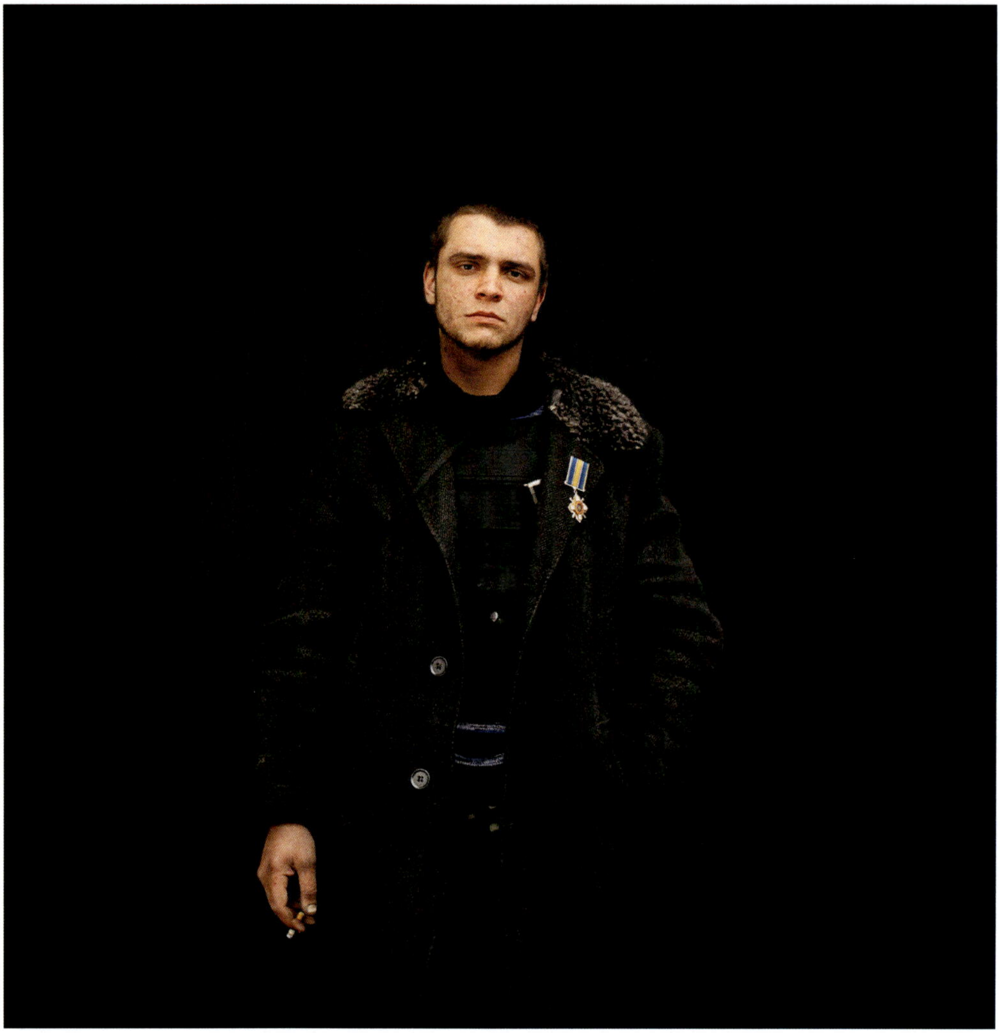

3.11

Title: from *Maidan – Portraits from the Black Square*

Photographer: Anastasia Taylor-Lind

These two images come from a series of portraits of anti-government protestors and mourners made in a makeshift photographic studio in Maidan Nezalezhnosti (Independence Square), Kiev, during February 2014.

The portraits have been uniformly shot against the black backdrop of Taylor-Lind's improvised studio, removing them from the context of the barricades just a few feet away. The 'fighters' are identified by their homemade body armour, and the 'mourners' by the bunches of flowers they have brought to pay their respects to the dead. Captured with an air of stillness and reflection, these photographs show the individuals involved in, and impacted by, the unrest.

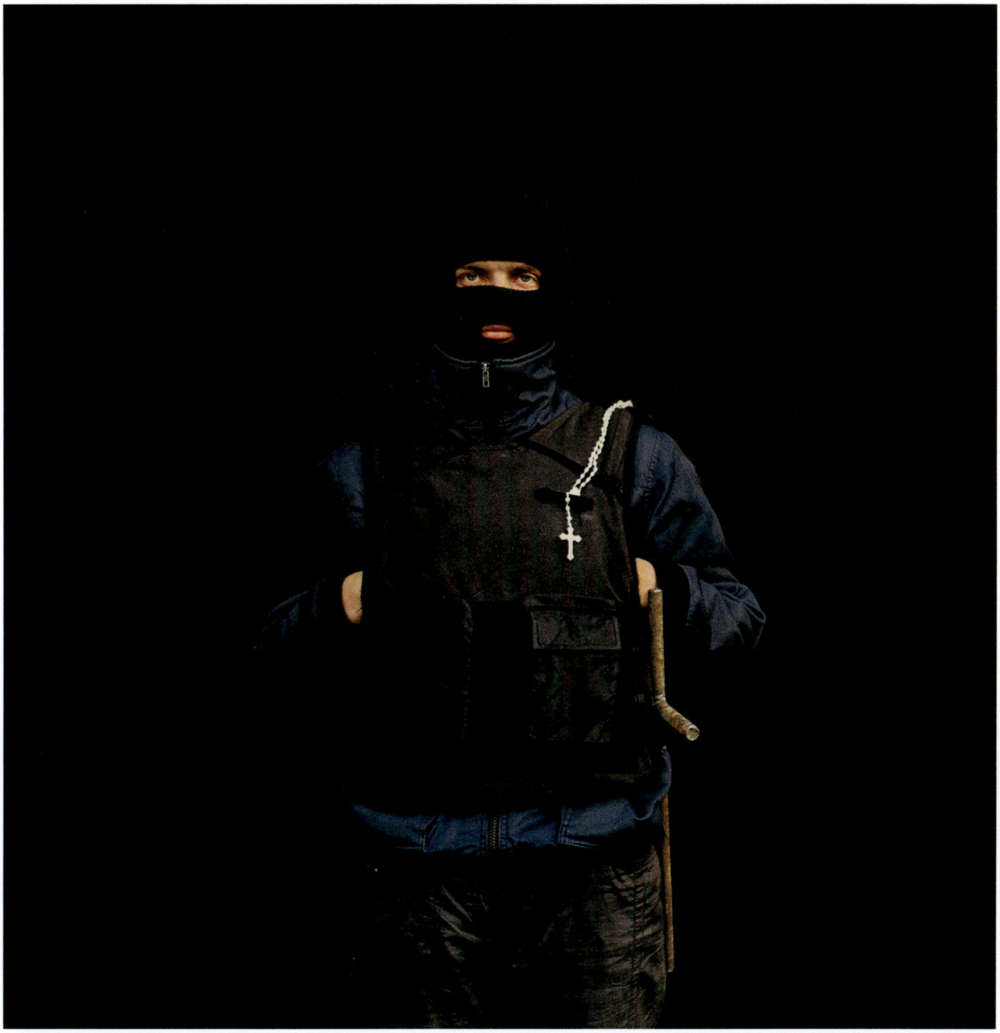

3.11

The field in which a photographer works is referred to as a particular genre or style. A genre of photography is essentially a type, such as landscape or documentary. Some photographers work in one genre for the whole of their career, while others will move between different genres. Within each genre there can be numerous different styles of working. An aerial landscape photograph looks completely different from a landscape photograph shot by someone working on the ground: these are different styles within the genre of landscape photography.

The land

Like most photographic genres, landscape photography comes in many guises. A landscape may have a documentary intention, observing social, historical, and economic change; be part of a campaign to protect the environment; or be concerned with beauty and the sublime.

The process in landscape photography is likely to be slower than, for example, street photography. Taking test shots and observing how a place looks from different viewpoints at different times forms an interesting part of the practical research for this genre. The landscape photographer may consider where shadows will fall, how the sky looks, and/or what happens to the light in different seasons. For example, in the UK, distinctive golden morning light tends to appear during the winter only.

If you are using colour film, the colour temperature changes at different times of the day and year: this affects the tone of the final work. Images can appear blue or yellow in colour or have a high/low contrast in black and white; colour temperature and lighting conditions often create these effects. Many landscape photographers will use medium- to large-format cameras to record their image in fine detail and enable them to retain this detail in large-scale prints.

Nature and the rural landscape have been fascinating for both amateur and professional photographers since the invention of the camera. Many questions have been posed about the tendency to romanticize the landscape through photography (and other art forms); these are interesting debates and familiarizing yourself with them will contribute to your research process.

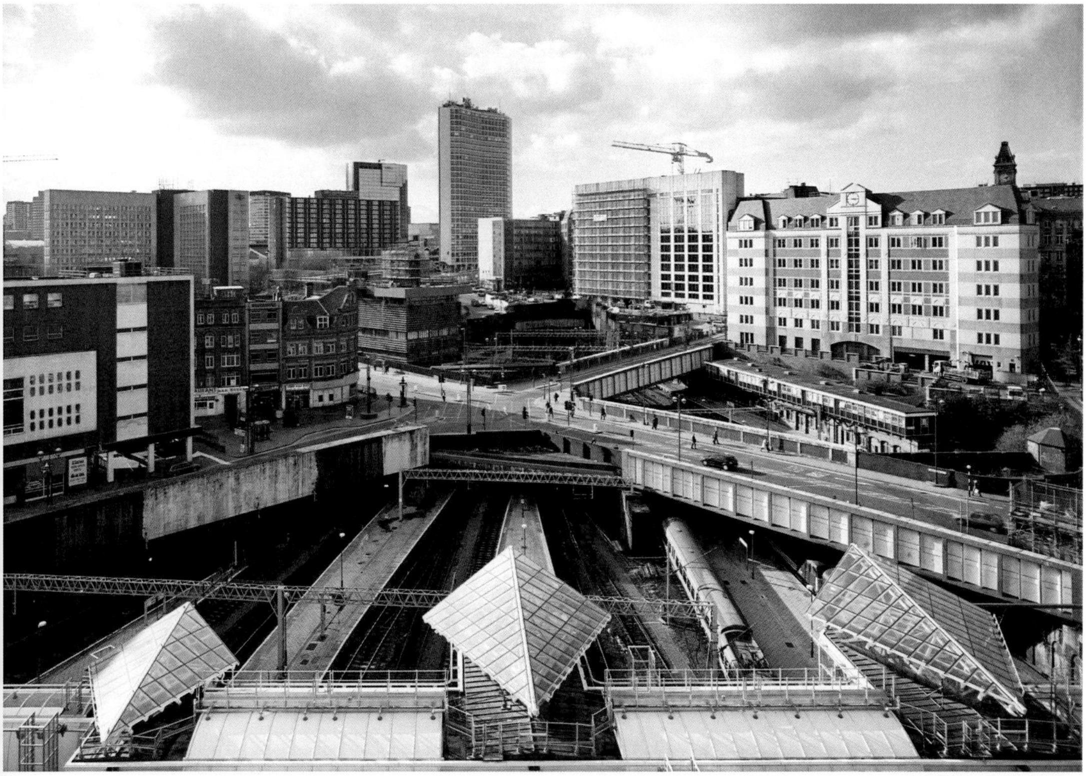

3.12

Title: New Street Station, Birmingham, UK

Photographer: John Davies

John Davies, a landscape photographer, is well known for his extensive documentation of the British urban environment. He frequently takes his photographs from high viewpoints, revealing the territory almost as if it is a map. The Birmingham photographs are from Davies' project *Metropoli*, which documented the changing face of the post-industrial cityscape in the UK.

Documentary and reportage photography

Documentary photography is popularly understood as a story told by a photographer about an event, person or place. It has sometimes been misrepresented as a genre that simply records events and represents the real world. In the last 30 years, the use of the term and understanding of the genre has expanded greatly. Documentary photography is now found in many different places, including in photographers' monographs, on gallery walls and in magazines. Today's documentary photography can be complex and multi-layered and often demands time, on the part of the viewer, to digest its meanings.

Reportage photography, or photojournalism, generally reports on significant, newsworthy events, people and places. Reportage stories are regularly found in magazines, newspapers, books, on the Web, and sometimes on gallery walls – notably at the annual World Press Exhibition. Photojournalists aim to communicate the significance of their stories as clearly and powerfully as possible. Their photographs have often provided disturbing evidence of world events, and information about lives outside of our own. It is important to remember that both reportage and documentary photographs are mediated by the ideas of their producers and also by the agencies that represent the photographers or by the curators and editors who direct exhibitions and magazine page layouts. All of these people influence the selection of images for a series and the context that it finally appears in.

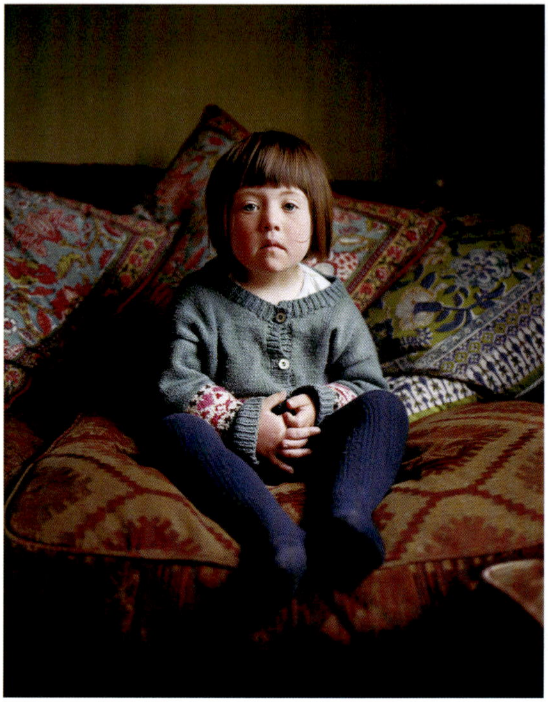

3.13

Documentary photographers and photojournalists may specialize in a particular subject or region, and they may work on a story for many years, being sure to research and investigate as many aspects of it as they can. They need to be well informed in order to negotiate the access they require and to shoot in an informed manner. Arts-based documentary practice has scope to be more complex in terms of its narrative and often deals with subjects in a more subtle manner.

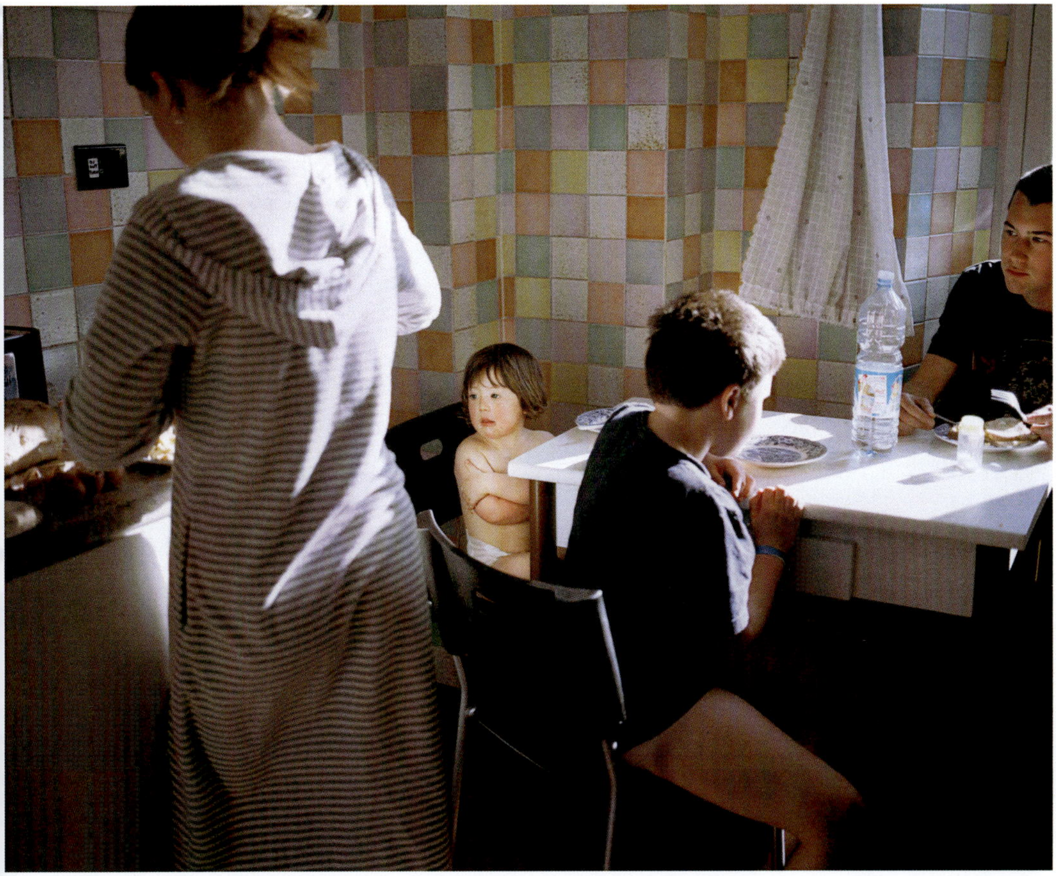

3.13

Title: from *Looking for Alice*

Photographer: Sian Davey

This body of work is about Sian Davey's daughter Alice and her family. Its story is centred around Alice, who has Down Syndrome. The everyday feel of the work lends it power: this could be any of our lives, and the subjects are treated with dignity and love. How photographs are made affects the way stories are understood: the very ordinariness and intimacy of these images allows us to relate closely to the people in the images, giving them a normalcy that becomes part of the message of the work.

Art practice

Art practice in photography is one of the most difficult types of photography to define; it is an incredibly broad category that could potentially include many different ways of working. There are numerous junctions where both the history of art and the history of photography meet or cross over. *The Photograph as Contemporary Art* (2009), written by Charlotte Cotton, gives an overview of photography that, today, is considered to be art.

Some people who work with photography as their prime medium define themselves as artists; this is generally because they want their work to be seen within an art history context, which influences the way it is interpreted. There are also artists who use photography (alongside other media) when it is appropriate for a certain project. For example, the artist Gillian Wearing works with video and photography alongside other media, while Rachel Whiteread, who is best known as a sculptor, has also made photographic work.

There are also artists who employ photographers to execute an idea; an artist might do this if they want a particular look to the work that only a skilled photographer can achieve or because the act of employing the photographer is a vital part of the conceptual process. In this case, the artist is operating like an art director or like the director on a movie set. In some cases artists have deliberately ignored both the technical and craft-based aspects of photography, instead embracing a vernacular approach, using a snapshot style to produce their work; again, this act will be purposeful and connected to the intended meaning of the work.

3.14

Title: 'Agnieszka' from *One Month*

Photographer: Maria Kapajeva

Maria Kapajeva made a series of before-and-after photographs during a trip to the National Institute of Design in India in 2009. She travelled with a group of students and photographed them all when they arrived, then again when they were about to leave. The resulting diptychs pose questions about identity and its relationship to time, travel and experience.

3.15

Title: Beyond the View 5

Artist: Helen Sear

Helen Sear is an example of an artist who uses photography. She has a fine art background in painting and sculpture and has also used performance and film in her work. Her series, *Beyond the View*, explores her interest in the relationships between culture and nature, and the notion of the body in the landscape, using digital layering and drawing to create striking images.

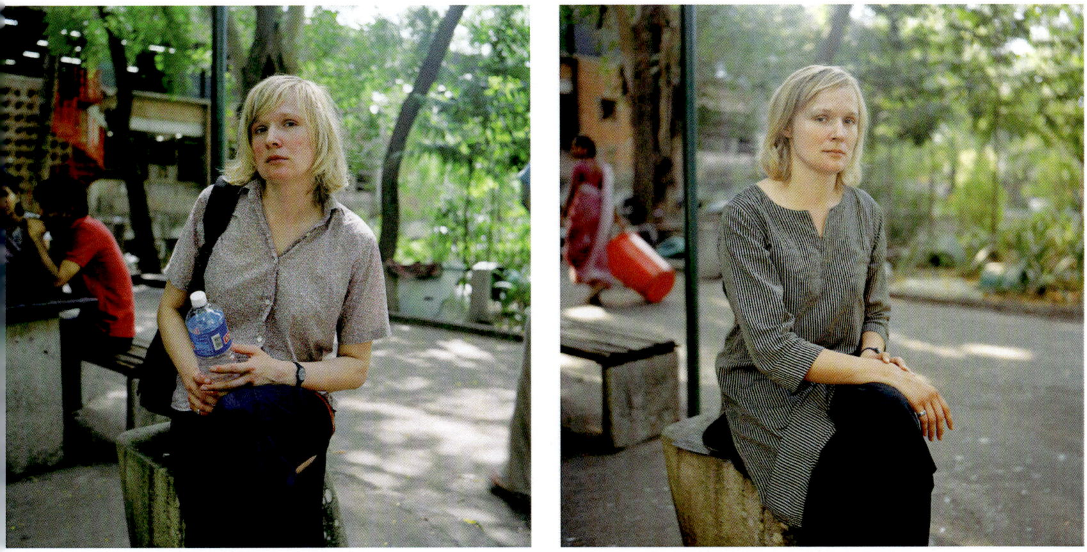

3.14

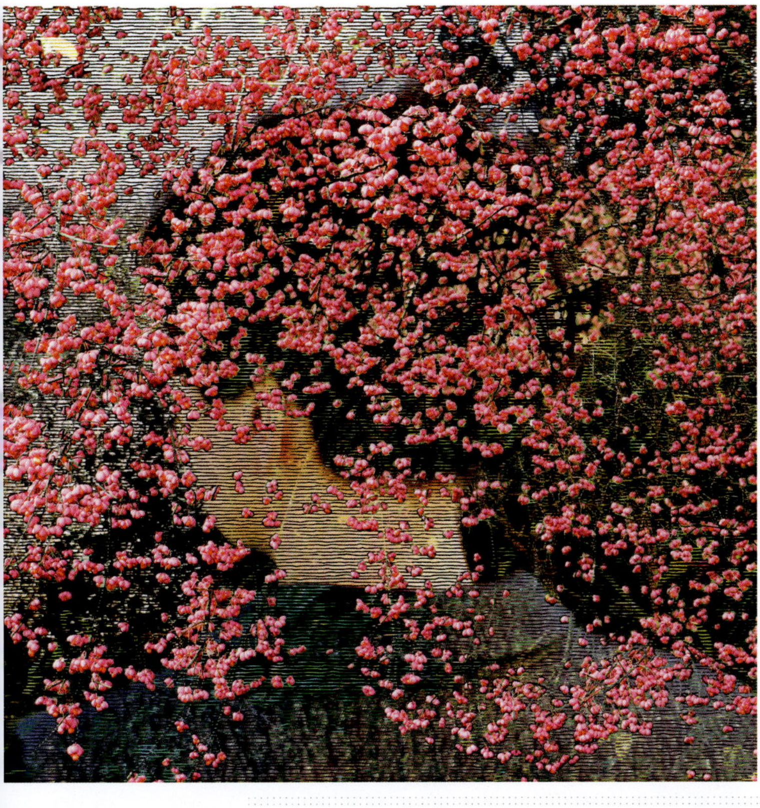

3.15

Technique, medium and style

Photography can be studied from many different perspectives: artistic, scientific, historical, theoretical, craft-based or philosophical. By looking at various genres of photography, we are concentrating primarily on the field of visual arts, crafts and media. As well as thinking about and testing out a particular genre to work within, it is interesting to explore the various technical aspects of photography.

The camera itself provides multiple possibilities for the ways in which a photographer can take photographs. Aperture, shutter speed, and camera type all affect the nature of the photograph produced. It is valuable to explore all aspects of the camera as part of the practical research process, as well as testing how your photographs work in different formats. The difference between shooting on 35mm and 10x8-inch film, equally the difference between a low resolution digital camera and a high-end digital product such as the latest Hasselblad HX1D II 50C, is vast, with the results being most acutely noticed when large-scale prints are produced for exhibition. The choice of aperture and shutter speed affect the look of an image; the depth of focus, the detail, and the exposure of an image can all radically change the impression created.

Photographers experiment with different types of film or different digital presets to find out which best suits the work they are making. Each make of film or digital preset has a distinct appearance when printed: one colour film may produce much warmer results than another. ISO ratings (film speed) also affect the resulting image: slower film has a finer grain, and will produce clearer detail in the print, whereas fast films often produce grainy results. You can also experiment with over- and under-exposure, as well as over- and under-developing (film) when processing.

When testing films, profiles and cameras you should keep detailed notes on what you have done, so that when the photographs are printed you will have a record of how they can be recreated. Bring the prints and the technical shooting notes together in your research documentation in order to archive the findings of your exploration.

When testing films and cameras, you should keep detailed notes on what you have done, so that when the photographs are printed you will have a record of how they can be recreated.

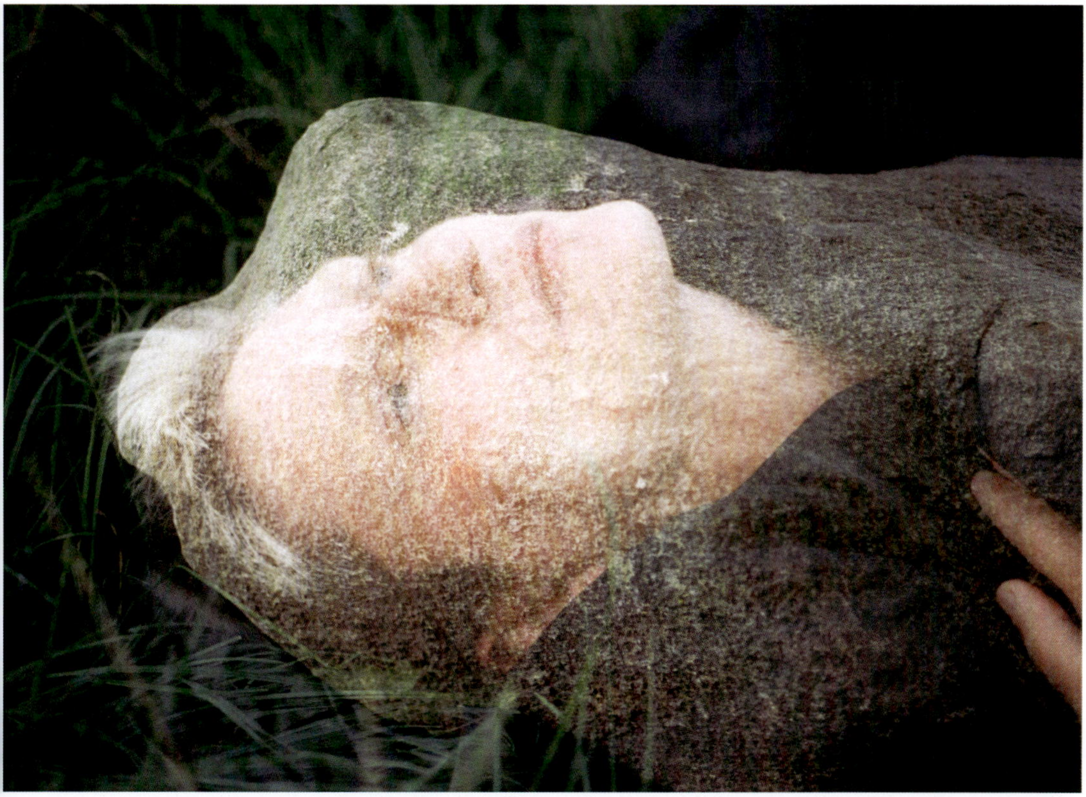

3.16

Title: Double exposure

Photographer: Taro Zaine

Double exposure can be used in a planned way, but it is always difficult to predict what will happen – and that is part of the excitement. This double exposure, by Taro Zaine, superimposes the sitter directly into nature creating an eerie portrait as the end result. The double exposure is used here to create a disorientating scene, referencing death masks and Victorian mourning portraiture. The series was created with Camilla Watson during a collaborative session as part of a Work-Show-Grow workshop aimed at interrogating the idea of a murdered sweetheart.

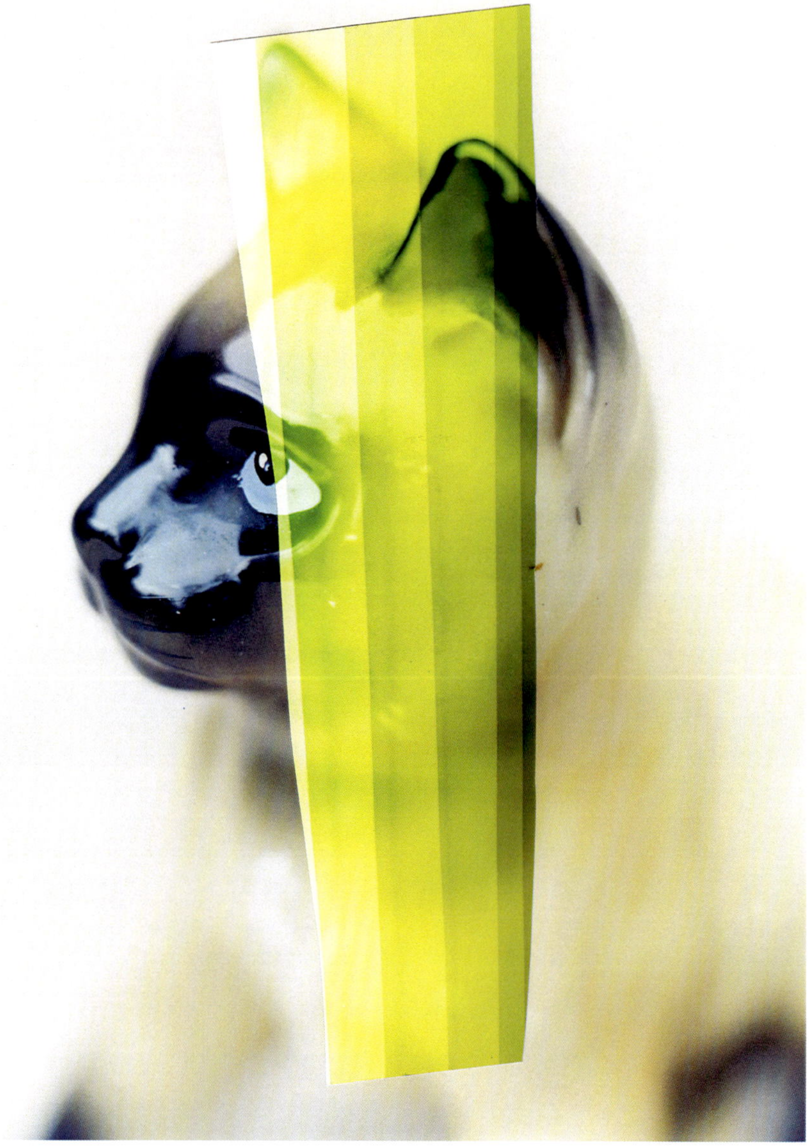

3.17

Title: Cat (Cyan 0, Yellow 60, Magenta 81), from *The Chase*

Artist: Dean Hollowood

Dean Hollowood's series, *The Chase*, was produced through experimentation with colour, tone and the layering of photographic paper in the darkroom. The positioning and exposure record of each test strip cannot be reproduced, so each image provides a new expression of the subtle variations in conditions that gave rise to it. Using an element of chance to create this work contrasts with the controlled predictability of digital methods.

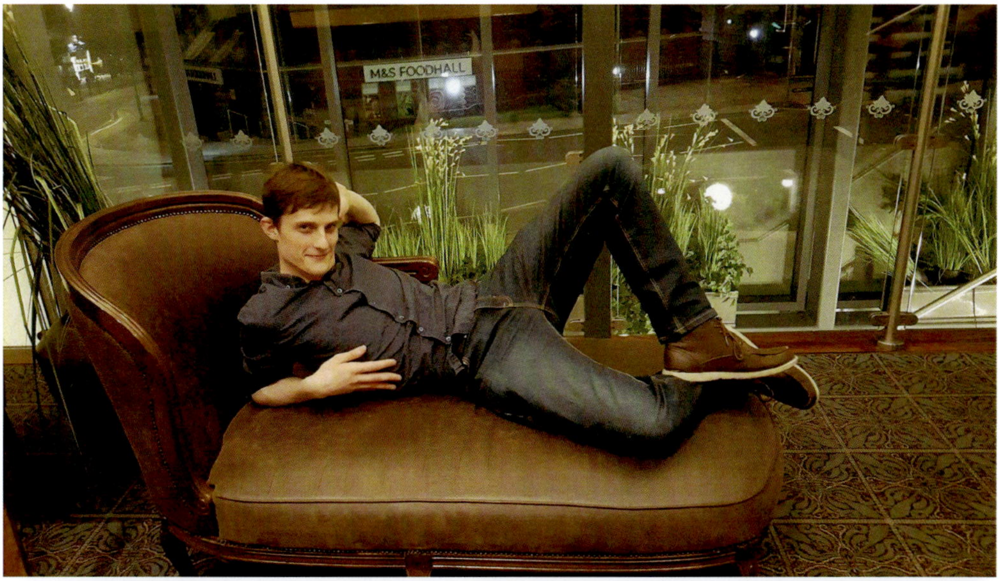

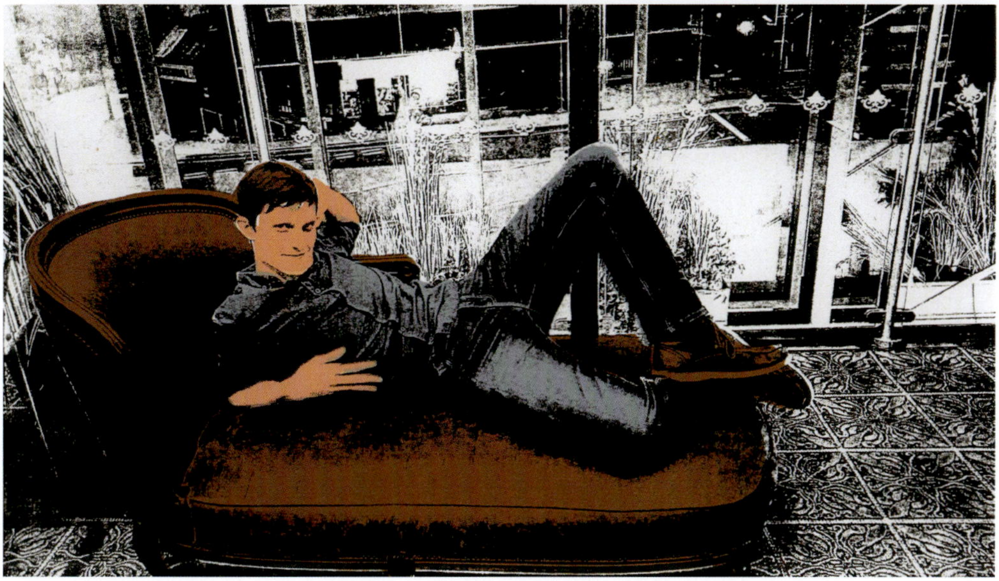

3.18

Title: Portrait of Rhys

Illustrator: Louis Fox

An art student transforms his photograph of a young man into a print through the screenprinting process. Louis Fox has been able to select parts of the image to add colour to, and through the sharp outlines of the figure and environment, he has added drama to an image that was quite a flat and less interesting photograph.

Any work done to alter a photograph after it has been taken falls under the term 'post-production'. Post-production can be conducted in an analogue darkroom or in a digital production suite, with adjustments being made to alter the look of the image and ultimately affect the way it is seen and understood.

In analogue photography this process starts with the development of the film: photographers can alter the way a film is developed to change the look of the resulting photographs. When working digitally, this can be done using a post-production program. During the printing stages of both analogue and digital photography, numerous changes and adjustments can be made.

The darkroom

Taking photographs at the start of a project is like executing the preliminary sketches for a body of work. Post-production work in the darkroom represents the later stages of this process where you finalize the look of a print or a whole body of work. There are endless possibilities in the analogue darkroom; testing different output techniques can transform an image.

Commercial analogue darkrooms are closing at a dramatic rate. In 2006, there were more than 200 darkrooms run by printers in London, but by 2011 there were only six left. It is still possible to set up your own black-and-white darkroom at a small cost and with little space.

Getting lost in the quiet and stillness of a darkroom is an exciting and enriching experience. To get an idea of the numerous printing techniques possible in the darkroom, it is well worth reading one of the excellent photography manuals, such as *Langford's Basic Photography* (2015; 10th edition). Michael Langford's *The Darkroom Handbook* (1990), gives you more detail on what to do in the darkroom.

There are endless possibilities in the analogue darkroom; testing different output techniques can transform an image.

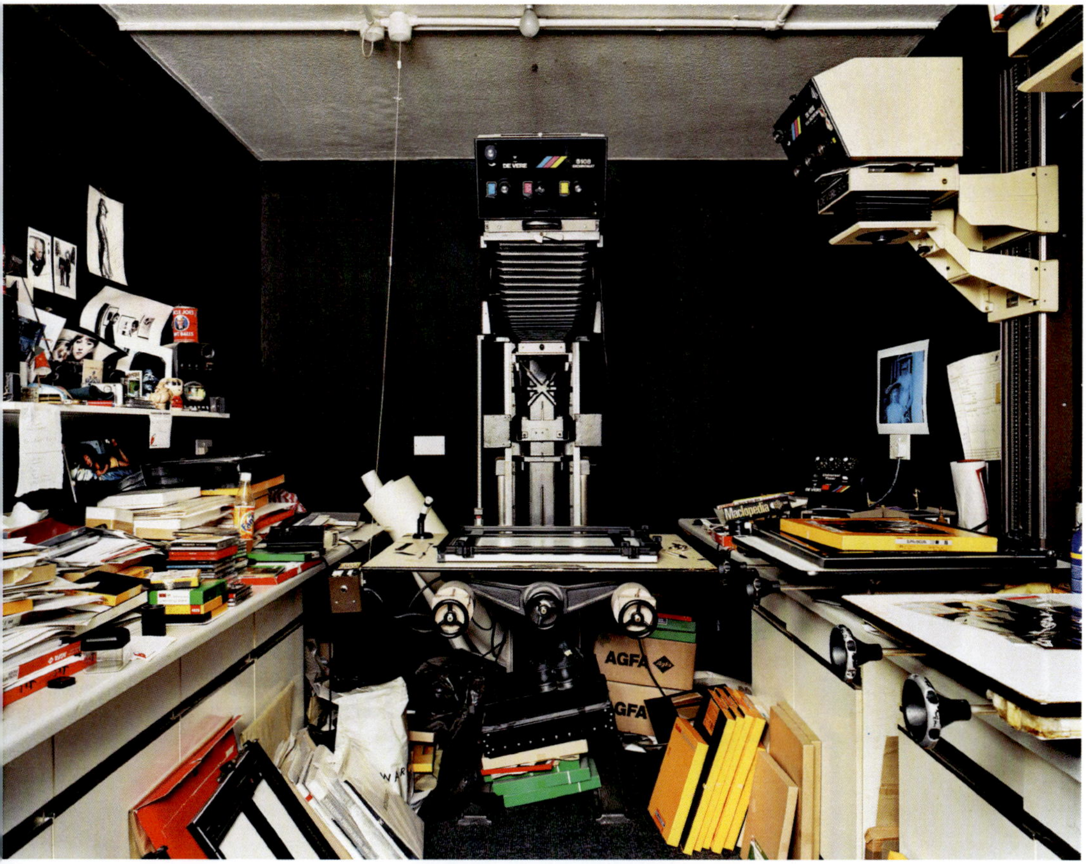

3.19

Title: 'Brian Dowling, BDI', 2006, from *Last One Out, Please Turn On The Light*

Photographer: Richard Nicholson

In Richard Nicholson's series of colour photographs of London darkrooms, he observes and records the slow disappearance of analogue production spaces. By photographing the darkrooms before they become redundant, he has created a valuable archive.

The images' vivid aesthetic is created by shooting with large-format film in pitch black, lit by a series of continuous flashes, which were made by moving carefully around the space with a hand-held flash gun.

Toning images

You may wish to tone or solarize an image as part of your post-production work. How will this affect the reading of the image? Test it out and ask people. Experimenting with toning can lead to a new and exciting end result. Toning can be achieved both in the darkroom or digitally.

Toning affects images in different ways. Sepia toning browns the image, making it appear aged, whereas selenium toning brings out the metallic silvers, therefore increasing the depth of tone in the blacks and whites of the photograph. Selenium toning is now prohibited in most colleges; if you do have access to it, instructions should be followed with great care.

3.20

Title: An Angel Appears

Artist: Richard Sawdon Smith

Many of Richard Sawdon Smith's photographs are created by experimenting in the darkroom with different printing processes and toning techniques. Influenced by the photographer Joel-Peter Witkin, he is not afraid to interfere with negatives – cutting them up, scratching the negatives to make black marks, building up texture or ageing the look of the images. The choice of models, backdrops, and hanging fabrics and the use of the toned black-and-white images with the various effects are all part of the process to create contemporary images that remain timeless.

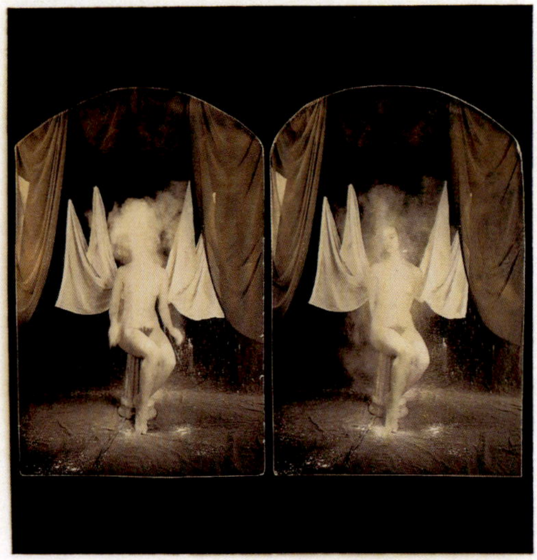

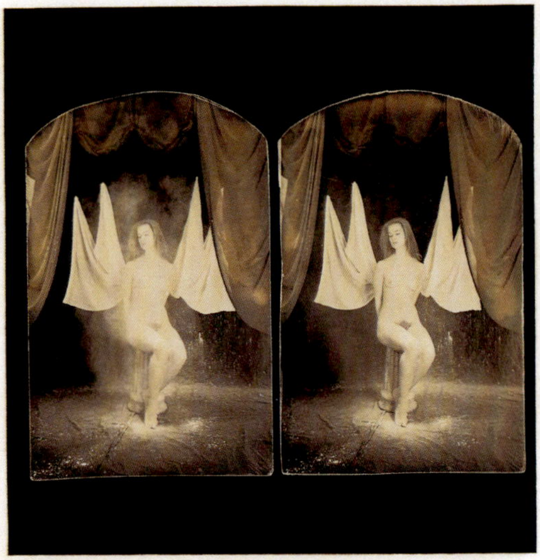

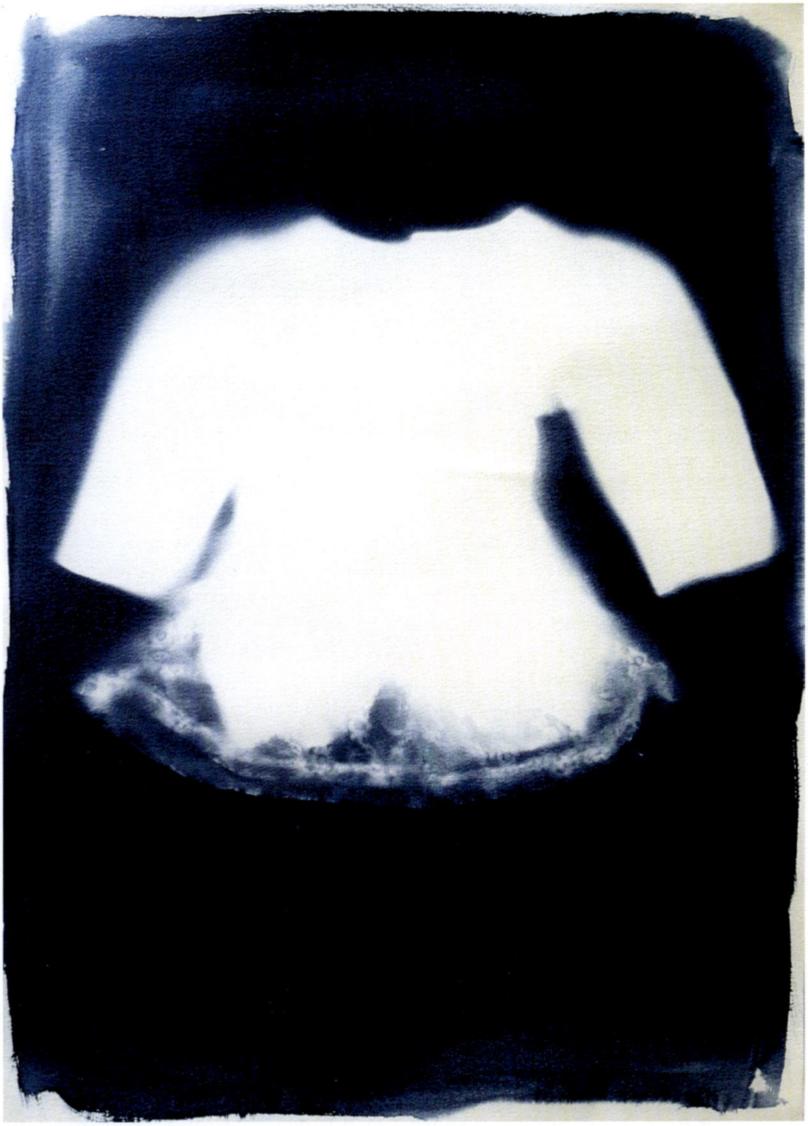

3.21

Title: Little Black Dress

Artist: Joy Gregory

This image is from Joy Gregory's series *Girl Thing*, for which she produced cyanotypes—an old photographic printing process that results in a cyan-coloured print. Cyanotypes were used by engineers from the early 20th century to produce large-scale copies of their work, called blueprints. The artist uses the process to explore gender construction through the association between an object and a 'feminine' description.

Digital post-production

Digital post-production is a key part of the contemporary photographic environment. Many photographers who shoot on film choose to scan and print their images digitally, allowing them to benefit from all the possibilities of digital post production.

A new wave of photographic approaches has come out of the innovative knowledge gained through digital experimentation. Images can be created and manipulated through various means: by digitally joining negatives, adding and taking away whole elements, replacing one thing with another, montaging different images together and simply experimenting with a whole range of digital effects. The digital post-production suite is a place where the most elaborate illusions can be constructed. There has never been a time where the blending of fact and fiction has been so potent and seamless.

Your early explorations in the digital suite will illustrate the huge number of possible outcomes; it is easy to get carried away and to 'over-do' digital effects. Try everything out in the various digital programs and then consider what meaning the altered image might have. If the digital effect or combination of effects dominates the image, it can take something away from the intention of the work. Tests can be collated in your research archive or workbook, and an analysis of these will help you decide what you should do and which program to use.

3.22

Title: *Flight to Freedom*, from India Song

Photographer: Karen Knorr

Karen Knorr created this image by digitally joining two photographs. We are easily convinced by the illusion that a white crane is walking through the palace. Knorr's work is concerned with the position of Indian women in society and with feminine subjectivity. The way birds and animals appear in this series, combined with the captions and titles, creates a sense of containment, domestication and desire to escape.

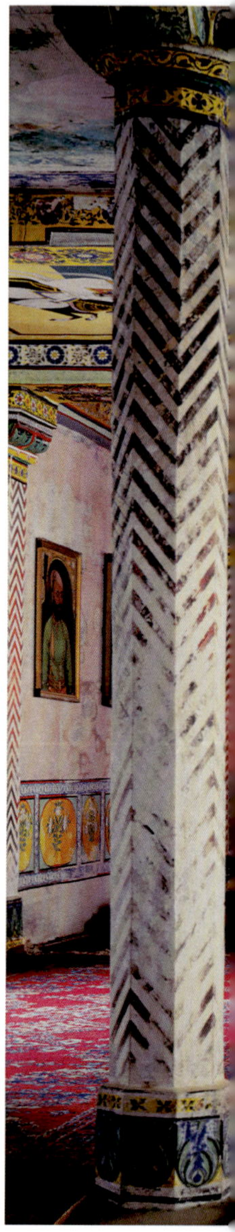

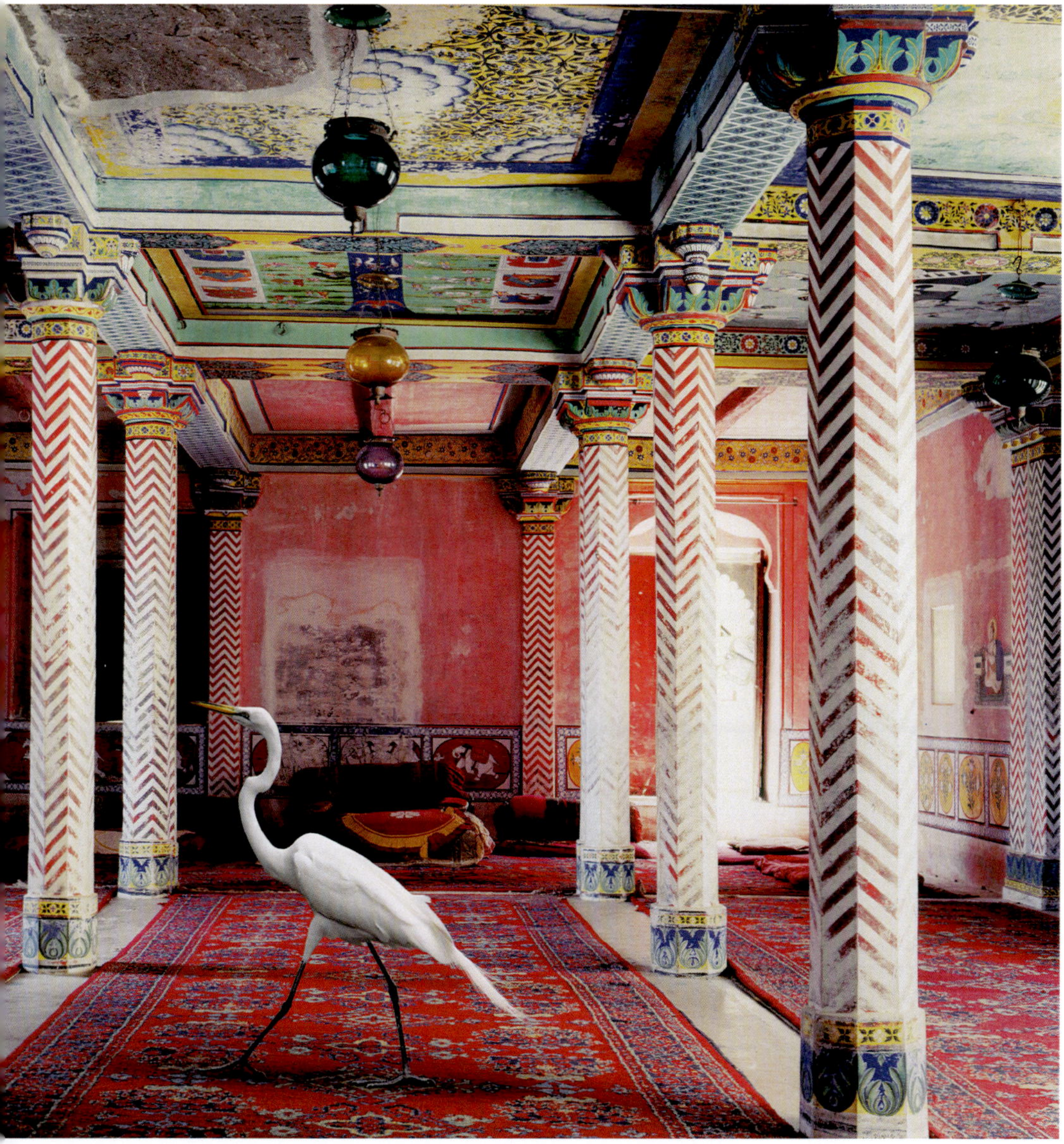

3.22

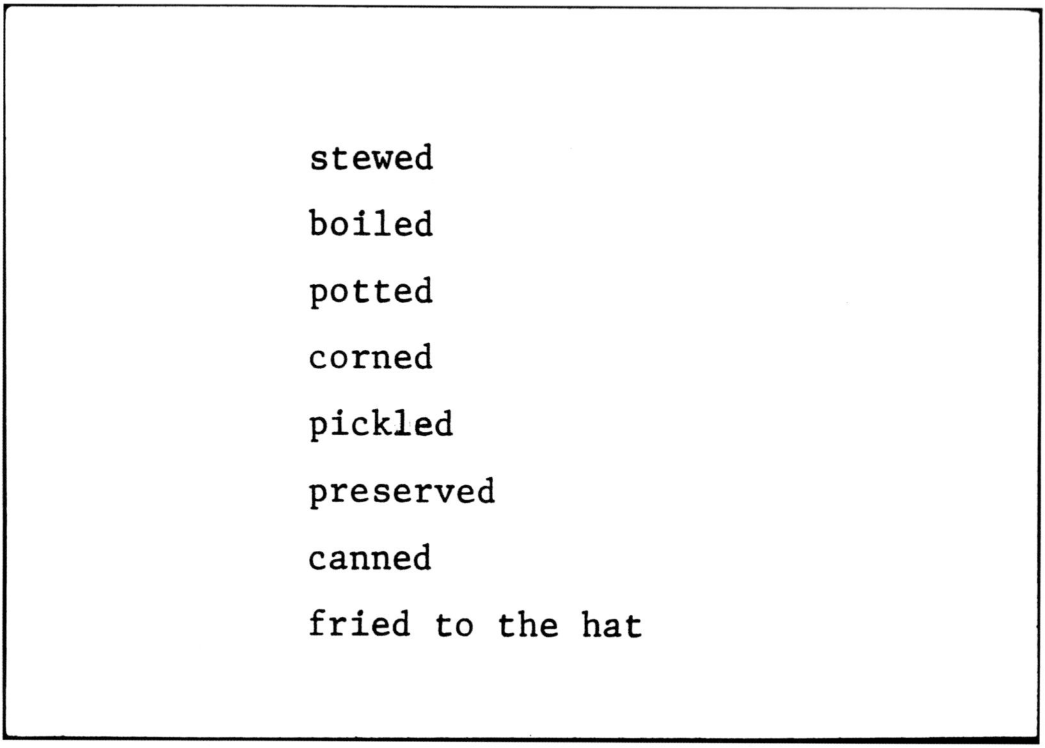

3.23

The exploration, experimentation, reading and thinking that you do through the course of your research will play a significant role in informing the way you resolve a body of work. Research does not usually lead straight into the making of the work; more often it sinks in slowly, over a period of time, subtly affecting and changing the way you work and what you decide to concentrate on.

Sometimes your research may affect your practice more directly: you may discover something that changes your opinion, idea or approach.

Archiving everything in a way that you can easily refer back to will help you apply the research you have done to your practice. Your project may start with basic research into a subject, theme, or technique, but equally it may start through taking photographs and realizing, on reflection, the potential for further work. You might be inspired by being somewhere or hearing something or through reading, looking or watching. Essentially, recording how a project or body of work develops allows the photographer to see how different types of research have informed and affected the work, and shows that all aspects of a project are part of a research process.

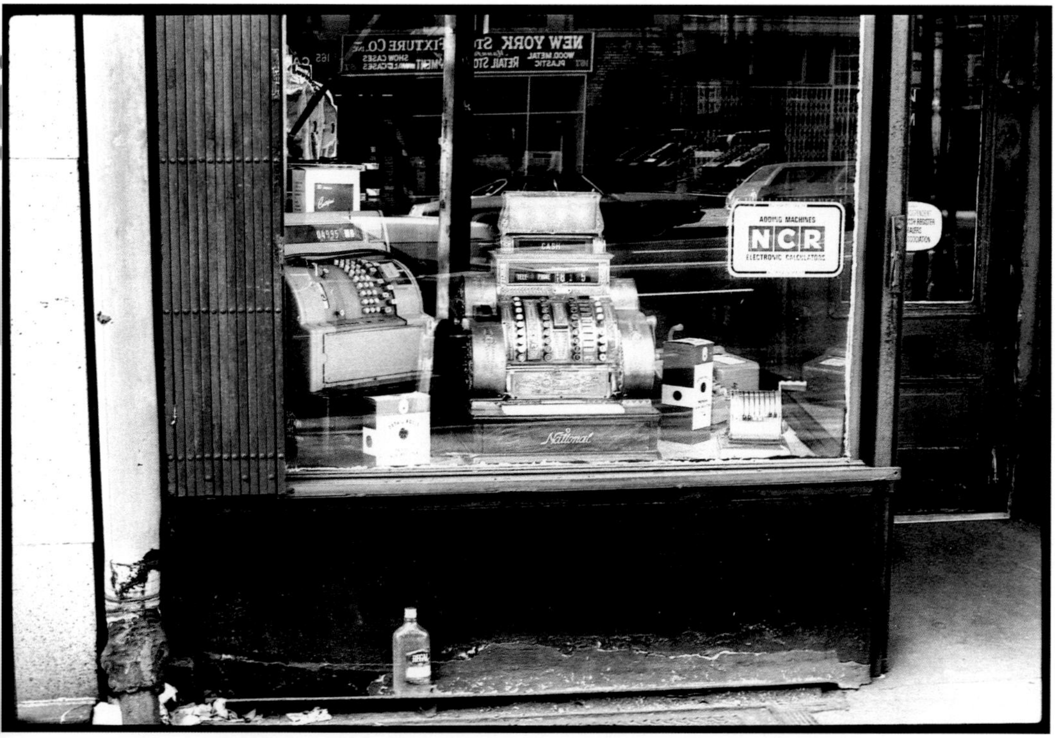

3.23

Title: The Bowery in two inadequate descriptive systems

Artist: Martha Rosler

Martha Rosler's work is informed by her keen commitment to questioning politics (both in society and in representation) and to creating awareness of social issues. Through her strategy of combining text (in this case: stewed, boiled, potted, corned, pickled, preserved, canned, fried to the hat) and image, she highlights the problems of documentary practice, both visual and text-based. The title plays a key role in directing the viewer to the meaning of the work. The Bowery is the oldest thoroughfare on Manhattan Island, New York. In the 1970s it was very run down, a typical area for documentary photographers to record. Rosler questions both photography and text as methods of recording such a place.

Time

Time is an important part of the research process: we all look at things differently as time passes and the direction of a project can change radically when it is made over several years. Many projects have to be finished quite quickly. An editorial portrait, for example, may be requested by a picture editor one day, shot the next and published the day after: it is a fast-paced world. However, this does not affect the fact that your approach to photographing will change over time and is influenced by all of the different types of research you do.

Editing

Editing involves selecting final images from a larger body of initial work. It is a slow process that demands careful thought and often benefits from the opinions of others, both professionals and non-professionals alike. A professional editor or curator can provide an expert view on how to select work for a publication or a particular space. You can also experiment with editing in small groups by handing your work to someone else and asking them to select a meaningful series from the photographs. Once the trial edit is done, the rest of the group can explore through discussion how they understand the story or the meaning of the work. This process will enable you to think more clearly about how others react to and understand your photographs; you will gain a distance from the work that is invaluable in making editing decisions. Editing is discussed again in chapter 5.

Reflection

In order to successfully edit your work, you will need to reflect on it. Reflection is the process of looking back on what you have done: analysing, reconsidering and questioning what has happened and why. Strategies for reflecting on your own work could include asking yourself: Is it working? Which images are really saying what I want them to say? If there is only one image that interests you, concentrate on this image and try to determine exactly what makes it successful.

Think of alternatives. Look for other points of view. Look for hidden assumptions and challenge them. Look at the work from the opposite point of view. How does it look now?

Through reflection, you are able to create new knowledge that is born of old knowledge. This is achieved by giving yourself the space and time to look back on your progress.

If there is only one image that interests you, concentrate on this image and try to determine exactly what makes it successful.

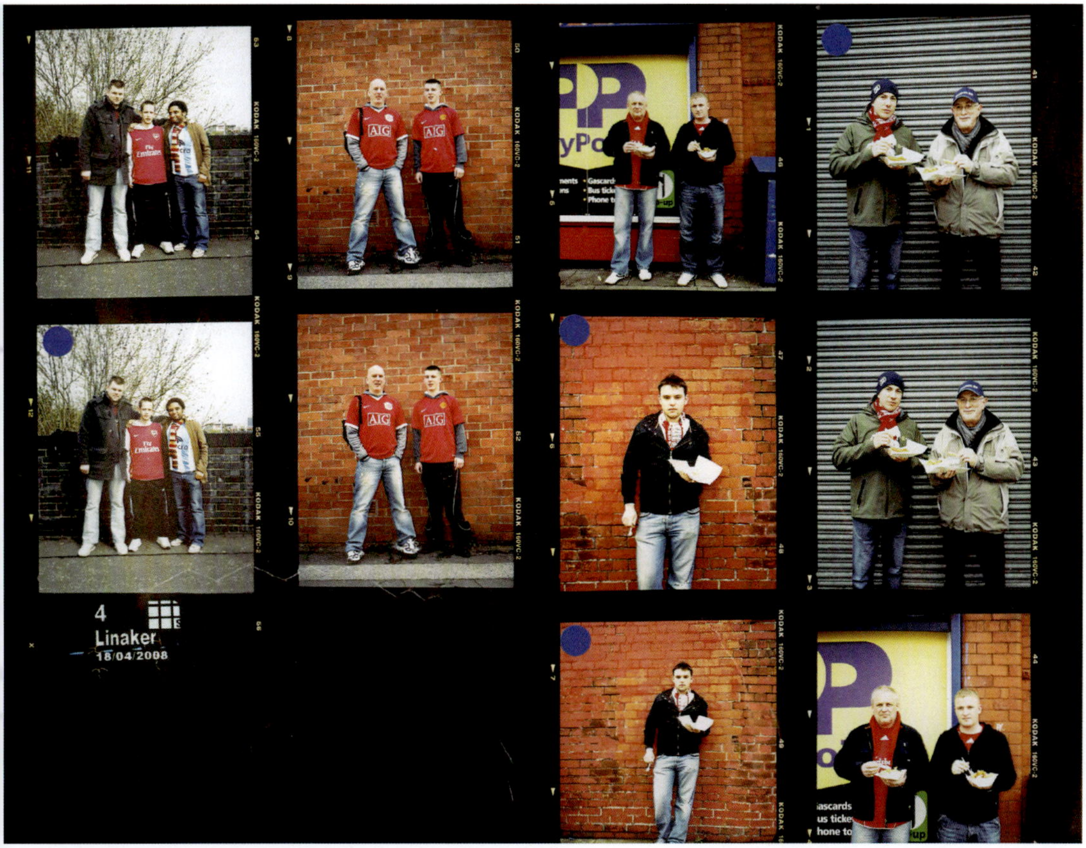

3.24

Title: *Match Day* contact sheet

Photographer: Chris Linaker

A documentary photographer will take numerous photographs and edit as they go along. This contact sheet shows how Chris Linaker uses coloured dots to indicate the images he is interested in for a first edit; he will then make working prints of the shortlisted images and use these to help decide how to refine his approach in the next shoot. The working prints become part of his archive and will be used in the second stage of editing, during which they are collected and laid out before the next draft edit is made.

Evaluation is part of the research process. Evaluation involves analysing what you have done, judging the evidence you have found, and then, most importantly, responding to the information and making appropriate changes. The process of evaluation can take place at regular intervals: you should do it after each shoot and at the end of the project.

It is helpful to evaluate the progress of your work against your proposal or your initial aims and objectives. By formally assessing and judging the value of a particular piece of work, you can begin to see what improvements can be made. We evaluate things all the time; it's part of everyday life. It can be difficult to evaluate your own work, however, so it is useful to ask yourself a series of questions that you can answer in written form.

Questions and answers

The following are examples of questions asked and answered during the process of evaluation:

- How well is the project going?
- What improvements can I make?
- How has it changed from the original project proposal?
- What are the strengths of the project so far?
- What aspect am I enjoying?

Appraise the weaknesses and strengths of the project. Keep a record of your answers. It is easy to focus on the areas you are finding difficult or to concentrate on what isn't going well. However, it is always important to evaluate the positive aspects of a project as well as the negative. Drawing attention to what is going well and what you are enjoying is a powerful motivator.

3.25

Title: Project evaluation form

Source: Natasha Caruana

Evaluation is a fundamental part of the creative process. The first few times you are evaluating pieces of your work, it is useful to follow the structure of a form such as this. The questions will help you to focus your thoughts clearly and get the most out of the self-evaluation process.

PHOTOGRAPHY PROJECT SELF-EVALUATION FORM

Project: Date:

---

1. **PROJECT TITLE**—How did this develop from your working title and what was involved in the decision-making process?

---

2. **SUBJECT**—Reflect on the subject matter of your project and the background research on this subject.

---

3. **AIMS/OBJECTIVES/CONCEPTS**—How, and to what extent, have you achieved the aims and objectives of your project? Describe the main concept driving your project.

---

4. **AUDIENCE**—Are you addressing a specific audience with your piece of work? For example: your peers, members of your family, or patients of a hospital department.

---

5. **CONTEXT**—What is the context of your project? Is it going to be viewed in a gallery space, a magazine, an artist's book, on the Internet, on a book cover?

---

6. **FORM/MEDIUM/PRESENTATION**—What is the final form and method of presentation for your work, and why did you come to choose these?

---

7. **RESEARCH METHODS**—Which research methods did you use to research this work and how did this research inform your project?

---

8. **REFERENCES**—How useful were the references you explored – the artists, writers or film-makers? How do you think your project would function in similar contemporary fields of production?

3.25

By thinking about practice as a research process, you are allowing yourself the space and time to be able to make mistakes and to make any improvements you feel are necessary. You should never be afraid of making mistakes or pushing yourself into unknown territory. This is often when image making is at its most exciting. Making improvements is a positive process; re-shooting is a healthy and worthwhile exercise. Or you may choose to improve single images from a series in post-production.

You are also allowing yourself time to reflect and act on your judgement or the judgement of others. It is important to learn not to take the judgement of others on your work as absolute: your own intuition is invaluable. The perspective achieved through taking time to evaluate and judge one of your projects can inform your approach to the next body of work. It is difficult for both emerging and experienced photographers to be fully satisfied with a body of work. However, there comes a time when your work needs to be revealed to an audience.

Arts funding

Researching funding is a vital part of any artist's business. University libraries usually have a section devoted to funding, and there are a mass of different organisations, trusts and foundations that one can apply to. It is important to learn about the various funders and what they will support so that any application that you make can be directed to the right place. In the UK one of the best known and most important funders of art is the Arts Council, which has departments in Scotland, Wales, England and Northern Ireland. The Arts Council produces a free newsletter with information about opportunities as well as a website listing grants to apply for and a phone line for help with applications.

The Arts Council have funded a wealth of arts projects in the UK and also have an important arts collection. Most funds will have clear guidelines (the Arts Council's are very clear) that you need to adhere to, and some will give you feedback (if you do not get the grant) helping you to re-apply in future.

Whilst it is disappointing not to get a grant you applied for, the feedback is often generous and always invaluable. To apply for a grant, you need to have a well-researched project and be able to understand the context that your work fits into (you will have some idea of this through the research processes that you have undergone). You also need to complete a budget and a timetable. At the end of a grant period, you have to do an evaluation of what you did and how you used the grant. It is advisable to keep any funder updated with changes that happen in your project.

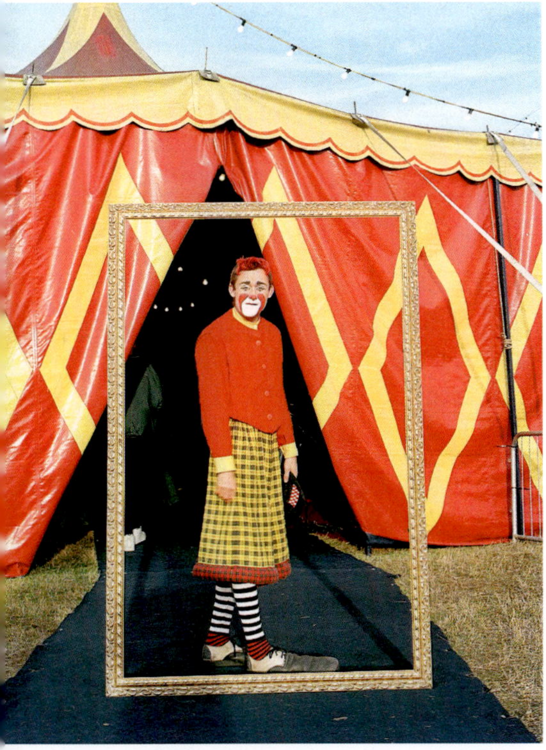

3.26

Title: ***The Clown*, 2004**

Photographer: Natasha Caruana

For the last seven years, Natasha Caruana has been making work around the clown community from a personal perspective: she is the daughter of a clown. She used props to try to capture the persona of a clown. She evaluated her first images and concluded that they were overly predictable. Through her research, she developed different ideas about how to represent the clowns in a way that challenged our perceived views.

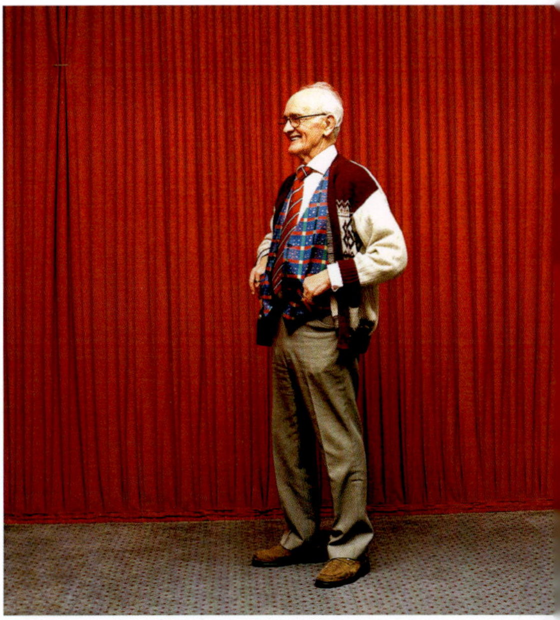

3.27

Title: ***Dizzy the Clown*, 2009**

Photographer: Natasha Caruana

Natasha Caruana continued shooting while researching and getting to know the older clowns beyond their performed personas. She documented unguarded moments at committee meetings, in dressing rooms and in living rooms.

This latest series of portraits captures the clown out of costume. Through the detail in the image, the audience is drawn to imagine how this man performs as a clown. This is a development from the more literal perspective she used in the previous portraits made in 2004.

Research materials need to be compiled in such a way that they are user friendly, so that you, as well as other interested researchers, can make the best use of them.

Each photographer will have a different method or system for compiling their research. There is no right or wrong way; you need to find the approach that works best for you. The way you choose to store or catalogue your research does not have to look pretty, but it does need to be accessible enough to inform your work; it will require some effort to organize and structure your research materials. If your research is in a manageable order, it will be easier to create a clear and organized project.

It is important to remember that, whatever method you select to compile your research, there must be space for it to evolve, grow and develop along with the project itself. Allowing the research to have significance will add authority to your practice as a whole.

This section looks at some of the methods that are available to you for compiling your research materials, and also for storing them.

A visual journal, workbook or sketchbook is a physical manifestation of your thought processes. It is a space to play, a sounding board for developing different ideas, and a place to track developments. You need to decide if your visual journal is a travel companion: if it is, it will need to be a suitable size. It may be that you use a small journal to record everyday thoughts that can then be transferred to a larger, master journal. The process of transferring this information may also invite further reflection.

Thought processes can be tracked, and all sorts of materials, such as photographs, photocopied and found images, written fragments, quotes and interviews, letters, lists, technical details and real or fictitious notations, are potentially relevant and can be included in your journal.

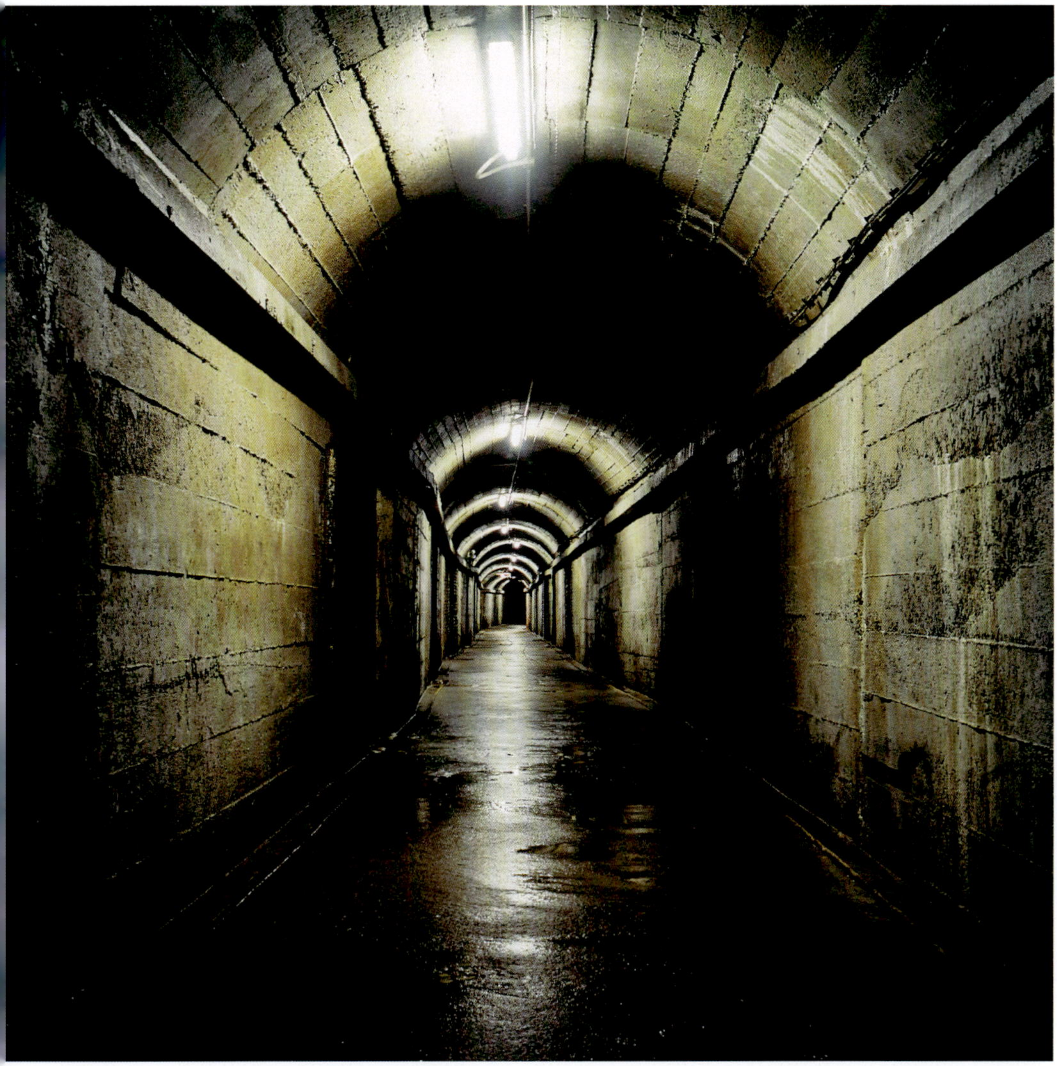

3.28

Title: Abteilung Nr/L, from the project Subterrania 2009–10

Artist: Fiona Crisp

Artist Fiona Crisp's image of an underground World War II hospital on the Channel Islands, which is now a tourist destination, questions the complex relationship between leisure and heritage. The image was featured in Crisp's monograph *Hyper Passive*, and Crisp describes the making of the book as a defining moment in the organization and dissemination of her stored research. She uses different methods and locations to compile her work, with large-scale prints in storage, and other materials such as objects, data, negatives and working prints stored at home.

Digital workbooks

Keeping a digital workbook may be more appropriate if you have collated a lot of digital materials and images. You can add your thoughts in the form of typed notes, rather than transferring them to a handwritten sketchbook or journal. The Internet is a wonderfully liberating research resource, although you do have to analyse the material you find there to determine its credibility and relevance. Digital workbooks allow you to seamlessly collate your Internet research.

The results of using a digital workbook are quite different from a physical workbook, and you should consider which way is most appropriate for your work. Although it seems environmentally unsound, you may find it helpful to print out a digital notebook or workbook in order to see the pages side by side. Alternatively, you may be able to view all the pages on screen as thumbnails. Measuring where you have been and forecasting where you are going can be difficult if you cannot view several pages at the same time.

In a digital workbook, links to relevant subject matter and images can easily be added between the text entries. For example, you can copy gallery opening times onto your research page or drag across interesting images. You can collate screenshots and add video clips.

If you have a laptop computer, keep a folder on your desktop and carry it around with you. Create document pages with Adobe InDesign or Photoshop or with Microsoft Word; these are transportable between laptops, studio desktops and some mobile phones. The information on your digital workbook can easily be shared; it can be emailed or added to your Facebook page. You can also invite online reviews from peers, giving you a response to your work in progress.

Keeping a workbook

Workbooks should be made in a way that suits you: there is no set formula. You may come across a completely new way of recording your research.

A workbook can be private or public. It is a place for personal reflection, so it should not be overly self-conscious; it is not necessarily for public consumption.

Make your workbook a pleasurable space to explore your thoughts and ideas.

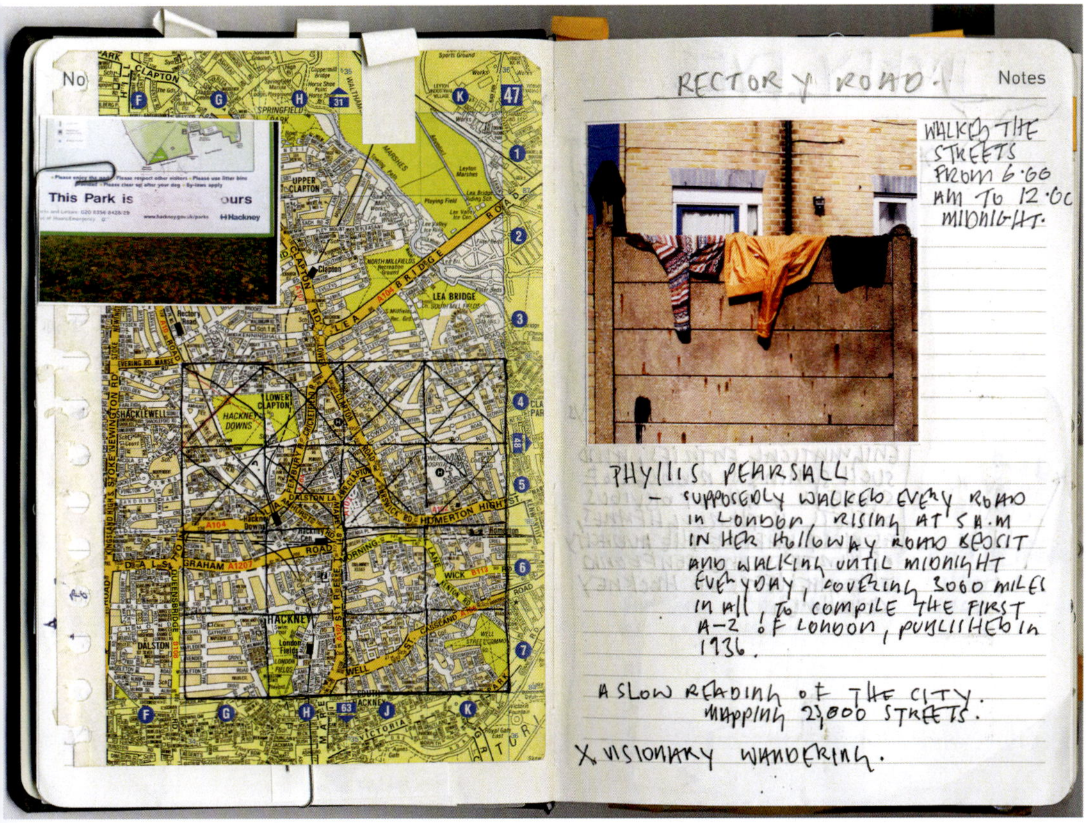

3.29

Title: Sketchbook page from the project *Hackney Eyes*

Source: Simon Aeppli

Keeping visual journals such as this has been central to Simon Aeppli's practice as a film-maker and photographer for the last ten years. He uses his visual journals as a starting point for his finished work, which interweaves video footage with images from books.

Creating a blog allows increased functionality above simply digitizing and compiling your research material. The thought of setting up a blog can be daunting, as they are often perceived as being solely text-based. On the contrary, blogs are highly flexible and can be whatever you want them to be.

Following an online blog template gives you full control over all of your materials, whether you want them to be visible on the Internet or hidden. A blog can have private sections or, when you choose a 'closed' blog, which can only be accessed via a password, it can become a completely private working space. A blog can also be an open working space with access for all. Consider whether your research will be enhanced by allowing people to comment on your entries or by allowing them to share your entries with the rest of the Web.

3.30

Title: Screen shot of a blog

Source: Work-Show-Grow

This blog offers accessible information for emerging photographers on how to get ahead within the photographic industry.

WORK-SHOW-GROW ABOUT TESTIMONIALS **BLOG** EVENTS CONTACT

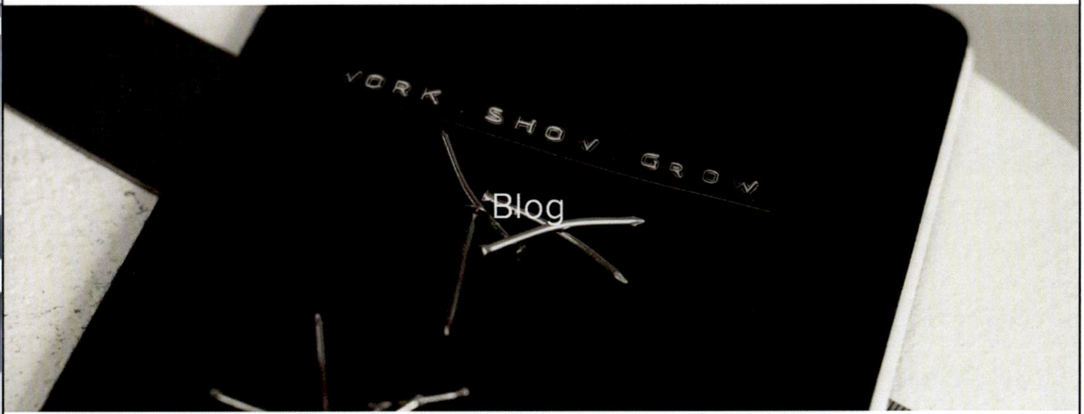

Arles opening week I Advice I How to do it

July 11, 2018

Opening week Arles 2018

Les rencontres de la photographie

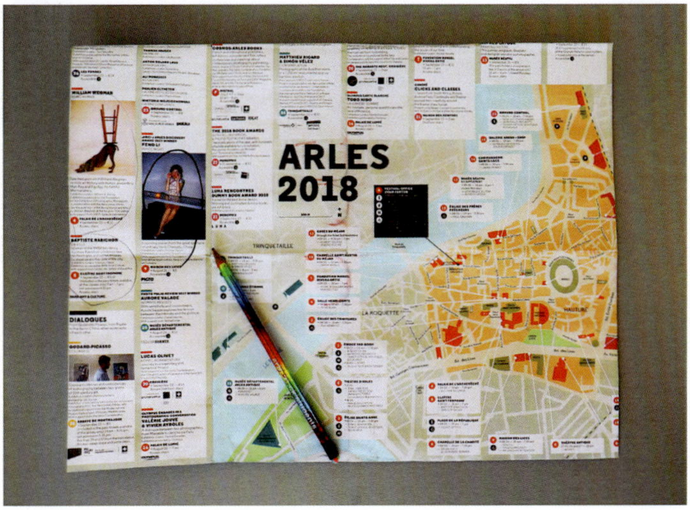

OFFICIAL FESTIVAL MAP, 2018

3.30

The advantages of blogging

Using a blog makes your research fully transportable between working environments and even countries: as long as there is Internet access, you can have access to all of your research material.

By creating different online entries, you can model the structure of your blog on the pages of a physical workbook, creating an online journal.

One of the key benefits of using a blog is that you are able to tag each entry with keywords. By using this tag system, you can organize all of your information and, over time, create your own catalogue. The blog archives become more valuable over time. Using a search function, connections are made between entries that might not otherwise have been obvious.

Blogs for organizing and compiling research

Blogs can also be used in a more public realm. Unlike the diaristic use of blogs previously discussed, photographers can use their blogs to help compile research that is then structured by subject matter. The subject-specific sections of the blog encourage you to reflect on the relevant compiled material whilst sharing it with your online audience.

If you are choosing to compile your research using a blog, it is good working practice to make regular backups of your blog entries to protect your work. There are numerous issues to do with hacking and servers crashing that could affect your blog and cause you to lose work that has not been backed up.

Photography blogs/resource websites

Try to familiarize yourself with as many different photography-related blogs as you can. Compare how they each present and organize their information and images. Examples of interesting blogs are included below, and some of these have links to other blogs that you may also want to investigate.

Alec Soth is an American photographer who set up a blog for his publishing company, Little Brown Mushroom: littlebrownmushroom.wordpress.com

Photoworks is a UK-based photography organisation aimed at practitioners worldwide. The site offers inspiration of viewing new works, videos of artist interviews, and news of commissions: https://photoworks.org.uk/

Light Stalking offers guides and tips on the practical elements of photography: lightstalking.com

Flak Photo showcases the best photography from artists, curators, bookmakers and photo organizations around the world: flakphoto.com/

Work-Show-Grow is an insider guide to photographic professional practice focusing on how to get ahead: www.work-show-grow.com/blog

David Campany is a writer, curator of exhibitions and an artist. He has published several books on photography, cinema and art, and generously shares over a hundred essays from a range of projects to read on his website: davidcampany.com

Once you have completed a project, you will have collected a significant amount of physical research material that you may only need to access from time to time. It is therefore important to give some consideration to the storage and organization of this material. Some photographers use a system of boxes or folders during the course of their project. It could even be as simple as a collection of open shoe boxes in the corner of a workroom.

You will need to keep your material well organized so that it is easily accessible for future reference. The items will also need to be stored safely. As a basic rule your items will need to be kept in a dry environment and out of direct sunlight in order to avoid fading or bleaching.

Forms of storage

Archival boxes are used both by individuals and organizations: they provide an efficient means of storage as well as an appropriate amount of protection. Typically, archival boxes are made out of corrugated plastics or acid-free material. They are normally crushproof and water resistant. Choosing an acid-free material will ensure that delicate contents, such as manuscripts, newspapers and maps, will not degrade too severely over time.

Negatives and prints should be kept cool to keep them in good condition. In the US, archives of negatives and colour prints are frequently frozen. Researchers who want to view the material have to book appointments and the work is taken out of the freezer in advance of their arrival at the archive.

3.31

Title: Basement Archive, Wiener Library

Photographer: Ali Mobasser

The Wiener Library Institute of Contemporary History in London holds more than ten thousand historically significant photographs, as well as books, pamphlets and other materials. Very careful consideration has been given to the safe storage and archiving of each of these items. Considering appropriate forms of storage is key to all archiving, whether you are preserving a large, historically significant collection such as this or organizing your own project research materials.

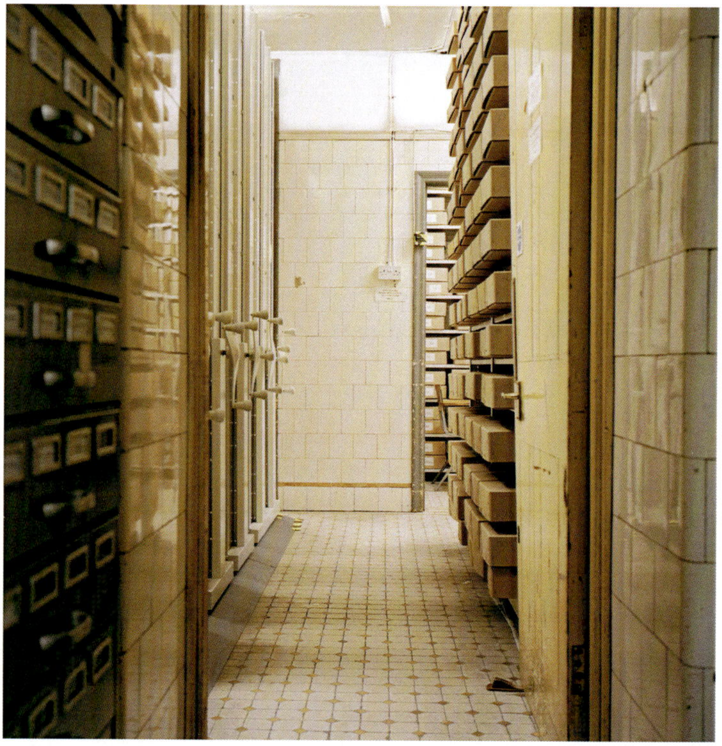

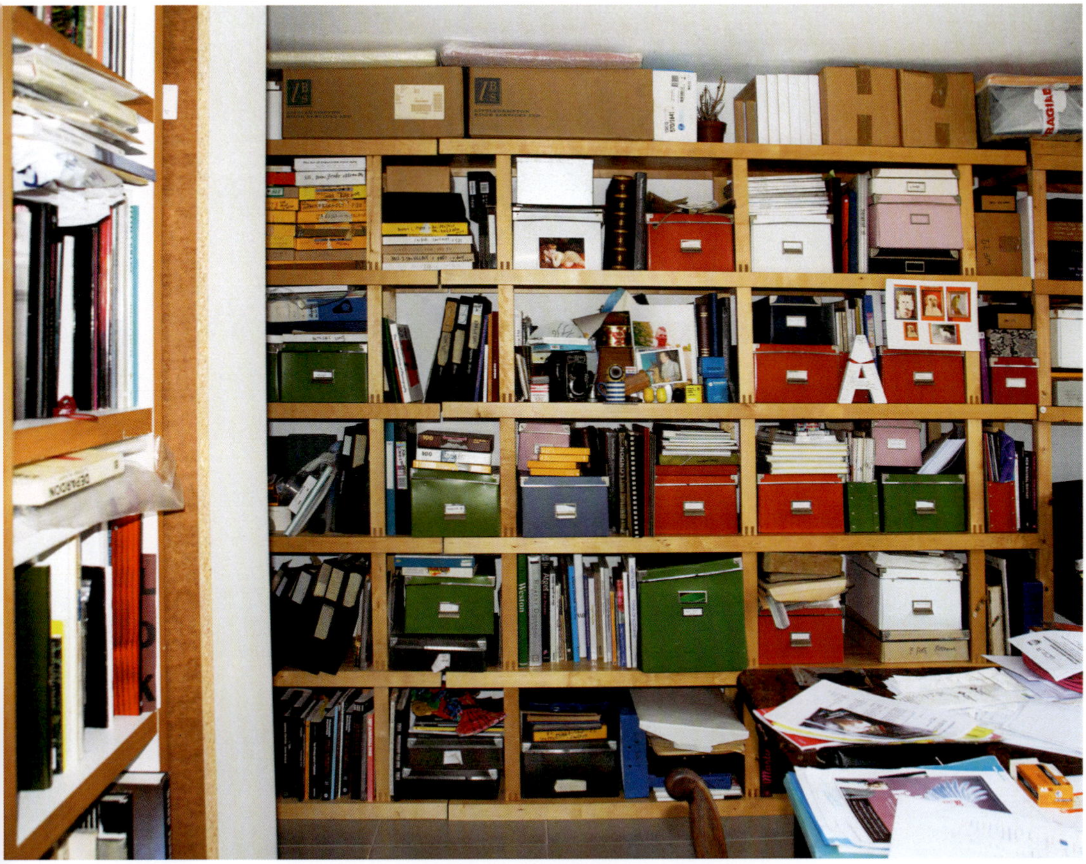

3.32

Title: A photographer's archive

Photographer: Anna Fox

This archive demonstrates a range of approaches to securing and organizing research material. In a small corner of the studio, negatives are stored in acid-free negative boxes; a system of named folders organizes the material, and green archival boxes store a valuable collection of vernacular photography, magazines, newspapers and old family albums.

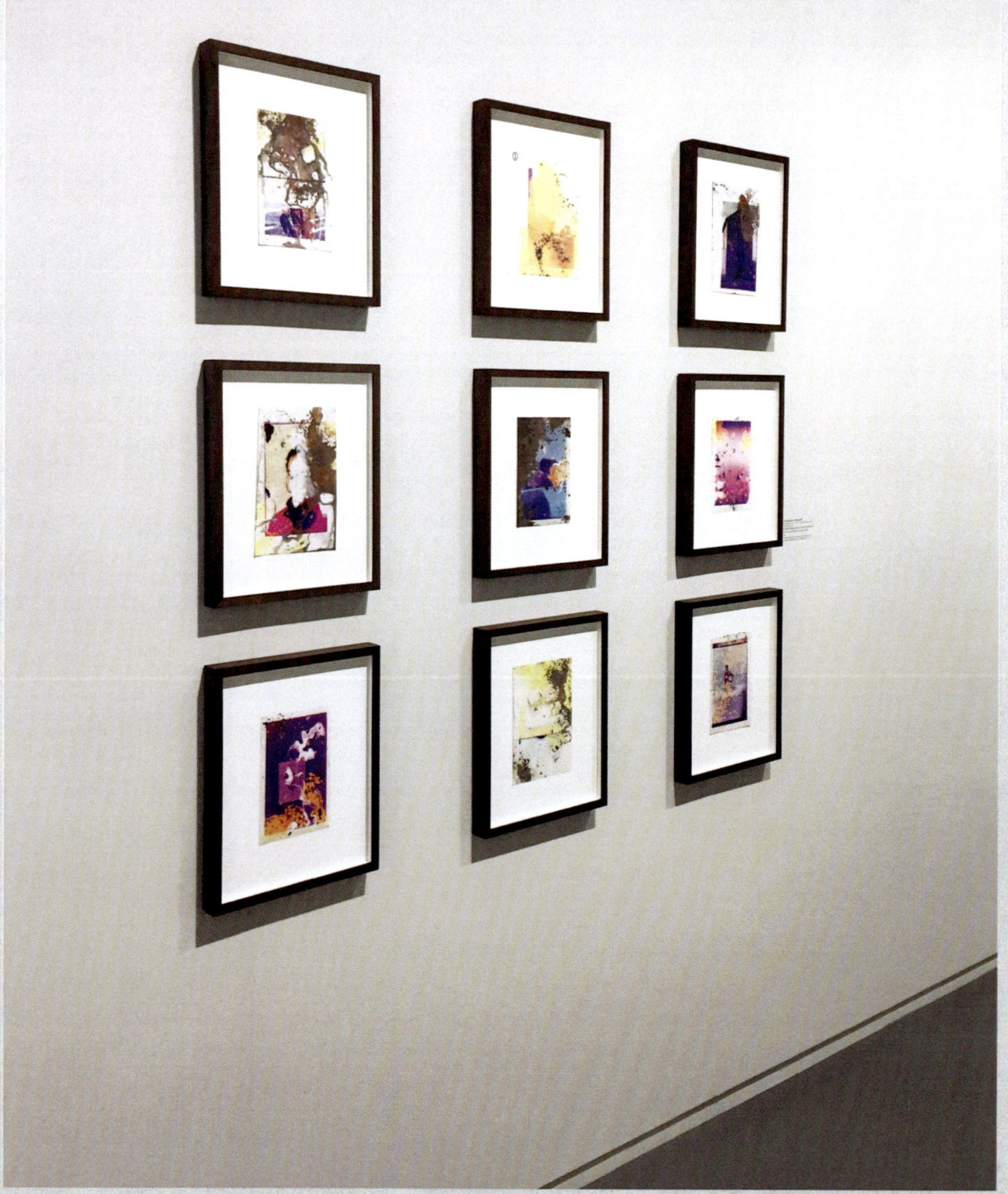

3.33

Title: Lunar Caustic, (*selected works from the series*) Unique C-Type Prints, Acid, Silver Nitrate, 2014

Source/Artist: Melinda Gibson & Thomas Sauvin

This is an installation shot from the exhibition *Surface Tension: Breaking the Plane of the Photographic Image*, FOMU, Belgium 2017.

Case study 3
Melinda Gibson

Melinda Gibson's interest in photography developed from an early age. Her father was an avid amateur photographer and her mother a keen family archivist who regularly created traditional 'family albums'. Throughout her childhood, family trips to galleries and museums were frequent, and this helped Gibson to develop her creative vision.

Whilst studying for a degree in photography, Gibson realised that her interests in 'traditional' photography were changing, and by the end of her degree she had started to find her new voice. Drawn to the ideas of reproduction, experimentation and the multiple, she began to produce imagery that questioned existing codes and practices within the medium of photography itself.

After graduating Gibson began assisting a number of different photographers, finding a thriving alternative fine art community away from what she previously described as her traditional photographic education. She was deeply inspired by the energy and spirit of these artists, who were using photography in a poetic way. During this time, she continued her own practice and started a new body of work reworking Charlotte Cotton's seminal text, *The Photograph as Contemporary Art.* Within this series, Gibson deconstructed the canon of photographic education by playfully appropriating the photographs found within Cotton's book.

Gibson was inspired by each of the photographers she assisted. Her time working at Martin Parr's studio gave her knowledge and understanding of how to make photography a business and potentially create a brand for oneself. Working with Gareth McConnell assisting on commercial shoots exposed her to his profound appreciation for light, composition, and, importantly, how to work with clients. Her time at Wolfgang Tillmans' studio heightened all of this; also, seeing how he worked, what he believed in, deeply touched her. These influential experiences enabled Gibson to think differently about her practice and really consider the materiality of the photograph as an object.

Gibson's practice experiments with installation, collage and alternative processes while always maintaining a strong commitment to the idea of the multiple and photography's malleability. In 2012, the French photography collector/artist Thomas Sauvin contacted Gibson to see if she would be interested in reworking his archive, *The Beijing Silvermine*, to form a new collaborative project. Sauvin spent many years sourcing found negatives, predominately 35 mm colour and vernacular images, from a recycling unit on the edge of Beijing city. The finds were rescued from destruction in kilo rice bags (Sauvin paid to save them), and the archive now amounts to a million images.

During an initial ten-day residency in Beijing, Gibson viewed and edited half a million found photographs and categorised them under twelve different headings. In this period of sifting, she found herself intimately drawn towards the mysteries of these decaying images and the possibility that without Sauvin they would all have been lost.

Flying back to London, Gibson began to research into processes of decay and destruction. Her parents' garden shed became Gibson's 'laboratory' for working out ideas and experimenting in the old alchemic ways. She wanted to use the very same chemicals that destroyed the negatives, caustic acid and silver nitrate, to make the new series.

Gibson returned to Beijing to make the work, armed with the knowledge (because of her experimentation) of how those two compounds, acid and nitrate, could be interwoven within the work. Melinda and Thomas worked with a Beijing-based student to print just one image of each of her edited selections. They began by enlarging the found negatives traditionally and printing them by hand. Once the prints were ready, Melinda and Thomas submerged each print individually, upside down, in a tray of hydrochloric acid. At this point neither had an exact idea on how much of the print would be affected and if the colour shifts would be the same as Melinda had tried and tested hundreds of times before. After removing the print, a small amount of water was added to dilute the acid before sprinkling the silver nitrate on top of the surface, using a peppershaker.

The prints would then be placed in archival sleeves and placed in sunlight; this action created suction between the plastic and the wet print, speeding up the reactive process. The white silver nitrate would then turn to black from the sunlight, resulting in an uncontrollable emergence of curled patterns. When the artists felt that the print had reached an optimum point, it would be taken out of the sunlight.

During the residency, Melinda and Thomas bottled and stored their urine in a fridge; this was collected to act as a neutralising agent to the acid on the prints. The prints were washed with the urine and then left to dry. The alchemic effect of the urine is that it temporarily sets the image; however, the prints are still in a constant state of change which will eventually result in their demise.

All photographic prints are subject to deterioration, but these fragile works disappear at a much faster rate than a properly fixed photographic image. To avoid the difficulty of how these disappearing images might fit into the art marketplace, the artists offer print buyers the opportunity to have a scan made of the print at a point in time. The buyer simply has to take the image to the artists for them to make the scan, which they then also own.

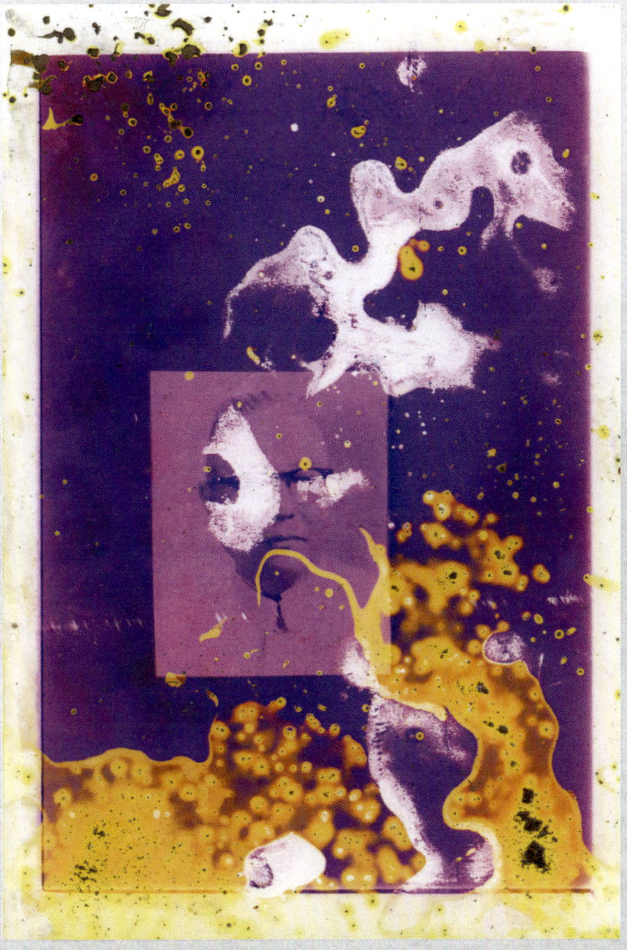

3.34

Title: Untitled XII, (*Lunar Caustic*) C Type, Acid, Silver Nitrate, 2014, 215 mm x 144 mm

Source/Artist: Melinda Gibson & Thomas Sauvin

Each print is unique, shifting in colour and tonality as the sunlight reflects on its surface.

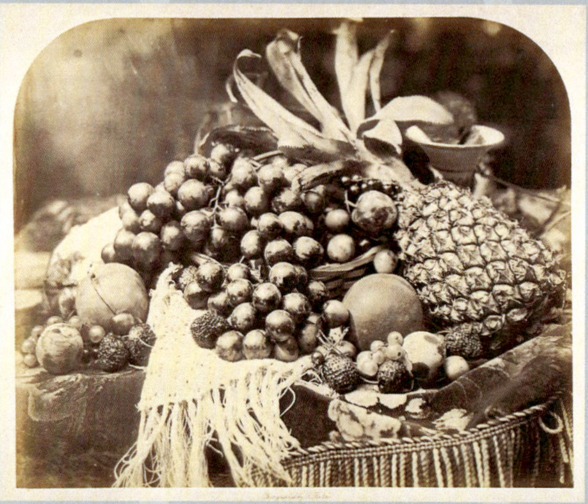

3.35

Title: Still Life with Fruit, 1860

Source/Photographer: Scala/Roger Fenton

Fenton's original 'Still Life With Fruit', shot in his studio in 1860.

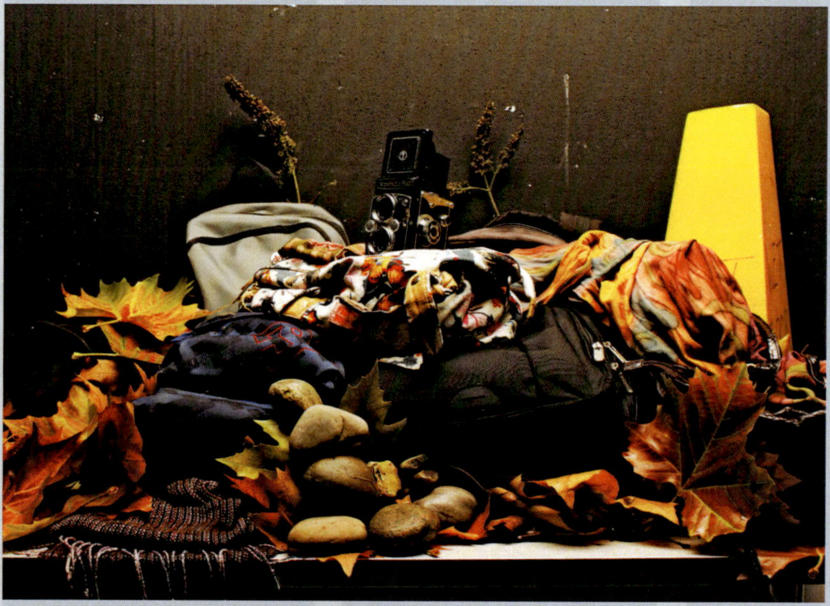

3.36

Title: Remake of Fenton original, 2010

Source: Photography students, UCA, Farnham, UK

This image is a remake of the Fenton image. Shot on a digital camera, it replicates the lighting Fenton used. However, where Fenton used natural light from large skylights on the roof of his studio, this new scene is lit using a large soft box placed directly above the set. The photographers worked as a group to replicate the form of the fruit in Fenton's image, using autumn leaves, backpacks and other available materials.

Activity 3 Pioneers of photography

For this activity you need to gather a series of examples of other photographers' work. During your research process you will have looked at both contemporary and historical work. By looking back at one of the pioneers of photography as a reference, you can relate your work to the history of visual practices.

The pioneers of photography can be found by searching your local library, an archive, or by looking online. Try to find a variety of styles and techniques within the work. Look for images that are linked to your interests through content, lighting, style or context.

Now select one image to work with; study this image more closely. Take notes describing how the photographer has used lighting. Reflect on what you think they are trying to say. Evaluate the strengths and weaknesses of the image. What makes it work? Write down all of your thoughts.

Look back at your notes and consider how you could begin to visually interpret the photographer's image and use this information in the making of your image.

Using the information you have gathered, remake the image that you selected. It is good practice to recreate the image precisely before reinterpreting it. It is also good practice to work in the studio with professional equipment in order to imitate precisely the lighting used. By remaking the image, you will notice details that you might otherwise have missed.

Think about how you can update the image. What modern-day props could you use? Could you apply the same technique, but use different content? Or use the same content, but a different technique? Now you are not trying to reproduce the image; instead, you are trying to reinterpret it.

Remaking a great work of photography gives you an appreciation of how far photography has evolved. It will give you an awareness of the energy and effort used to produce images in the early days of photography. It may seem a speedier process today, but we still need to invest time, energy and thought to make interesting images.

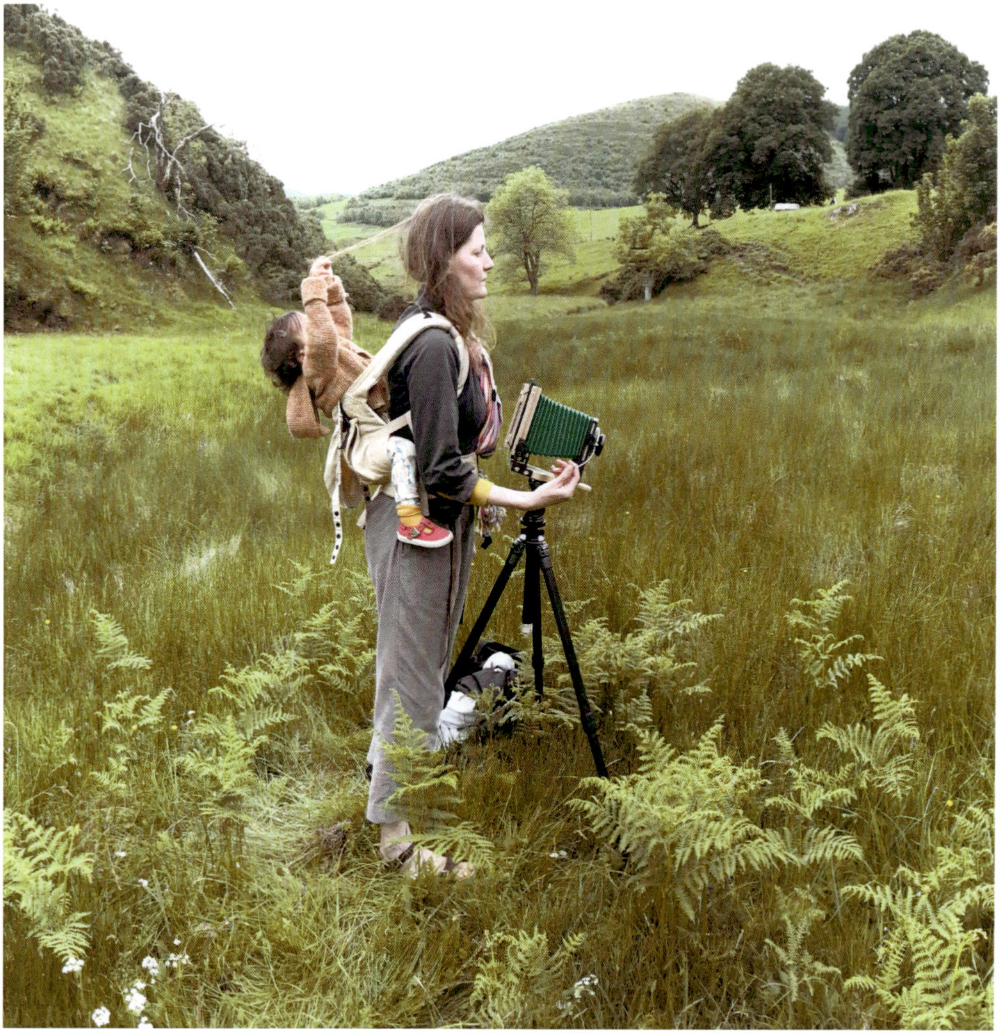

4.1

Title: Laura Hynd at work

Source/Photographer: Simon Hynd

Laura Hynd is a photographer who works across art and commerce. She is largely known for her elegant portraits shot using only natural light and her editorial stories. This image comes from a project she is currently developing with curator Rodrigo Orrantia. The project invited Laura to revisit her work, *Lady into Hut*, under the title 'Live Forever', working in Scotland at the place her grandparents met. Pictured with her daughter, Bonnie, at 15 months old, during the summer of 2017.

4 Practice as research – commercial photography

An arts-based practice and a commercial practice can sometimes look quite similar and might even have gone through similar processes in the way that they have been made. Boundary lines that exist between these two fields can be quite blurred, and frequently commercial work grows out of one's own artwork and personal projects. This is useful in one way as it means both art and commerce can co-exist and regularly inform one another. Working methods can be similar, although timing of work is quite different. In other words, a commercial project may only last one day or one week whereas an arts-based project can span months or even years.

As a commercial photographer, you need to be as equally well informed about arts-based practice as you are by commercial-based practice. The research process has some similarities and some differences. In this chapter, we will look primarily at the areas of research that are most specific to practicing commercial photography.

Networking in the industry

Networking can be considered part of your research process because it is through networking that you will be able to speak to agents, photographers, art directors and designers face to face. This is an important means of learning and hearing opinions and ideas first hand. You might also meet essential team members at networking events such as assistants, stylists and lighting designers. Networking generally means events connected to the industry that could include special exhibitions, trade shows, awards nights, fairs and festivals. You need to find out when and where these things happen; they are usually centred around major cities. A shoot will be affected by who you are working with, and working for, so it is vital to know who's who in the business.

Networking can be considered part of your research process.

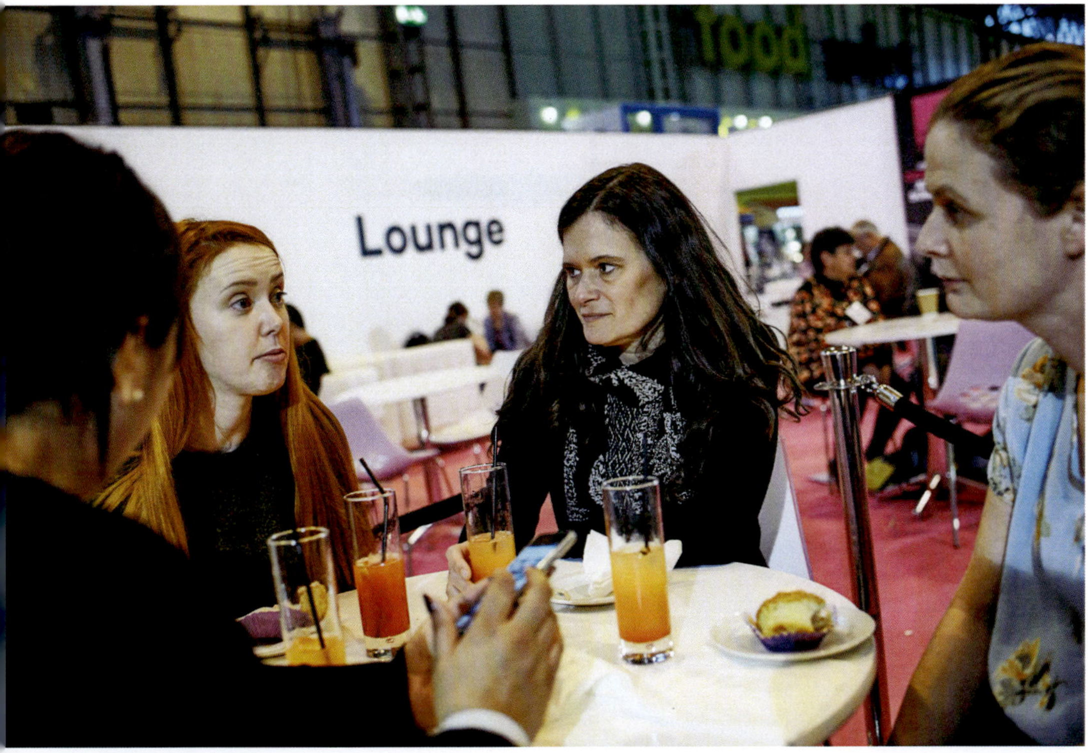

4.2

Title: Fast Forward, a women in photography networking event at The Photography Show, Birmingham

Source: The Photography Show

The Photography Show is an annual trade show held at the National Exhibition Centre in Birmingham, UK. The show brings together a variety of companies from the photographic industry to demonstrate and sell their new products, as well as hosting a series of events and talks. This image shows the Fast Forward networking event, designed to enable networking for women photographers.

A shoot will be affected by who you are working with, and working for, so it is vital to know who's who in the business.

Magazines as research sources

There are a wide range of magazines that publish commercial photography, and getting to know them and what they do will help you to understand the breadth of the industry. Magazines include those from specialist businesses, like architecture and graphic design, through to fashion magazines and Sunday supplements that publish both advertisements and editorials using photography. Photographic work in magazines is incredibly varied, and you may want to collect particular editions as research references. Magazines help you to understand what is happening here and now; they are different in different parts of the globe. A typical commercial photographer might collect hundreds of magazines as part of their inspiration archive.

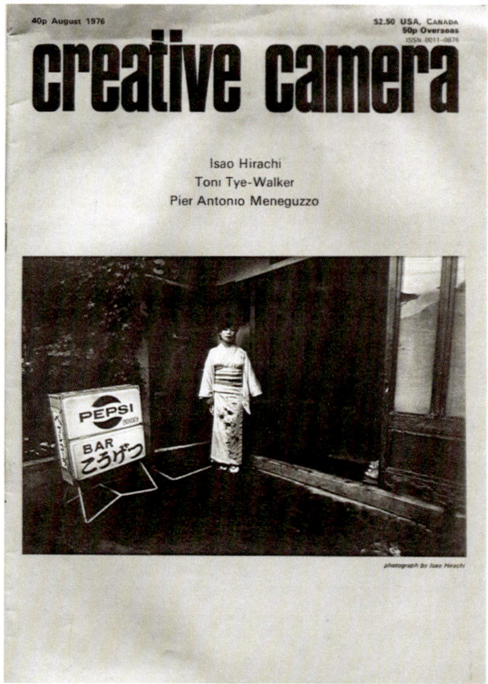

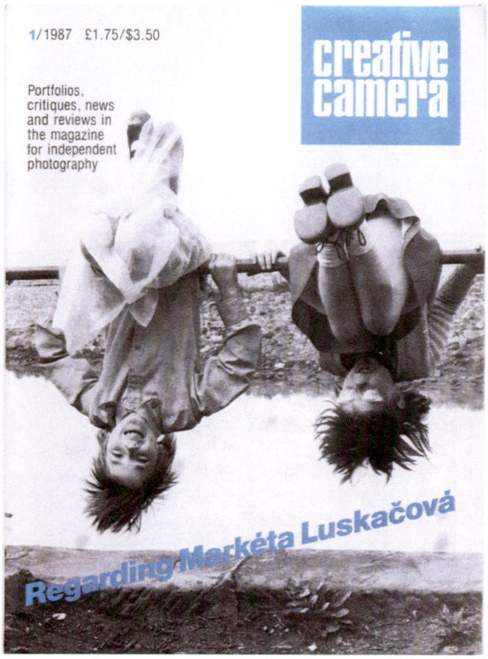

A typical commercial photographer might collect hundreds of magazines as part of their inspiration archive.

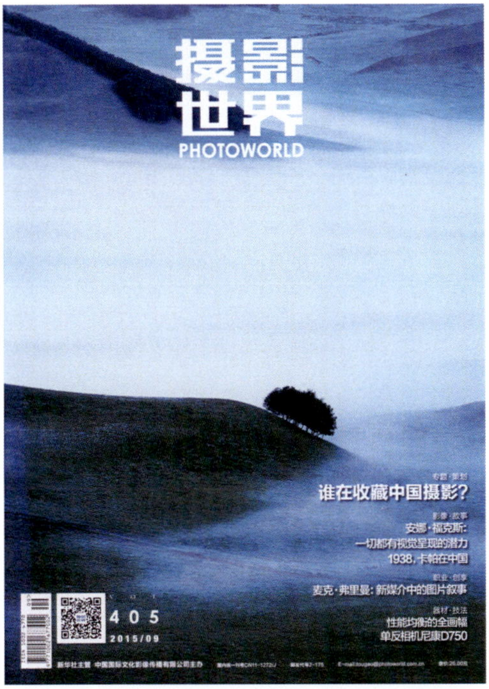

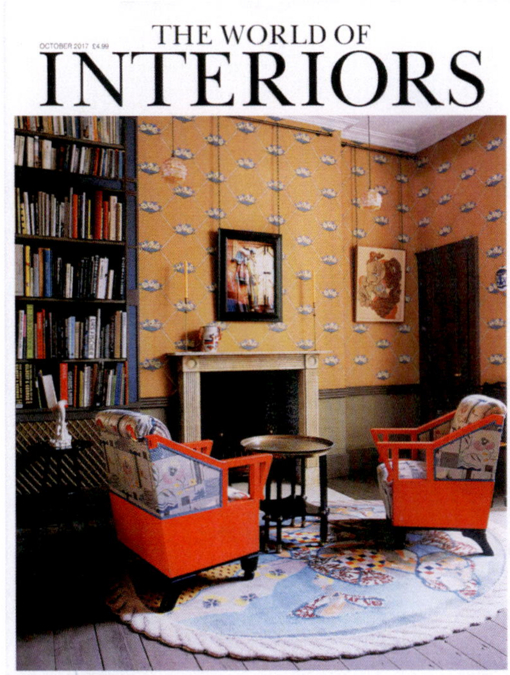

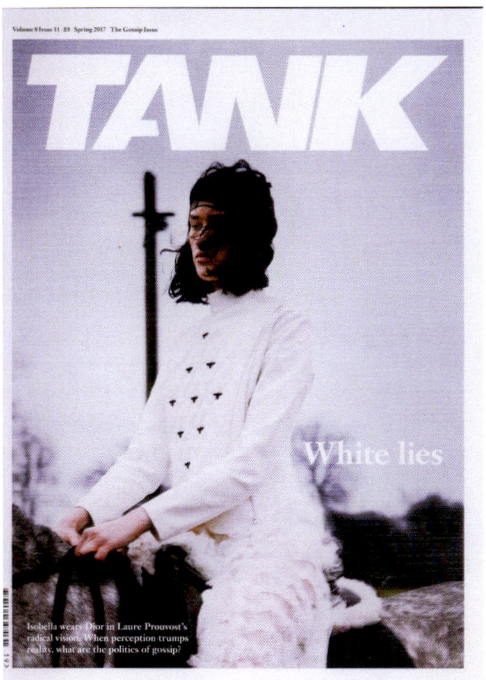

4.3

Title: Various magazine covers

Source: Anna Fox archive collection

The World of Interiors, *Creative Camera* (old editions), *Tank*, *Photoworld* China. Magazines are an excellent research source and give a more current perspective on specific aspects of photography (and the world). A photographer will look at a variety of magazines, including weekend supplements, and not just photography magazines in order to inspire and develop ideas.

The Internet as a research source

The Internet is a vibrant and vital research source and really there is no limit to where one might look for inspiration and ideas. Test various ideas through search engines, looking at all the images that come up when you put in specific words; this can be enlightening. It is valuable when trawling the Internet to make sure you know where the images you look at come from as the context will have determined how the image was made and what it means or says. The Internet is also important when you want to find people to work with. There are various websites that will give you information that you need for your shoot, including things like which assistants and stylists are looking for work, what they have done in the past, and contact information. Websites such as The Association of Photographers (AOP), The Freelancer Club, People per Hour and the Dots can be incredibly useful to freelance photographers and can help you to set up your network or your next shoot.

Instagram and Pinterest are commonly used by commercial photographers; they are popular ways of making public mood boards, collating research (in images and text) and showing your potential clients a flavour of who you are. Pinterest is an ideal platform for pitching for a job or sharing ideas with your team as you can make specific boards tailored to the brief. Instagram is more of a diary to show your sense of style; if you look at a few photographers' Instagram pages you will see that they build up stories that seem quite personal, often poetic, and above all feel very definitely authored by one person. Snapchat is useful for documenting the actual shoot and sharing the behind-the-scenes news and information, and it is also useful for storytelling.

4.4

Title: Website of the Association of Photographers (AOP)

Source: The AOP

The AOP is an excellent starting place for emerging photographers and assistants looking for information about the commercial world of photography. One can also research commercial aspects of photography on this site, and they have a good annual competition.

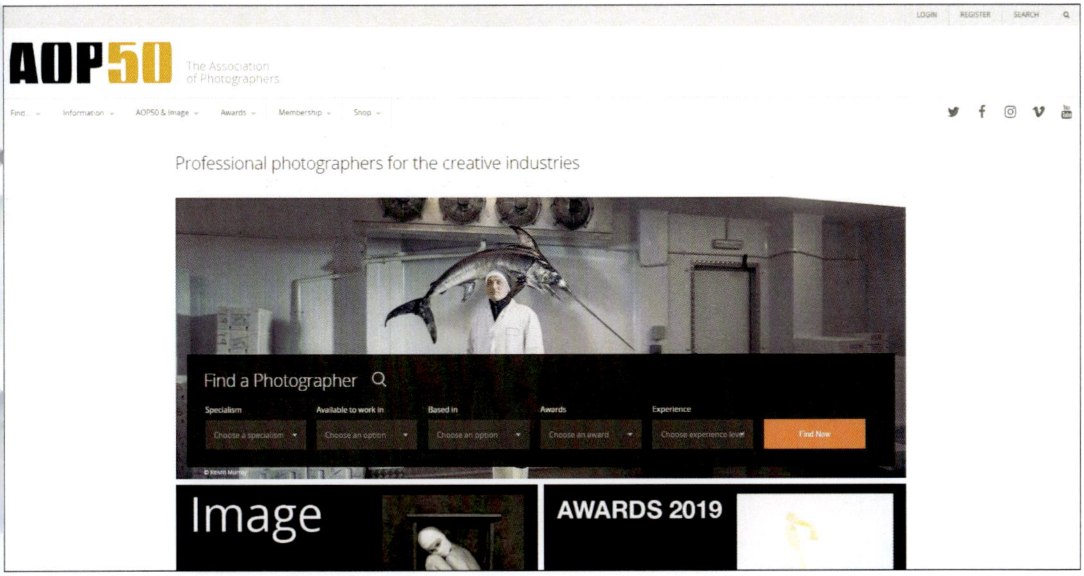

If you look at a few photographers' Instagram pages you will see that they build up stories that seem quite personal, often poetic, and above all feel very definitely authored by one person.

The best place to start testing practical ideas is in a space that you can control easily – a studio, for example – where you can add props and lighting and create an image or series of images as if from a blank canvas. Start simply, with one or two elements, and add new things bit by bit, building up your image tests in layers.

Another good way to start is to take an image you have seen and like and try to emulate it: you can never do this exactly, in the sense that, if models are involved, it is hard to get exactly the same look, but you should perhaps try to match the lighting and positioning of objects and models and then add your own twist by changing some elements. By copying an existing image, you learn a lot about how things are done and how even the simplest-looking image can be quite complex to create.

You would do well to follow a good lighting guide like chapter 7 in *Langford's Basic Photography* and learn the basics first before you try breaking the rules and inventing new things. Record all your tests and keep them on a blog or in a workbook/file of some type. This is the kind of testing you might do to build your initial portfolio.

When you are thinking about ideas for briefs that have been set, look for images that already exist (Internet or library) and start a mood board for discussion with the client and your team.

Location hunting

As you develop your practice, you will start to think about locations and how significant they are in a commercial image. You need to take photographic tests in various locations and discover what you can do with different photographic approaches and different lighting sources. Finding locations may

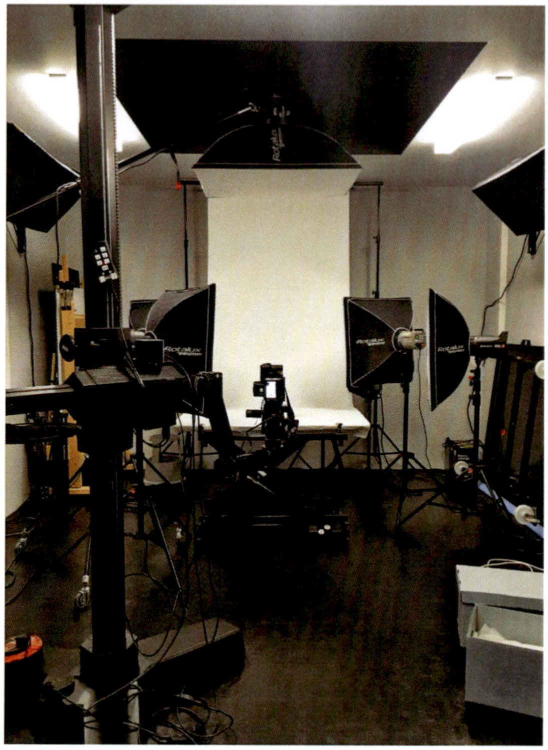

4.5

Title: The digitisation studio at The Postal Museum in London

Photographer: Andrew Bruce

The Postal Museum has its own photographic studio where their photographers can accurately document the objects and items in the museum collection. The studio is used to photograph objects and produce marketing material for the museum. Cameras are also used to 'scan' posters, books, slides and negatives; they also make 3D object scans using the process of photogrammetry. The studio offers its services and expertise to other museums, galleries and institutions.

involve getting permissions to enter. This is an important part of the research process, and if you are using the work you make on location in any commercial context, then you must get permission in writing as well as verbally to get in and use the site.

There are professional location hunters and numerous locations that are well known shooting spots, such as Bourne Woods in Surrey in the UK, that are often used for fashion shoots. (This was also the location for the opening scenes of the film *Gladiator*.) Shoot Factory is a location agency and library that provides a service for photographers and film-makers to find the place they want to shoot in. A simpler and cheaper method might be to search the Flickr site or Google Images.

Location is vital and affects the whole mood of an image, but with imagination it is possible to create numerous locations within a studio setting. You can also collaborate with set designers in a studio or on location; the more people involved and the bigger the studio space, the more the shoot will cost, so budgeting is an important part of the research process for a commercial shoot.

4.6

Title: Gucci. Cruise. Cannes, France

Source/Photographer: Magnum Photos/Martin Parr

One of Martin Parr's favourite shooting locations is the beach for both commercial work and his own personal projects. This shot was taken as part of a fashion shoot for Gucci on the beach in Cannes, France in summer 2018. In between shooting the looks Parr would photograph whatever he fancied and saw. The woman in this photograph was an extra that he photographed while waiting for the next outfits to be ready.

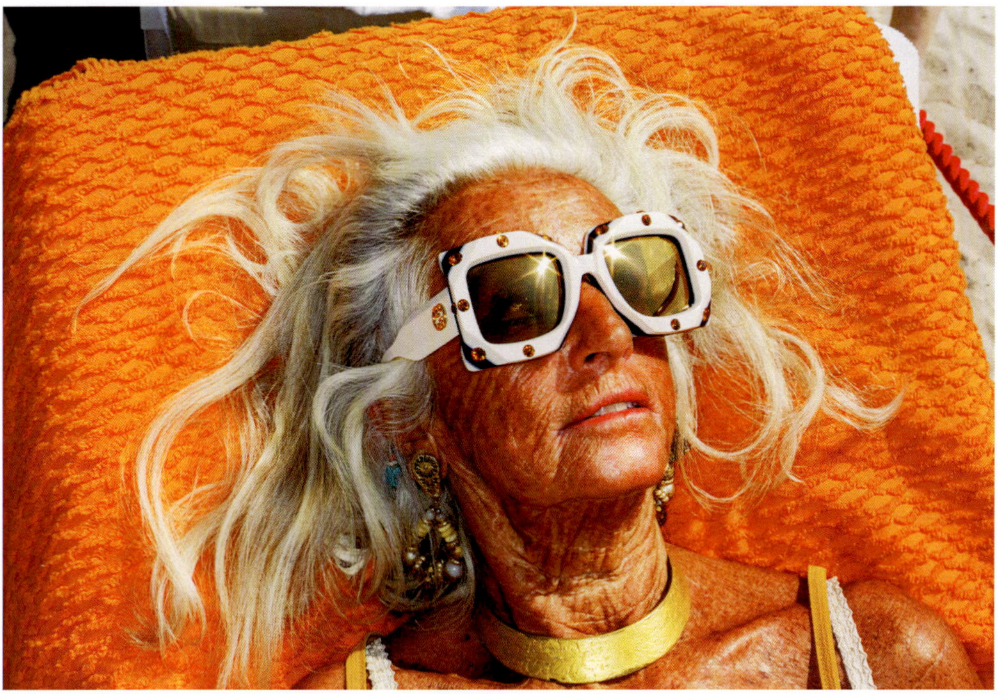

Model spotting

Models can be researched through model agencies and websites, or you can use your friends or start looking for models wherever you go. Model Mayhem is one of the main websites promoting collaboration between professional models and photographers. The Freelance Club also has a models section on its website. Frequently photographers model spot themselves in the street and have managed to persuade numerous ordinary people to be part of their shoots.

4.7

Title: Double page spreads from *PYLOT* magazine

Photographers: Anna Fox and Andrew Bruce

This double page spread is from a fashion shoot by Anna Fox and Andrew Bruce for *PYLOT* (the only UK fashion magazine that works solely with analogue photography). Bruce and Fox used real Morris men and women as their models.

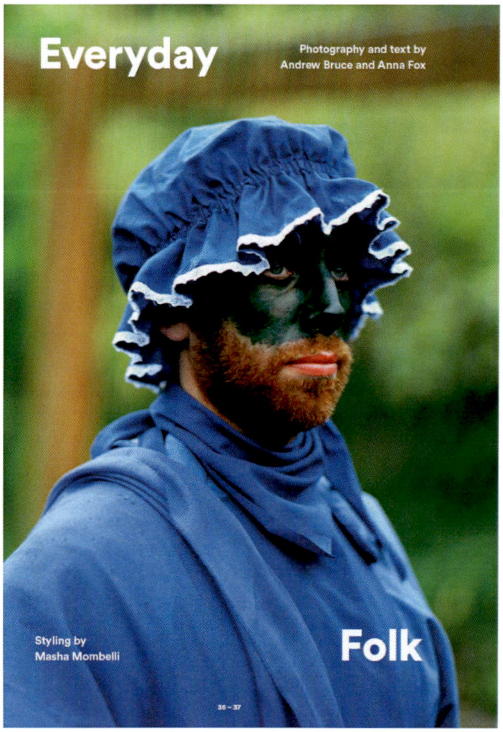

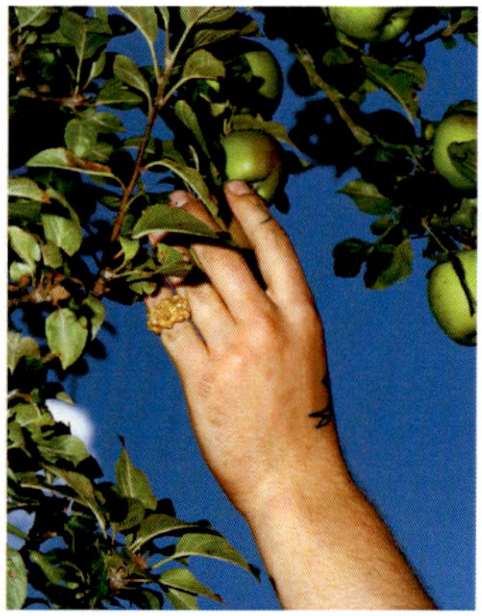

OPPOSITE BEN from *The Seven Champions Molly Dancers* wears his own clothes, bonnet and neckerchief model's own and scarf by **Richard James**
ABOVE SHALIN from *The Seven Champions Molly Dancers* wears ring by **NIZA HUANG**

Everyday Folk

Creating a mood board

A mood board is the way that you communicate your initial ideas to the art director/designer as well to your team. You might ask other team members to create their own mood boards and then use the combination of these to develop ideas further. As mentioned above, you can easily use Pinterest for this or you might simply want to create a PDF of an arrangement of images, text and colours. Making a mood board is a way to evoke a certain feel in a set of images. It is the feel or style of this set that you want to convey in your shoot.

4.8

Title: Mood board for Cold Cases

Source: Juno Calypso

This mood board has been created collaboratively by artists Natatsha Caruana and Juno Calypso in preparation for the workshop 'Cold Cases' that they ran with Work-Show-Grow (https://wsg.bigcartel.com/product/cold-cases). The workshop involved the artists making work alongside the workshop students and was exhibited in the Old Police Cell Museum as part of Brighton Photo Fringe.

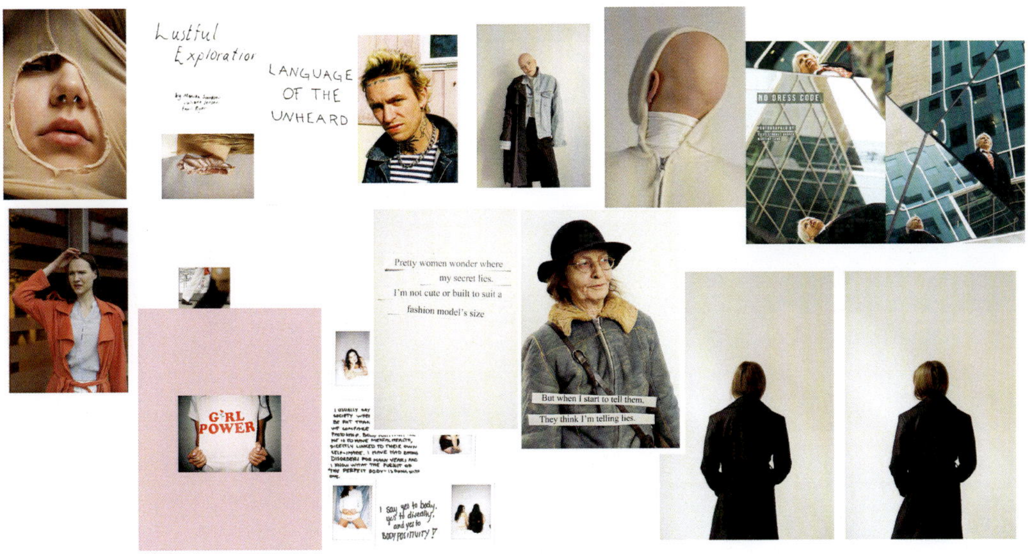

Writing a proposal

Sometimes you will need to write a proposal for your commissioner; this could be a picture editor or an art director in an advertising agency. The proposal generally needs to be upbeat, informed and easy to read. Your style/approach should be evident in the mood board. A proposal may also be the basis for a short editorial commentary in a magazine that could be published with your work. You can ask for guidance from the magazine for the word length and style of writing. You can ask them to edit the writing for you if you want help with it. A proposal may also include a budget and timeline for the work. Writing is both a creative and technical skill, and it takes practice; you should practice writing alongside your photography.

If your proposal is selected and you are hired to carry out the project you will enter into a contract with the commissioner. A standard contract will include details of the job such as name, location and fees. The proposal will also include information on the material such as format and deliverables. This is why it is important to research and test the shooting style outlined in your initial proposal before entering into a contractual agreement.

4.9

Title: Photographer's agreement

Source: Natasha Caruana

This is a copy of a standard contract a photographer would have to sign for a commercial job. Both the photographer (or the agent on their behalf) and the commissioner will sign before the project starts. Following the summary page of the project specification there will be a number of pages of terms and conditions. These are in place to protect both parties and set out the terms agreed in relation to the project.

PHOTOGRAPHER AGREEMENT (INCLUDING FILM/MOVING IMAGE)

PROJECT SPECIFICATION

Company	[redacted]
Agent	
Photographer	
Client	
Project	
Job Number	
Shoot Location and Time	
Materials	*[insert details of artwork, format, deliverables to be provided by photographer]*
Fees	*[insert shoot and where applicable usage fees payable, if no fees payable then state: "£1 (One Pound Sterling) receipt of which is hereby acknowledged"]* *[SPECIFY IF INCLUSIVE OR EXCLUSIVE OF VAT]* *[SPECIFY IF FEES ARE TO BE PAID TO AGENT OR PHOTOGRAPHER]*
Maximum Agreed Expenses	
Usage Start Date	
Territory	*[Specify territories, e.g. UK]* The parties acknowledge that the internet is by it's nature Worldwide
Term	*[insert term of licence]* *{IF THERE IS TO BE A FULL ASSIGNMENT OF ALL RIGHTS SPECIFY THIS HERE]*
Media	
	The Materials may be used by [redacted] for its own PR and promotion including use on its intranet and website. The Materials may be used by [redacted] to enter Creative Awards. The Materials may be used for academic textbooks on the advertising industry and advertising industry websites.
Extended Use	[*insert agreed fees* for each extended use in the Media in the Territory for each consecutive period of [insert] months after the end of the Term].

Date: .... Date: ....

Signed: .... Signed: ....

Name: .... Name: ....

COMMISSIONER **PHOTOGRAPHER/AGENT**

Testing

As in any form of practice, testing should play an important part of the research process. A commercial job often has a very tight deadline, so you should be constantly testing out new visual ideas in every spare moment that you have so that you will be ready with something new for the next job. You need to think about new ways of representing people, objects and places, as well as trying out new techniques.

You could say that the commercial world of photography is more conservative than the art world, but it is a hectic arena where new ideas change rapidly and traditions can be continually challenged. The best work can be shockingly new. Try using different types of model, ones that are not normally used, when you test for a fashion shoot: the fashion world has plenty of space for thought-provoking and often politically driven work.

4.10

Title: *Because your eyes won't see*, 2015

Photographer: Lisa Carletta

Because your eyes won't see by Lisa Carletta was published in *Material Girl Mag* in 2015. The shoot revolved around the idea of waiting – waiting for love, friendship or success – and how inaction leads to invisibility. Lisa worked with a small team for the shoot. Lisa will pick her own team from those she has worked with in the past. Normally she will retouch the images herself, but if time is tight and there is budget to do so, she will use a re-toucher. The team for this shoot consisted of photographer (Lisa), stylist, set designer (for advice only), makeup artist, hairstylist and re-toucher. The shoot took two weeks for preparation and one week shooting, followed by one week of post-production.

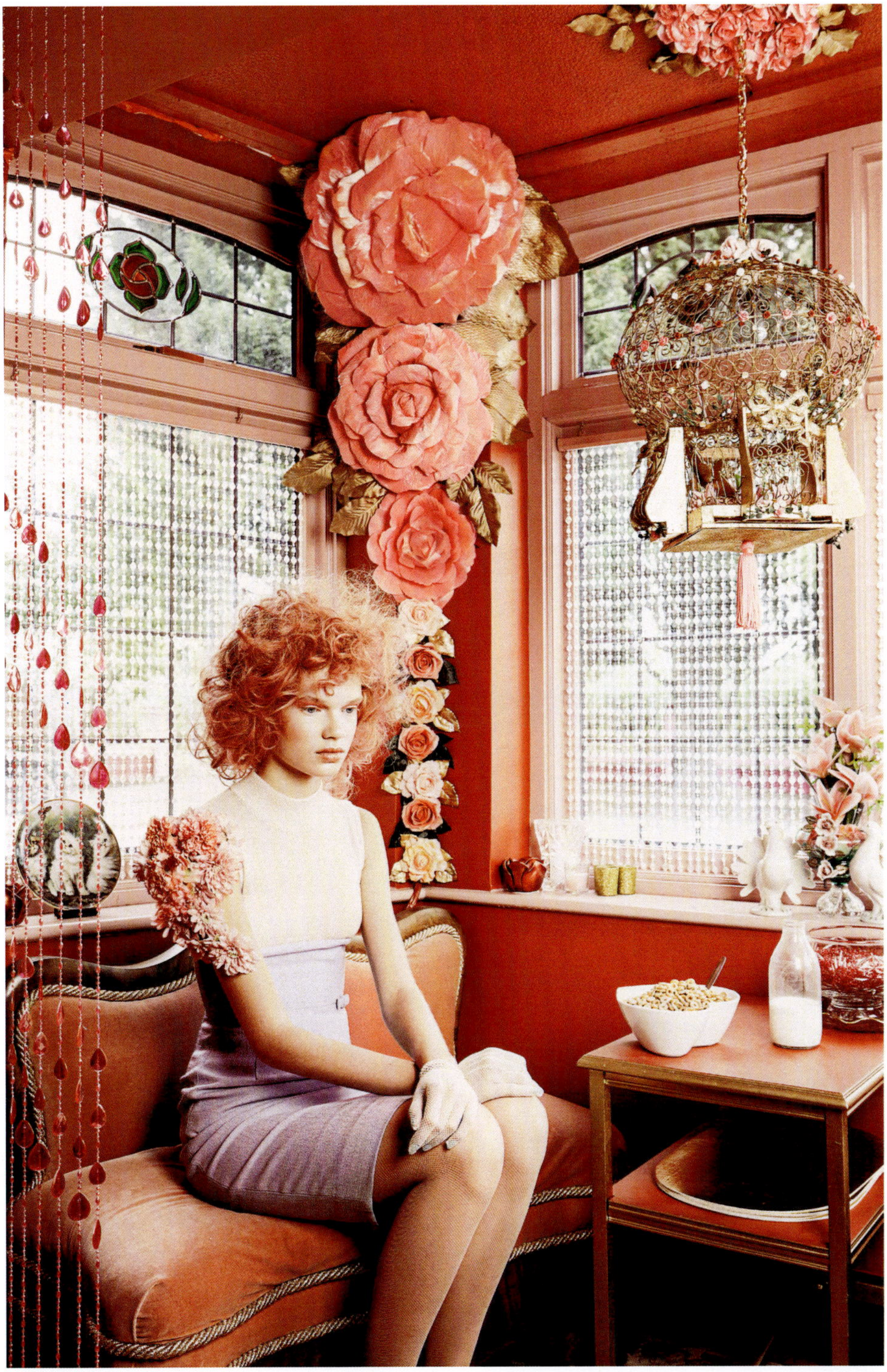

4.10

You may be art directing your own shoot; this means your research will be more extensive as you would need to know much more about the company/magazine you are working for. If you are working for an art director or a picture editor, try to get to know them and find out what they have done before. If you are keeping up with your networking activity, you will already know about certain people in the business and what their reputations are. Magazines such as *Creative Review* will give you background knowledge about art directing and who does it best.

The team

In the commercial arena, you will often be working in teams. You might have met stylists, assistants and various technical people at university and through networking events. You need to research what they are working on and who they have recently worked with. You can do this via the Internet and through speaking to other photographers. Sharing knowledge is helpful, although historically many people in the commercial world of photography like to keep their knowledge to themselves (it can be a very competitive environment). Keep information on potential team workers as part of your research archive.

It may be new to you as you leave your photography course to think about working in groups; you need to be open-minded, able to communicate ideas and able to trust in other people's ideas and knowledge. Being friendly is also a vital part of team work. There are whole teams already formed whom you can hire as a group, which can be very helpful if you are working away from home and do not want to take a big team with you.

4.11

Title: Cover, *Creative Review*

Cover image art direction by Gem Fletcher. Photography by Aaron Tilley.

Creative Review is an important reference for those in the commercial photography, advertising, fashion, music and design industries. The magazine started in the 1980s and focuses on offering analysis, advice, insight, leadership and inspiration.

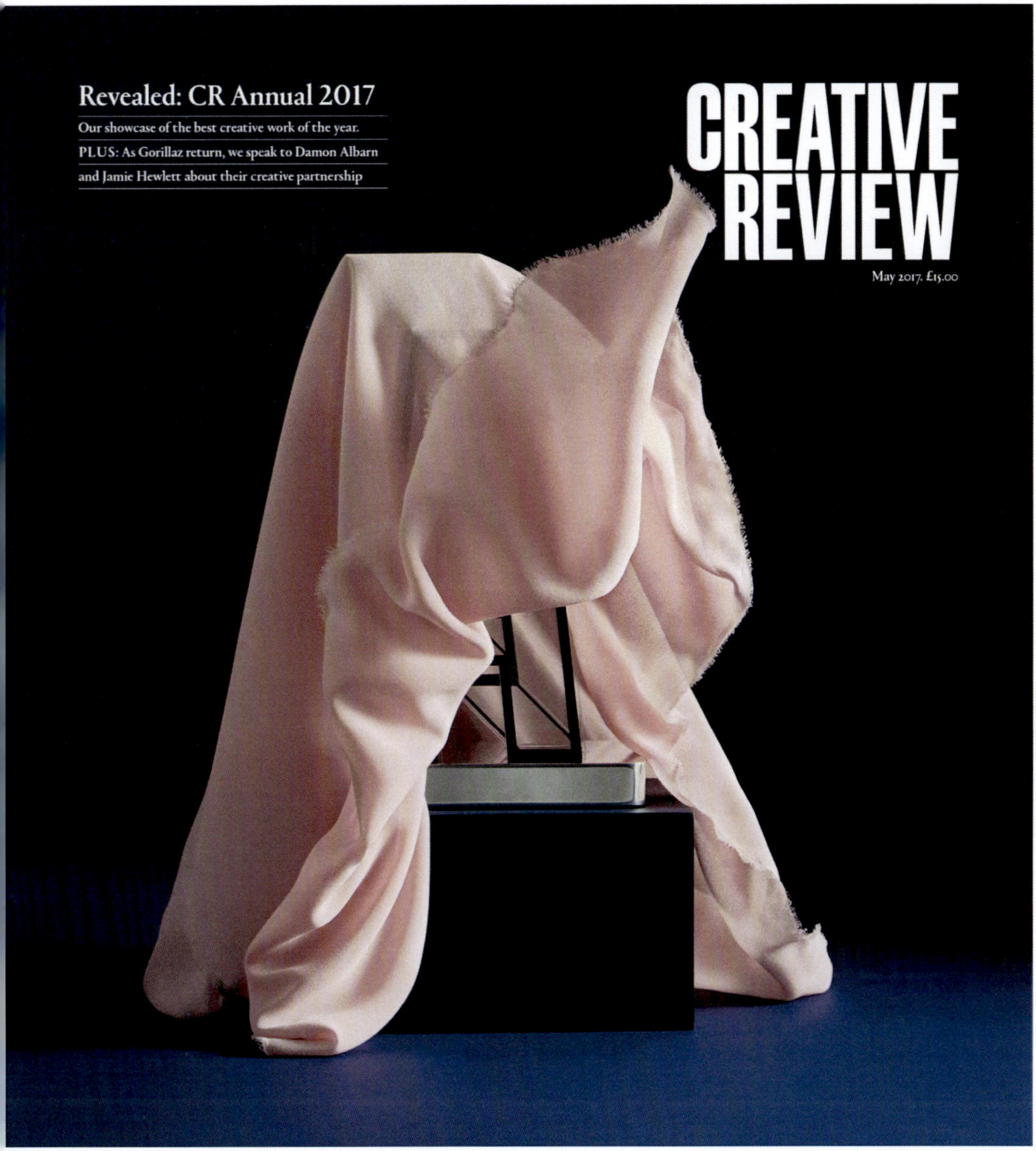
Revealed: CR Annual 2017
Our showcase of the best creative work of the year.
PLUS: As Gorillaz return, we speak to Damon Albarn
and Jamie Hewlett about their creative partnership
CREATIVE
REVIEW
May 2017. £15.00

4.11

Equipment and techniques

In the commercial world, you need to have a wide a range of knowledge when it comes to equipment – not only what to use but where to hire it or buy it from. The Photography Show, an annual event at the NEC in Birmingham, is a great place to find out about all the photography companies and the various equipment that they sell or hire. At the Photography Show you also find out about competitors in the field, and there are numerous talks scheduled that demonstrate new equipment and showcase various photographers' works. Finding out about equipment is as much a part of your research as testing it. Some companies look for students and graduate ambassadors to test new equipment. Make contacts with people in the business and see what they can offer.

4.12

Title: OTMFC – 'Their Little Black Truck'

Photographer: Vicki Churchill, photographed on a Nick Meek Beetle Campaign, shot in California. Lighting: OTMFC. Production: Happy Harley Production.

Photographers book road crews as well as fixers/production companies to assist them with shoots abroad so that everything is worked out before they arrive and to avoid the expense and trouble of transporting all their own equipment. OTMFC (One Tight Mother Fucking Crew – otmfc.com) trucks carry all the studio kit and lighting equipment for location shooting, with assistants who not only know all about lighting but look after the gear too. If a photographer takes their own equipment into a different country, they sometimes have to arrange travel carnets and this is usually done through ATA Carnets (see https://www.atacarnet.com/carnet-countries, which lets you know which countries demand a carnet and how to get one). A fixer or production company is a person or a group based in country who will assist the photographer to get access to what they want to photograph. The photographer Nick Meek uses Happy Harley (http://happyharleyproductions.com/clients) as his production company. A 'fixer' is a term more often used by documentary photographers, and contacts for fixers can usually be found in documentary agencies.

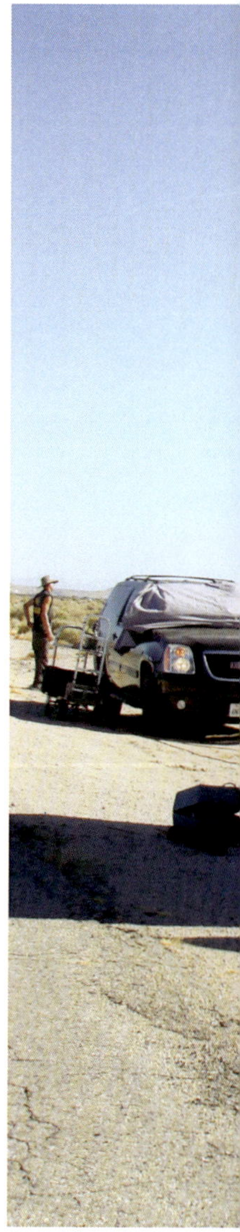

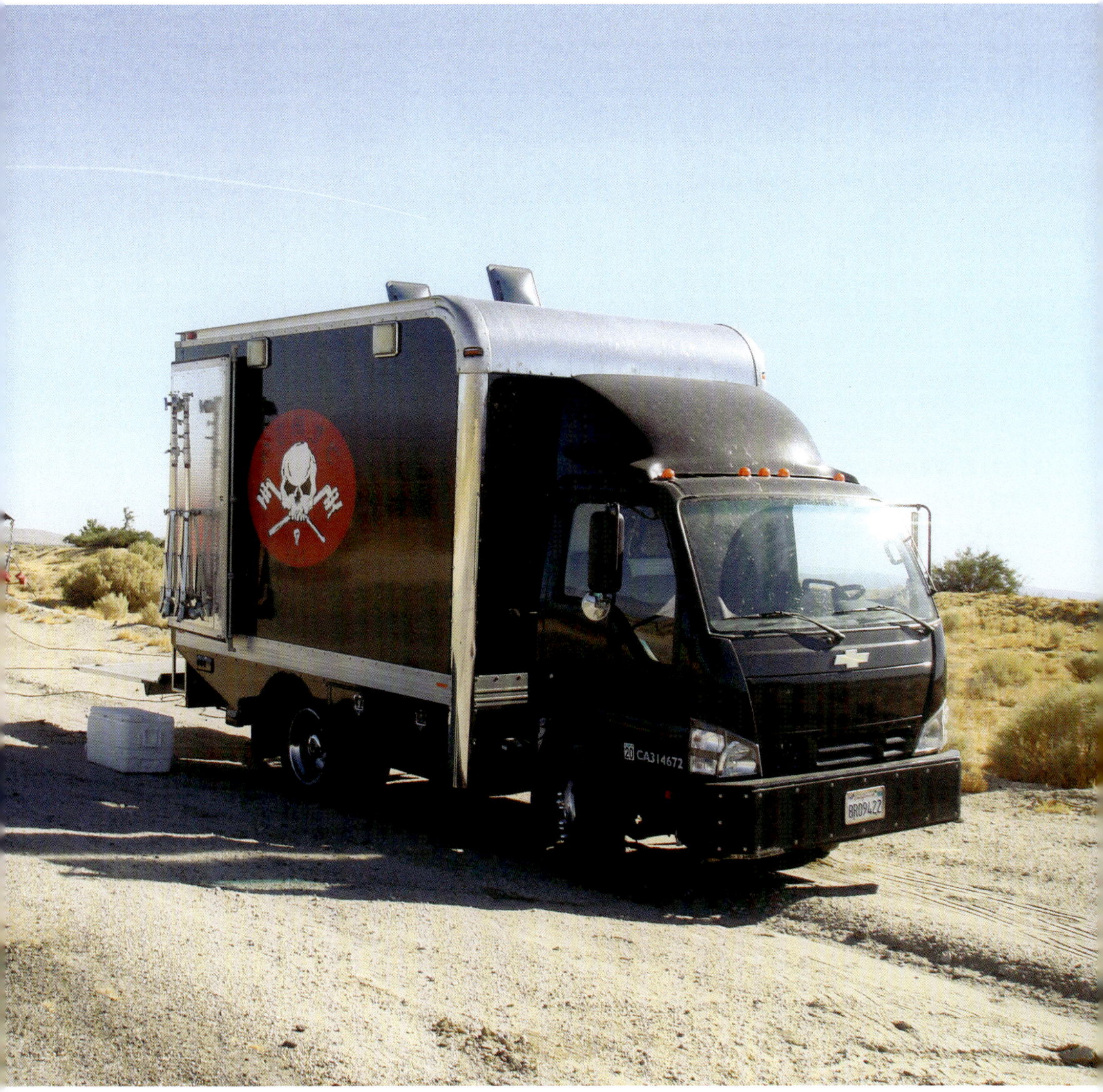

4.12

Editing and production

Editing (post-production manipulation) of your images may play a major role in their final appearance. You should be well versed in digital editing and design programs on your computer or know someone who might do the post-production work for you. This means that you will need to have done good research into how to use the wide variety of tools available in digital editing and how to become highly professional at using them. Post-production is an expensive business, so finding out who the labs are and who they have done work for will help you decide where to go with your images if you decide to ask someone else to do the work.

4.13

Title: example of post-production work

Photographer: Tim Savage

This studio portrait was originally made as part of a series to illustrate Tim's book about black and white photography, *Understanding Digital Black and White Photography: Art and Techniques* (2016). In the post-production work for this image, Tim set out to simplify the image through stripping out original colour overall (boosting the tonal response of skin tones to distinguish them from clothing and background) before adding a very weak split tone to add a sepia hue to the highlights and complementary blue to shadows. In terms of exposure, he increased the depths of blacks while boosting dark greys to retain pure black and also increasing detail in the shadows. He also boosted overall clarity to give the image some punch. Tim increased contrast to the model's hair to accentuate the light and shade and applied local dodging and burning effects to promote form (specifically around the neck and arm and filling shadows under the eyes). He also removed minor blemishes using the healing tool in Photoshop and added a subtle vignette. The image was finished with gentle sharpening to provide some additional crispness to the detail of beard and hair. 90% raw file processing in Lightroom. 10% finishing in Photoshop.

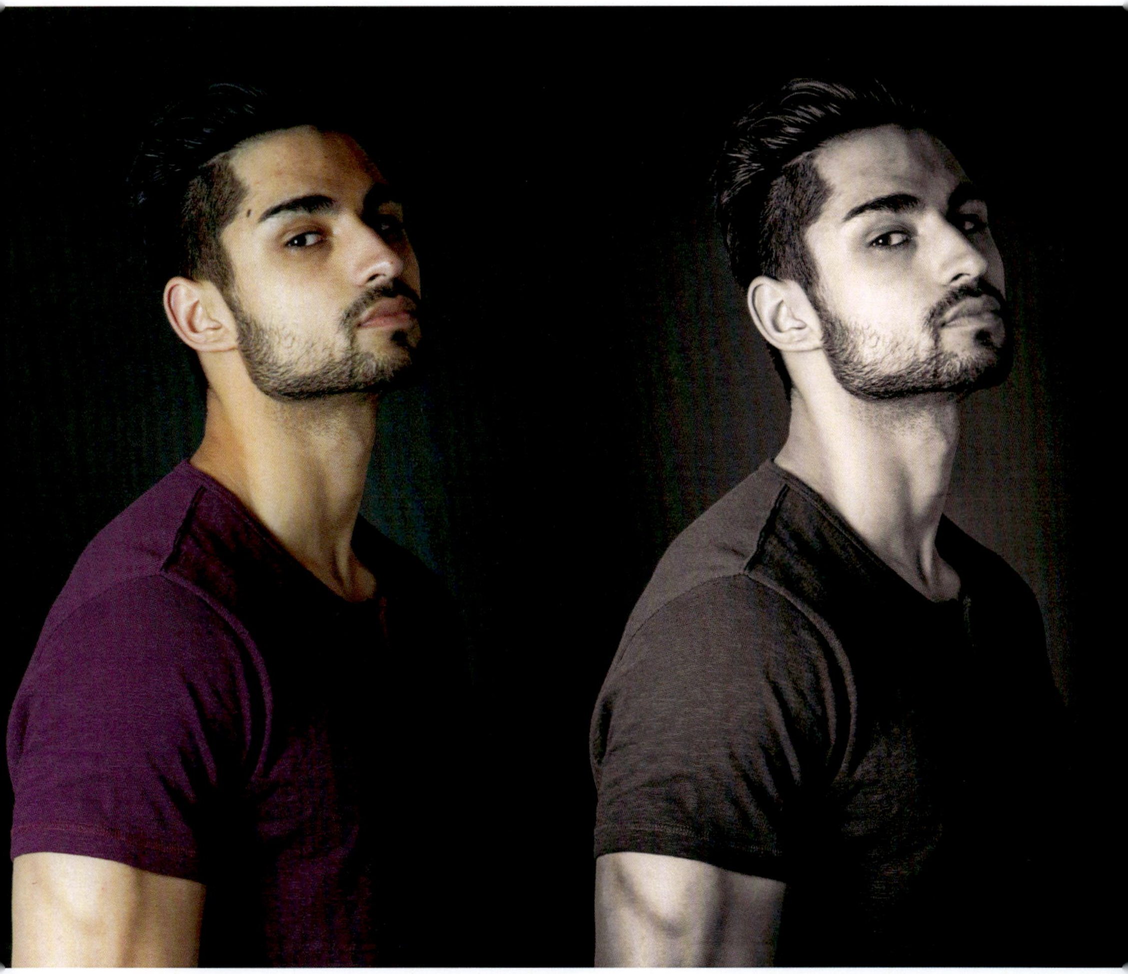

4.13

Editorial

The editorial world is huge, so you probably need to decide what type of storytelling you want to do if this is a field that interests you. Editorial photographers often have a niche type of story that they cover, such as photographing young people, stories around sport or farming life, or a particular region or country. What is exciting about editorial is the range is so vast that you can find things that really interest you and approach the magazines within that area. You need to find out all the magazine titles in the areas that interest you, find out who the picture editors are, and try to get to know more about them. Study the imagery and the narrative structure of the stories that interest you. Really think about how to make a set of images that say something interesting about a subject that may have been covered many times before. You need to find interesting and new angles on subjects that might already be quite familiar.

4.14

Title: Forte Sisters, *Town and Country Magazine*

Photographer: Sasha Hitchcock

Sasha Hitchcock creates editorial stories for a range of magazines and websites as well as making her own personal projects. This image comes from a series shot for *Town and Country Magazine* featuring the Forte sisters in Browns Hotel showcasing their Christmas Taste Menu.

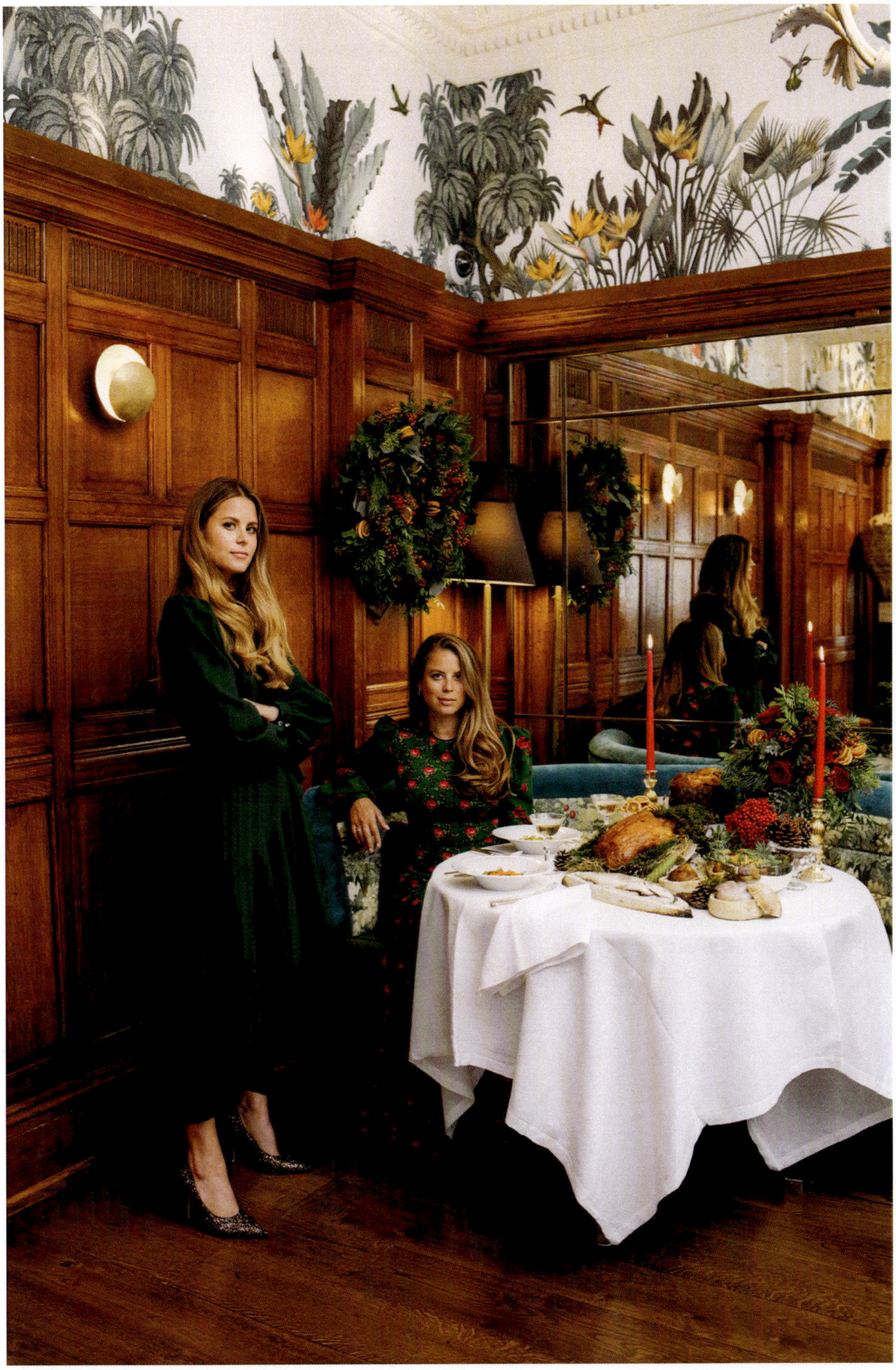

Fashion and advertising

Photographers working in fashion and advertising create some extraordinarily innovative images. These photographs are intended to sell products and lifestyles: a successful shoot will show these in such a way that they are understood and made desirable. Most fashion and advertising photographs are created through teamwork, and photographers in this field are likely to work alongside an art director, who will direct the shoot, and a number of assistants and stylists. These shoots can attract high budgets and the elaborate work produced often reflects this investment, as different levels and types of production can be explored with larger budgets. Fashion photographers often have to produce a large volume of editorial work for very little pay before winning commercial commissions.

Fashion and advertising photographers may also be recognized as artists in their own right. Artist and photographer Man Ray produced some groundbreaking fashion photographs alongside his artistic practice, and photographers continue to do this today.

Both advertising and fashion photography are clearly constructed, but they can veer from creating images in a documentary style through to images that are overtly fabricated, constructed either in a studio or on location. Constructed photography is created both by commercial photographers, in advertising and fashion, and by artists for their own work: art and commerce frequently influence one another.

4.15

Title: 'Power Suit' editorial, *Muse Magazine*

Model: Hanne Gaby; Photographer: Robert Wyatt

Robert Wyatt was a fashion photographer who worked for numerous high-profile clients, including Prada, Valentino and British Airways. He regularly had his work published in magazines such as *Vogue* and *i-D*. Wyatt started working as a gallery-based photographer and worked on his own projects alongside his fashion and advertising commissions. More of his work can be seen online at robertwyatt.net.

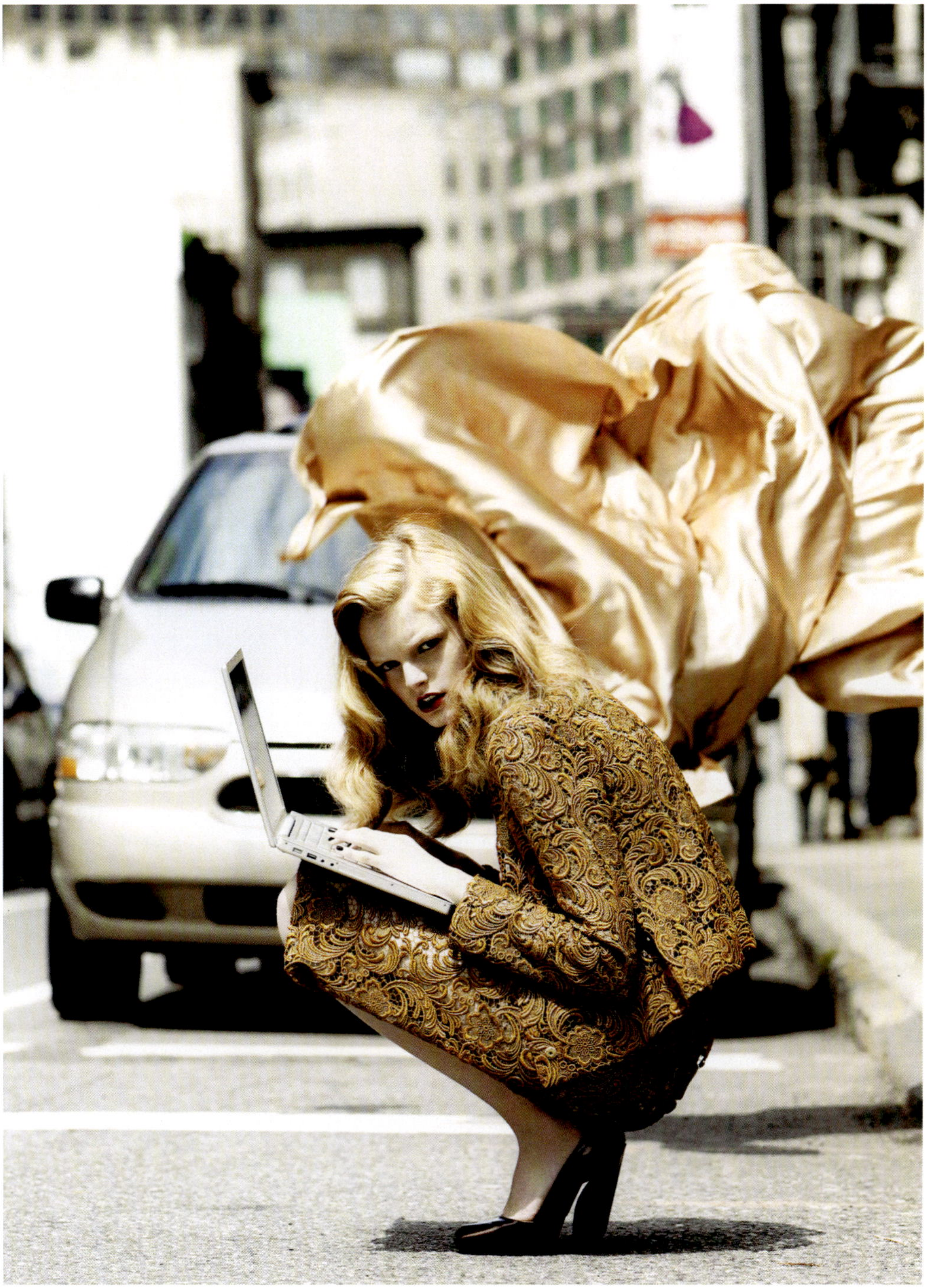

4.15

Other commercial fields

You might find that your commercial work leads you into photographing for company reports or working with designers or documenting projects for people. Again, this is an area of work that is incredibly large and diverse. It is probably best to start investigating designers near you to find out which clients they are working for and what they do for them. Start building up a database of people in the design world to contact. If it is DVD covers and the music world, for example, that interest you, find out which design company did the work for ones you like and investigate their other projects. You might also want to link up with design courses in your university and collaborate while you are still a student. This is an effective way of developing your network.

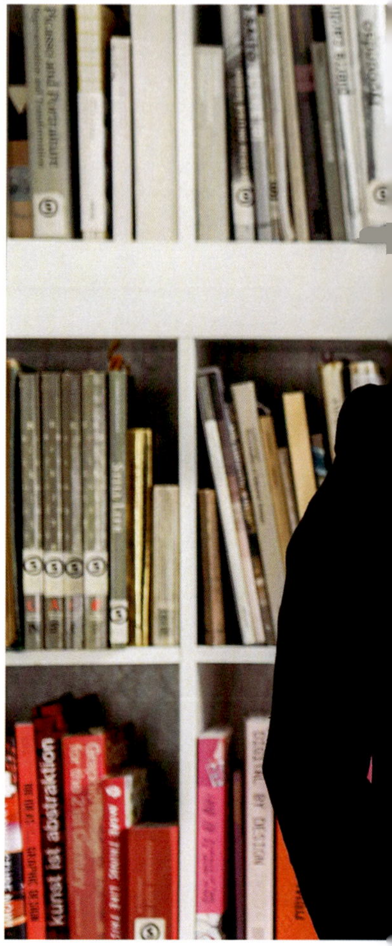

4.16

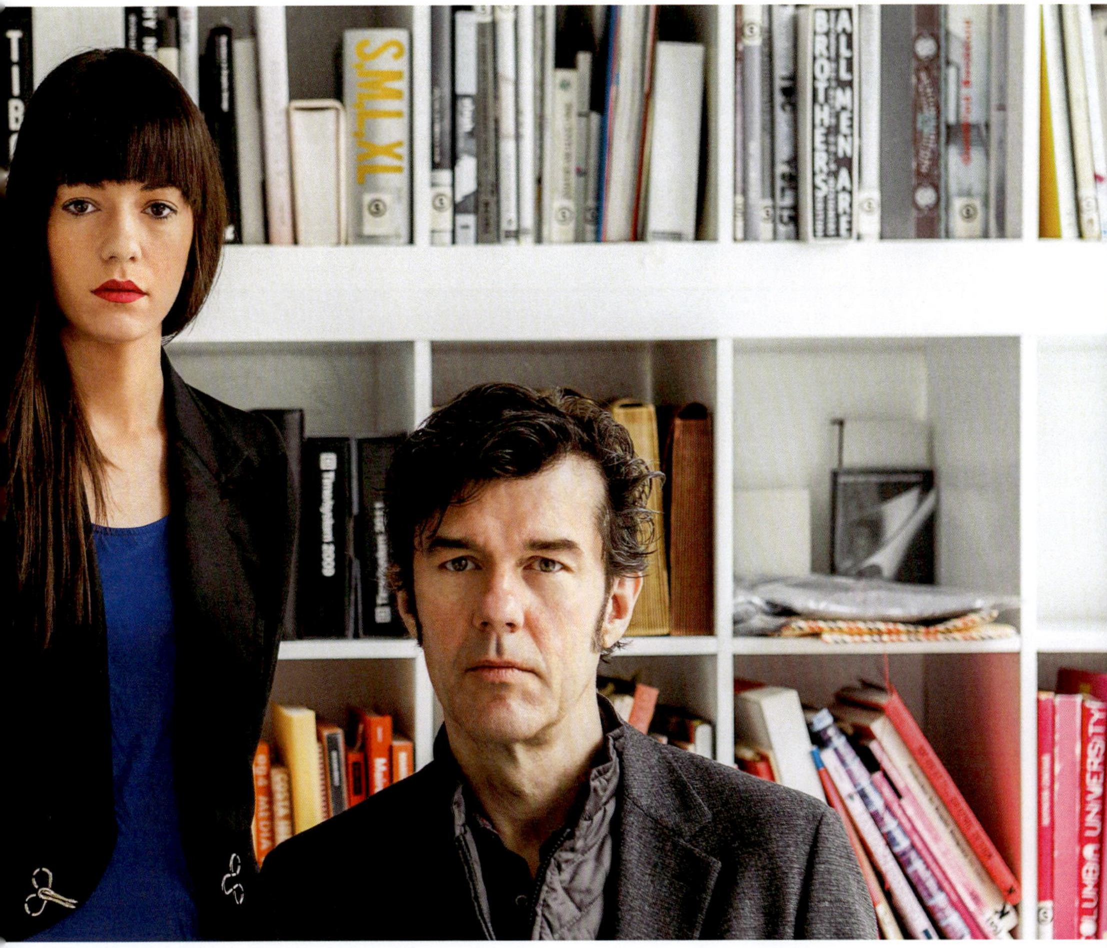

4.16

Title: Jessica Walsh and Stefan Sagmeister

Source: Marco Scozzaro

Designers Stefan Sagmeister and Jessica Walsh co-founded the design firm Sagmeister & Walsh Inc. in New York City. They have designed album covers for Lou Reed, OK Go, The Rolling Stones, David Byrne, Jay-Z, Aerosmith and Pat Metheny. Sagmeister & Walsh is an example of a design group that regularly use photography; they have a large scale exhibition currently touring European museums – 'Sagmeister & Walsh: Beauty'.

Case study 4: Nik Adam and Luke Norman

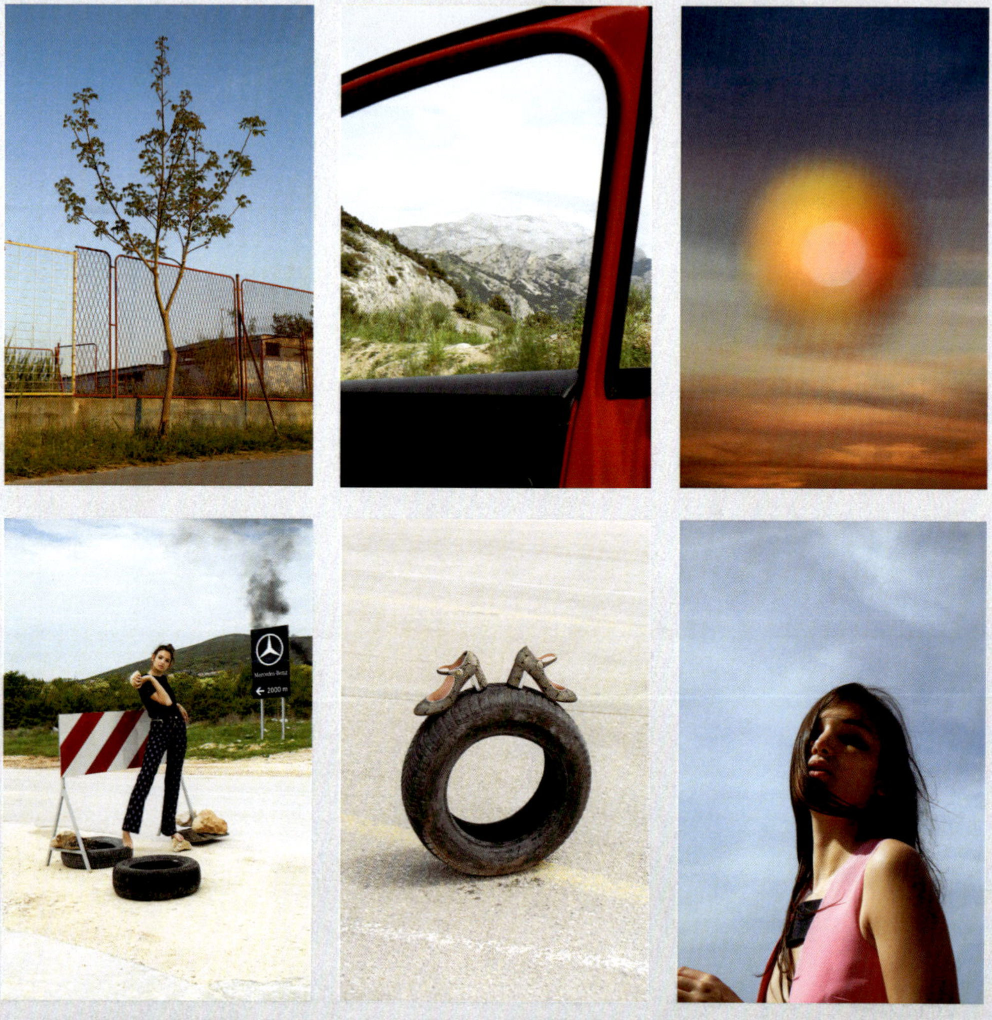

4.17a

Title: *Out of the Box* commission for *New York* Magazine, 2015

Model: Emory Ault; Assistant: Peter Haynes; Photographers: Luke Norman & Nik Adam

These images were shot on a commission for *New York* Magazine (2015). They represent the crossover between Adam and Norman's personal work and their commercial practice. "Often when shooting for a client there is a significant level of compromise to be considered, but from time to time an opportunity arises where the client offers us the creative freedom to really push our photographic practice and try out new ideas."

For this shoot, Adam and Norman had a small team (this is how they prefer to work): the two of them, their assistant, the model and the stylist. "We hired a car in Croatia and just hit the road, stopping wherever looked interesting. We find that we are most inspired when we are in a totally new environment, being left alone to explore and document our surroundings."

In between photographs of the model, they intertwined photographs that were more like images from their own art work: still lives of their sculptures and other interactions in the landscape. This combining of personal and commercial works helps to build the narrative of the series.

Case study 4
Nik Adam and Luke Norman

Nik Adam and Luke Norman first began working together in 2009, shortly after they graduated from the University for the Creative Arts, UK. They had like-minded ideas about photography and what they wanted to do with it, but also knew what a tough business they were getting into and so valued the idea of working collaboratively. In their personal work, Adam and Norman use photography to engage with the discourses of a variety of photographic and sculptural practices. They work on ideas drawn from contemporary life.

It is important to Adam and Norman that the division between art and commerce is blurred, and that today there seems to be much more acceptance of this than ever before. When they exhibit work, they like to bring together images from both their personal projects and images shot while on commission, though they always avoid including product in exhibitions. When they do commercial jobs, they frequently incorporate additional imagery that represents their personal work, developing the narrative of the sequence around a blend of commercial and art-based imagery. In an interview, they stated that:

> If you can see through the intent of an image which an artist took while on a commission, (for example to display a new branded shoe) then this will not offer much artistic worth in a larger discussion, but if the image is appropriated (in a different context) to comment on consumerism or something like that in a new and exciting way – we think this can be a productive blend of the two approaches of art and commerce.

Adam and Norman's commercial clients include *10 Magazine*, *Elle Magazine*, *Refinery29*, *System Magazine*, *New York Magazine*, *Jigsaw*, *XL Recordings*, and *The Financial Times.* Their arts-based projects have featured at internationally renowned photography festivals, such as *Unseen* (Amsterdam) and *SCHAU* (Dortmund), and have most recently exhibited work in London at both *Somerset House* and *The Photographers' Gallery*. Their work has been published in *FOAM Magazine*, *Art Review*, *Photoworks*, and *The British Journal of Photography.*

In 2010, Adam and Norman, together with former student colleague Peter Haynes, founded the collective group Wandering Bears with the idea of working together; organizing exhibitions, talks, podcasts and workshops; and showcasing and collaborating with both emerging and established artists from around the world to create something unique within the photographic community. Wandering Bears was set up as a centre for the making of new work, developing ideas and collaborative projects. It is a creative studio and photography-led community currently based in London.

The group are keen to connect to what they see as an international community of photographers: people who are enthusiastic about discussing and dealing with cutting-edge photographic practice. They are also interested in devising ways in which to engage a wider public community in the practices of photography, and were excited by the way that their show, *Inside Out Upside Down*, at The Photographers' Gallery in London, did this. During the exhibition, they foregrounded exciting new work by contemporary practitioners and presented it in an interactive way, inviting their audience to participate by responding to the art works on show and creating their own new images. Using their mobile phones, visitors had the opportunity to create and photograph their own unique personal interpretations, printing out the images to complete an individual take-away sticker album. The exhibition brought in children and teachers, who subsequently invited the group to run a workshop in a local school.

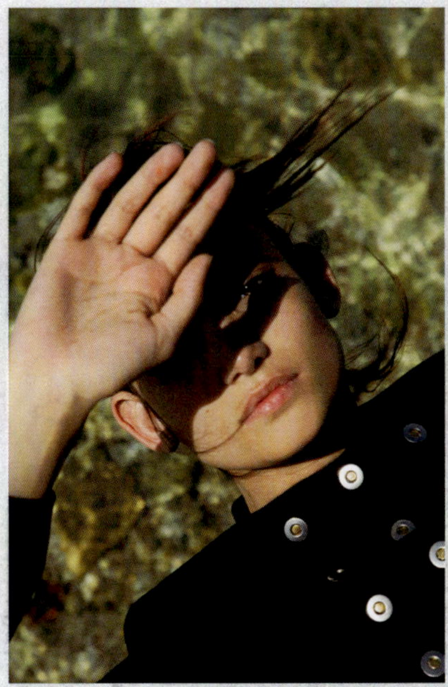

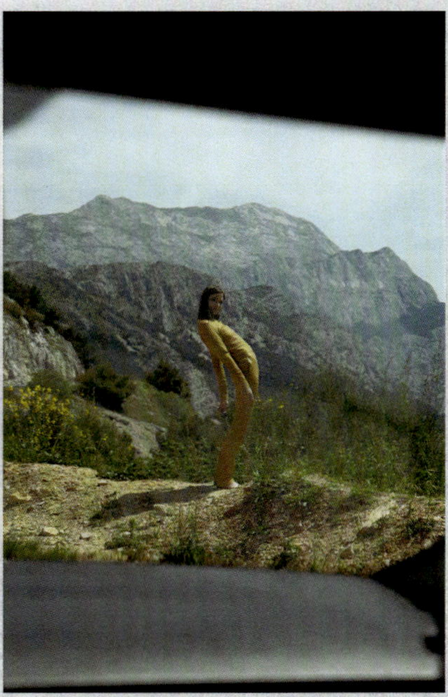

4.17b

Activity 4 Making a mood board

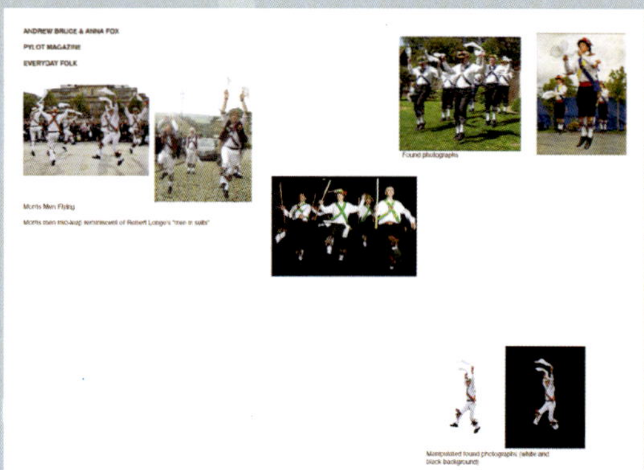

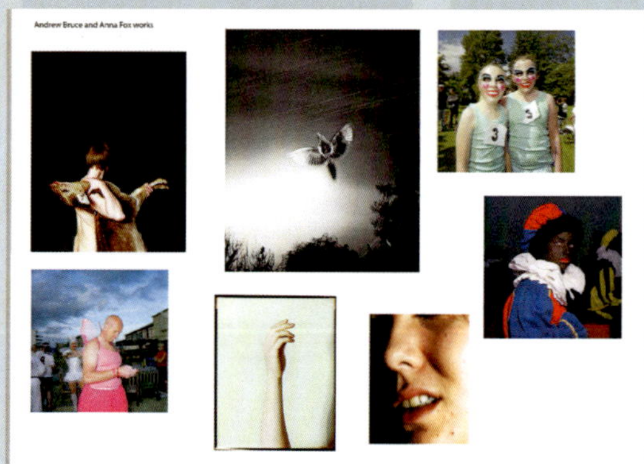

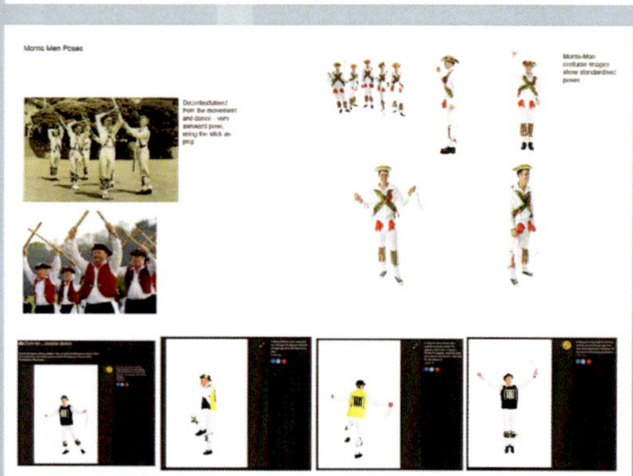

4.18

Title: Mood board

Photographers: Anna Fox and Andrew Bruce

This mood board was made by Andrew Bruce with image input by Anna Fox for a fashion editorial for *PYLOT* magazine. A mood board helps photographers, editors and stylists share a vision for their shoot.

A mood board is a vital part of the commercial photography research process. It is designed for you to gather ideas from disparate places and to share these ideas with your team, editor, art director or client. For this activity, you are going to design a mood board for a fashion shoot titled, *Restaurant at the End of the Universe* (reference Douglas Adams).

You can look for images for your mood board in different places. You should use the following list of sources to draw together as much imagery as possible: your own photographic archive, postcards, books, websites, television, magazines and going out to shoot new material.

When you are searching for images, you first need to think about the words in the title (*the end of the universe*, *universe*, *restaurant*) as references for your search. Then, you should try a wider trawl by broadening your research, thinking about different types of locations or times of day that might be of interest for the shoot. For example, if you put "American diner at twilight" into a Google search, you get a whole different set of imagery than if you put in "English Country Restaurant." Decide what will best suit your shoot (or what you want to test for the shoot) and start pasting images into a document, onto Pinterest or onto your mood board.

Next, you might want to think about characters. Who would be at a restaurant at the end of the universe? Perhaps you could look up science-fiction characters or a particular sub-group. Collect a stock of characters from different places to add to your mood board. You might also want to collect objects, animals and flowers; not simply for the literal things that they are, but also to think about colours and textures.

As well as using the Internet, you should be looking at other photographers whose work relates to the theme or mood of your board. It is vital to look at current photographers, from both art and commerce, to shape your mood board and to give you an idea of current works in the field of photography that have dealt with the theme you are interested in.

You are now going to look at the images on your mood board in closer detail. Start picking elements from the mood board that you might need for your shoot. Think about lighting, visualize the time of day and consider your location. All of the images on your mood board have been collected not to copy but to give you and the team an opportunity to realize the potential of your shoot – to get a flavour of what the shoot could be.

If you were actually designing a commercial shoot, members of your team (the stylist, for example) will look at what you are thinking about through looking at the mood board. The stylist (who may also have added images to a mood board) will then start to think about the clothes for each character, and so on. You would also start to look for potential models, either through a casting agency or from the street.

You may choose to make a cut-and-paste mood board, where you would need to re-photograph the board in order to send it to other people. You can photograph and screenshot the images to gather everything together as a digital file.

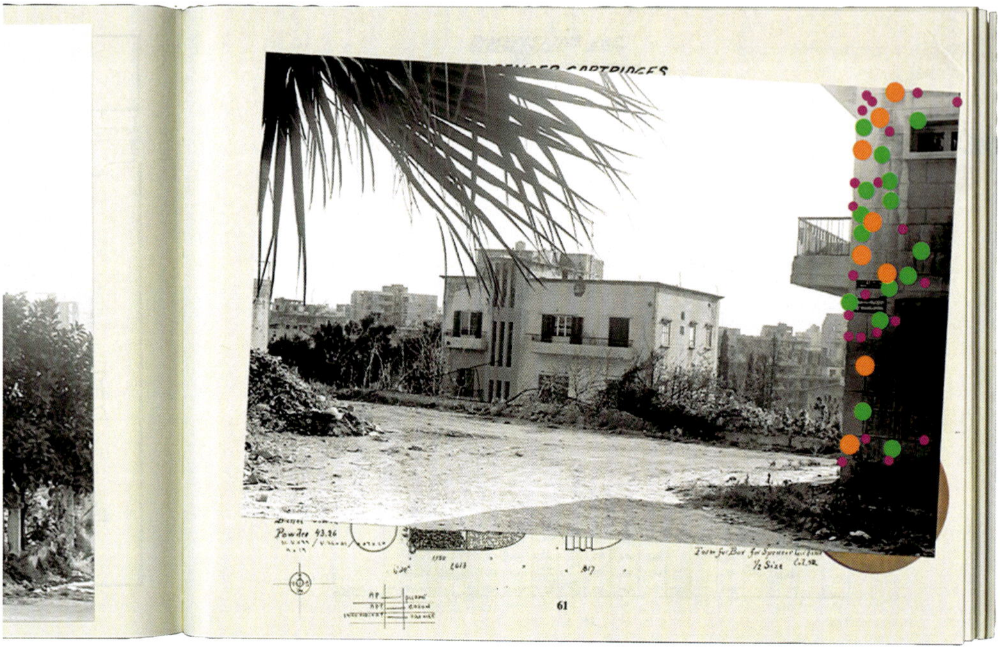

5.1

Title: *Let's be honest, the weather helped*, from The Atlas Group

Source/Artist: Anthony Reynolds Gallery/Walid Raad

Walid Raad is an artist who works with mixed media: installations, performances, photography and video. He is based in New York but grew up in Lebanon. Since 1999 he has explored the fraught contemporary history of his native country through a fictional research foundation, The Atlas Group. This vast body of photographs, texts, films and videos purport to chronicle Lebanon's protracted civil war of 1975–1991. Documents from within the series blend fact and fiction in a way that suggests the highly subjective and contested nature of historical memory. Here, photographs of Beirut's bombed-out and bullet-pocked infrastructure are overlaid with brightly coloured dots.

5 Research and practice

After you have been working as a photographer for a while, research becomes connected to practice in a way that makes the two hard to separate: the working process of undertaking research becomes second nature. A reflective practitioner automatically engages with research methods and a continuous process of critical analysis right at the start of a body of work.

Some photographers may state that they do not conduct research, yet everything they have learnt through years of practising and looking at other photographers' work is part of a research process and will have its influence. For example, an advertising photographer working outdoors may spend days measuring changing light conditions at the chosen location before the shoot: this is research. The location itself will have been selected through a careful research process.

From testing the relevance of your work, determining your audience and taking time to view your work from new angles, to the final production decisions on how to present your work, your research will continue to inform your practice.

Like a scientist, a photographer has to test whether what they are doing works in the way they expected and also whether it is effective for the audience they are intending to reach. Tests can vary from trying out technical methods – such as lighting, camera type, film or digital – through to examining the way the work is going to be produced and for whom it is being made. A photographer or artist concerned with theoretical discourses will test applying various theoretical concepts through their practice: a very specialized approach. Other tests can include looking at the relationship between the photographer's own work and other related work throughout history. Why does a particular project work at a particular time and what is its significance in relation to work that has been made before?

Methods of testing

Photographers frequently use a wall in their studio or home to pin or tape up images they are testing out. The photographs need to be big enough to be viewed clearly. The photographer may put up different sized prints next to each other to try to judge how changes in scale affect an image or series of images.

Different tones and colour balances may also be tested. Frequently, these images will be left for several weeks as the passing of time slowly affects how the photographer views the work. Visitors to the studio also bring their own comments and these, too, affect the photographer's thinking about the work.

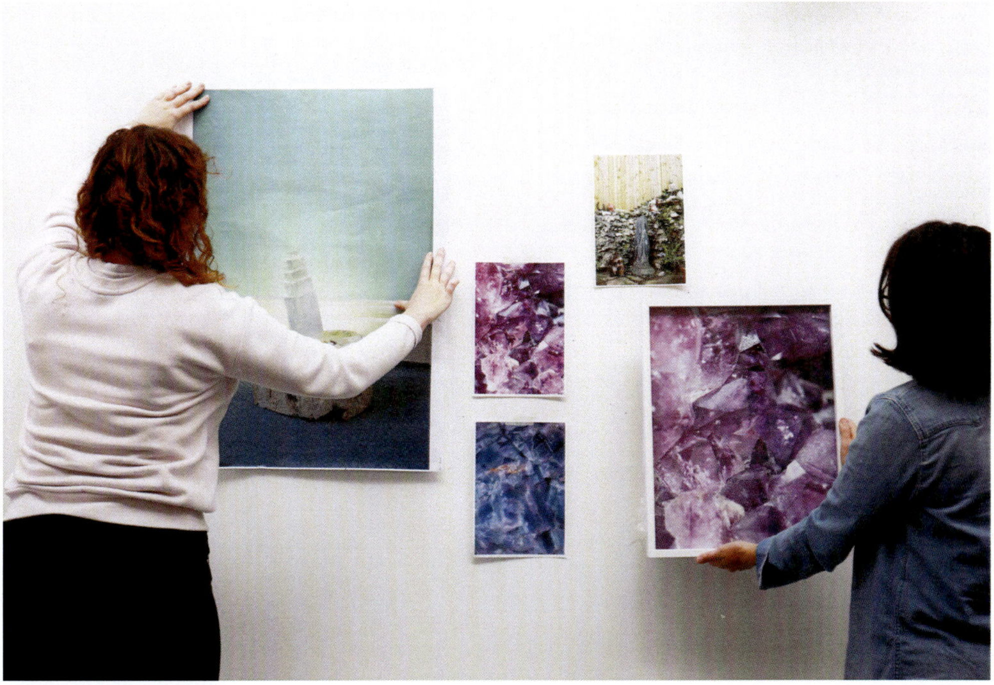

5.2

Title: Different methods of testing narrative and scale

Photographer: Alice Cooke

Photographers have various methods of testing: pinning work to walls, hanging it up or projecting images when testing large scale. Essentially the intention is the same: to test how photographs look next to each other, to work out the narrative structure of a sequence, to find out the optimum scale and to analyse the colour and tone of images.

Part of the research process that photographers continually engage with is considering where their photographs might go and who the audience will be. What type of venue or publication would be the best place to convey the meaning of the work?

There are so many contexts for photography that it may be that your work fits into more than one place. When a body of work is ready to have a public profile, you need to consider how the context will affect the meaning of the work and which setting will enable your work to be seen by an appropriate audience. A family album is made for family and friends; a billboard speaks to the masses; a framed photograph in a commercial gallery speaks to a select group of individuals from a world of art buyers and sellers to art lovers. A museum or public space tends to attract a broader audience and has a commitment to education.

Research ethics

Something else that photographers should continually engage with in their research and practice is the concept of ethics. If you are a student or researcher working within an academic institution, it is likely that the institution will have research ethics guidelines that you will be required to consider and apply to your practice.

When photographing people, you may need to use model release forms, which give you written permission to use a person's image. It is an important part of your working process to make your subject aware of what you are doing and the context in which their image might eventually be seen, although this becomes quite difficult for street photographers and some other documentarists. The same applies when conducting interviews: all interviewees need to have comprehensive information about the project and you need to confirm with them that they understand it.

Essentially, developing an understanding of research ethics means you have considered all the possible difficulties – personal, social or political – that your work might encounter when it is revealed to the world.

A professional photographer working outside of academia will not always concern themselves with the same kind of research ethics as academics, but it is likely they will have an ethical code of their own based on personal political beliefs and also informed by the relevant laws that apply where they are working.

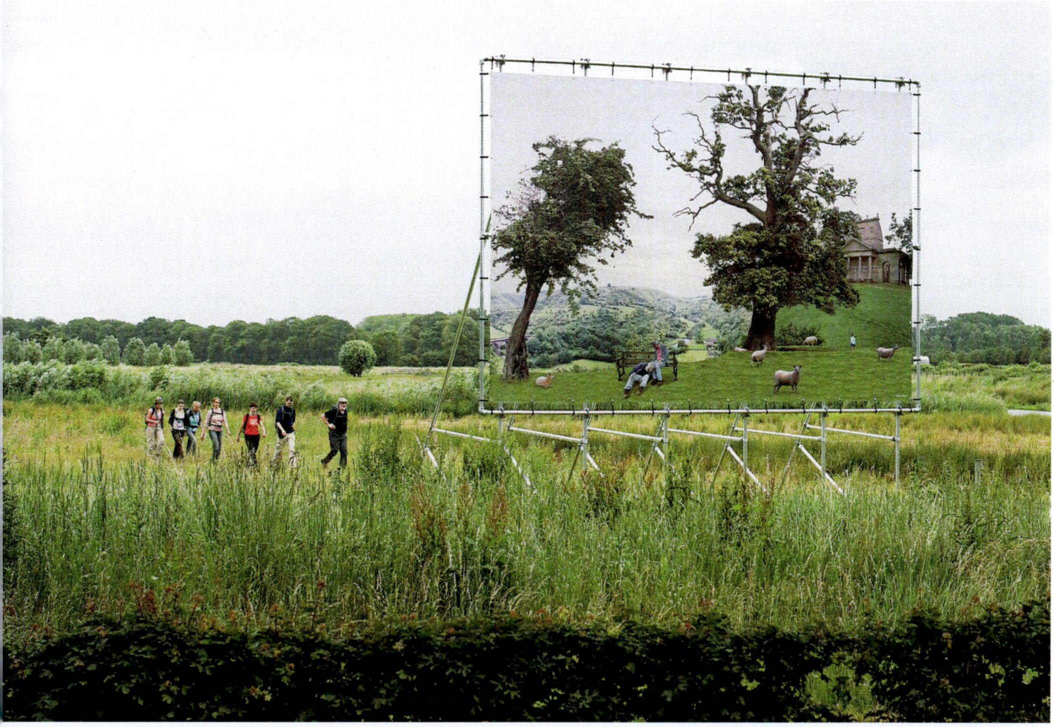

5.3

Title: 'Dreamers', from *High Summer*

Artist: John Goto; Installation photo: Ernie Buts

The curators of the Idyll and Friction in the Landscape project in the Netherlands took photographic artworks of landscapes back into the landscape itself, displaying the images on huge, specially constructed billboards. It was a form of montage: setting the idyllic or romantic images against the expansive Dutch countryside, near Sint-Michielsgestel. Visitors could walk or cycle a circular route to see all twenty exhibits in the project. In this case the artwork was placed directly into the community.

There are so many contexts for photography that it may be that your work fits into more than one place.

Past research, if filed in an accessible manner, is highly valuable. You may want to revisit a project that you feel was not completed properly, or a body of work that could have been developed further. In both cases, the original research material will prove invaluable.

Going back through your archive can be incredibly inspiring and gives you a sense of what has been achieved over a period of time and that a history is being recorded. New ideas can often be sourced from research archives as, generally, they hold more material than could have been used when they were originally set up. Photographers regularly revisit their archives and some have particular images or items that crop up as being significant for them time and time again.

New inspiration from old research

Karen Knorr has been photographing since the late 1970s. Her series, *Gentlemen*, documented life inside private gentlemen's clubs in London: highly privileged patriarchal settings from which women were excluded. Knorr gained access to these clubs and produced a fascinating series of images critiquing these environments.

Twenty-five years later, Knorr revisited the research she conducted for this series in order to create a new one, with a different focus: *Ladies*. This was made more achievable because Knorr had kept the original research material that sparked her idea many years before.

It can be a joy to revisit old research as you never know where it will lead you: by keeping original research materials, you keep open the door for revisiting, reinterpreting and re-appropriating your earlier work.

5.4

Title: 'Those Who Fear. . .' from *Gentlemen*

Photographer: Karen Knorr

One of the twenty-six images Knorr created in the 1980s which used image and text to create a humorous and critical perspective on the patriarchal values of London gentlemen's clubs and their members.

The text featured with each image is drawn from speeches made in Parliament or in the news:

> Those who Fear
> the Rule of Women
> but Love the Monarchy
> should reconsider their Prejudice;
> to ensure the right
> of his Firstborn to the Throne
> will create a better Climate.

Knorr made a later series, *Ladies*, as a fashion commission for *Pink* magazine. Knorr used the stylistic approach of the *Gentlemen* series to create a parallel series about women. The fashion is the handbags; Knorr played this down to some extent, allowing her images to echo the art-based staged documentary work she had made in the 1980s. See https://karenknorr.com/photography/ladies/.

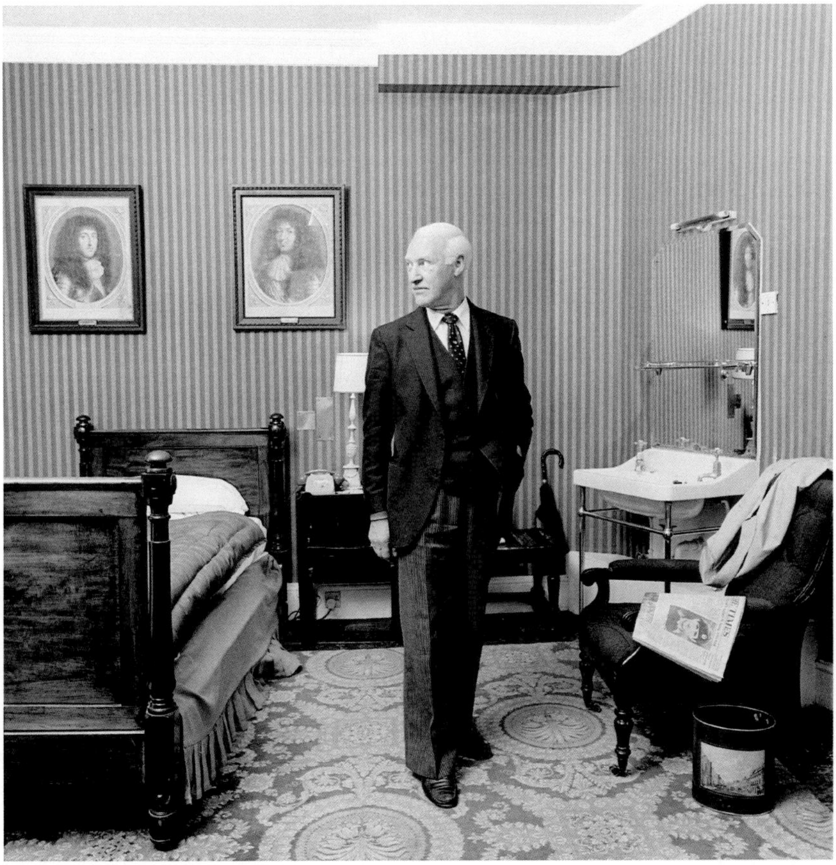

Those who Fear
the Rule of Women
but Love the Monarchy
should reconsider their Prejudice;
to ensure the right
of his Firstborn to the Throne
will create a better Climate.

5.4

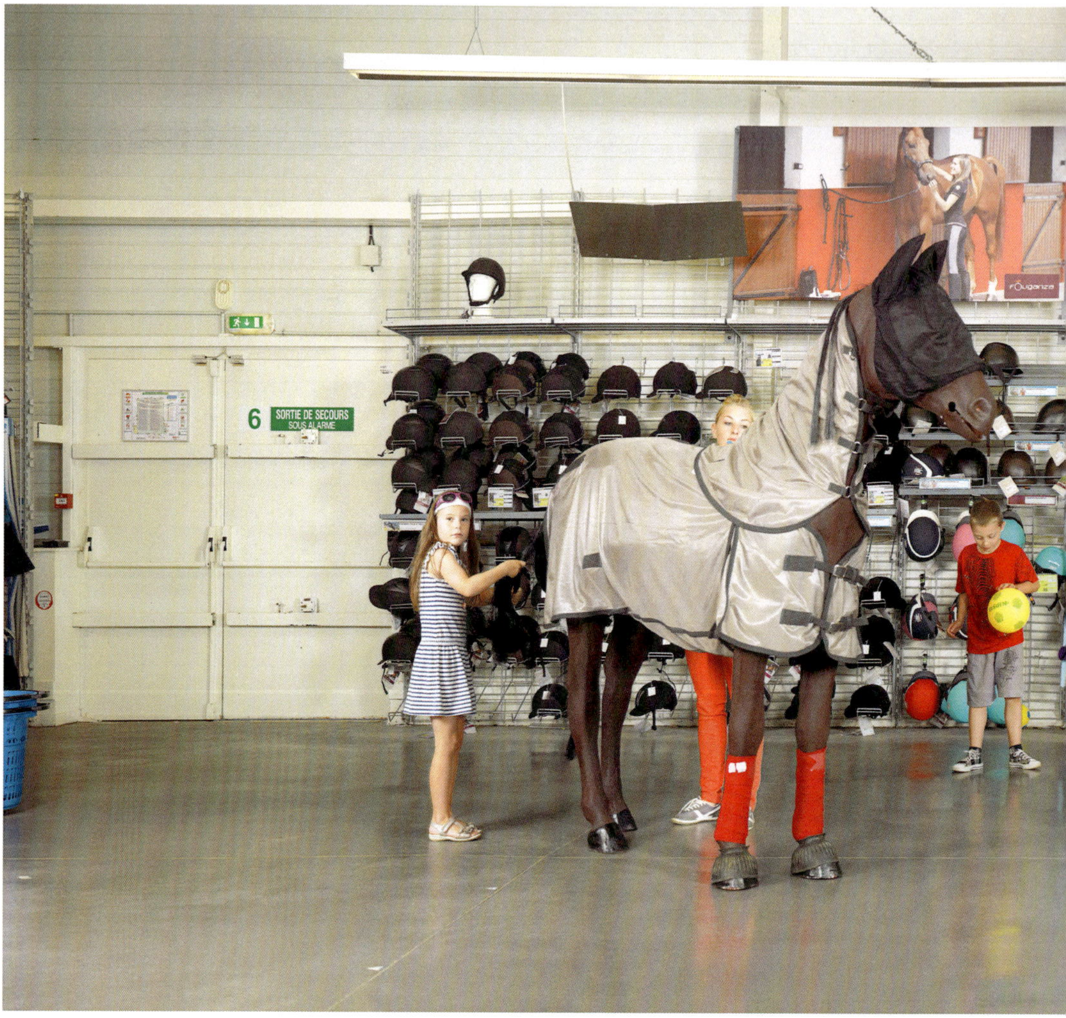

Thinking time is something that is often overlooked: it sounds like a luxury. However, it gives you an opportunity to look at your images from a different perspective. Taking a sideways glance is an important part of the creative process. It contributes to developing the approach that you take and the way you resolve a project. Try it out and take note of the kind of effect thinking time has on your photography projects.

Analogue and digital

If you are working with analogue film, there are periods of time between the shooting of the photographs, the processing of the film and the printing of the contact sheet that give you time to imagine how the pictures may turn out. This then mediates how you respond when you finally have a contact sheet in your hands.

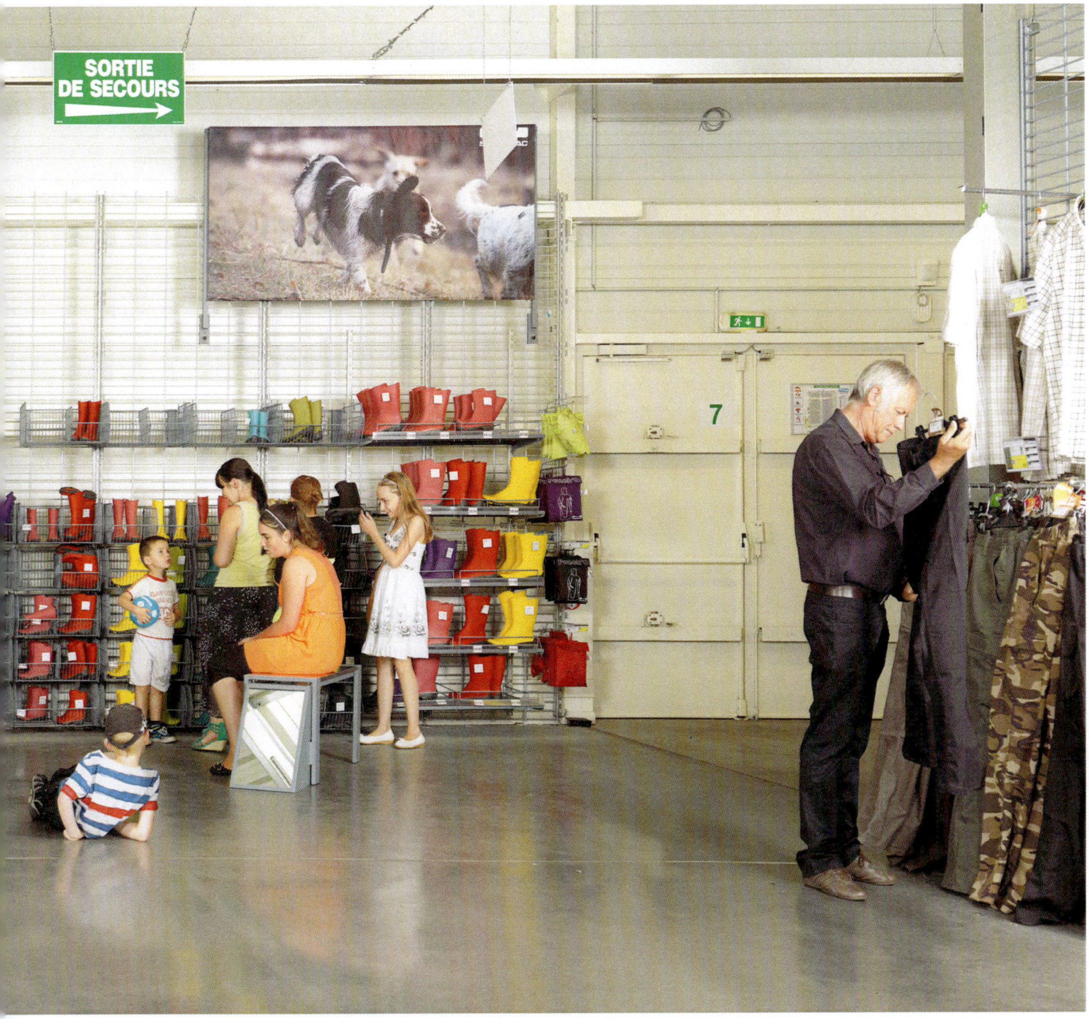

5.5

Title: From the series *Loisirs*

Photographer: Anna Fox

This image was part of a commission for Diaphane in France to photograph the contemporary leisure industry in Beauvais. Fox worked with a team of assistants to create these multi-layered images. Each photograph is shot over a period of two to four hours. First a back plate of the whole image area (the landscape) is created, and then Fox photographs people as they move in and out of the scene over a period of time. All the photographs are taken from one viewpoint (on a tripod) and then they are digitally joined after the shoot. The images look like "decisive moment" type photographs, yet they are made over several hours and each one is comprised of between eight and fifty single photographs.

It is very different when you shoot using digital as the result can be viewed almost instantly on the screen at the back of the camera. Photographers often delete their digital images quite quickly, sometimes a few seconds after shooting them, making decisions that they would not necessarily have made if they had waited and looked at the image a few days later.

Bearing this in mind, it is interesting to consider how the characteristics of photography could change in the next twenty-five or fifty years. If all photography is digitally shot, a certain type of photograph will have completely disappeared, particularly in the field of vernacular photography. Photojournalism and sports photography have already changed dramatically and are predominantly shot on digital.

Time and editing

Thinking time is also crucial when the photographer is reflecting on the potential edit of their project. Editing may well be done in collaboration with a publisher or a curator, but usually the photographer will have done an initial edit before the project reaches this stage. Potential edits that are being tested out often stay on the photographer's wall for weeks while decisions are slowly made.

Editing

Editing plays a more vital role than we imagine in forming the nature of a photographic project. It is a highly underrated skill, which is often hidden. Photographers do not generally like to show their discarded material; some photographers discard a large number of images while others shoot sparingly and discard few. It is best not to delete images when you are shooting digital until you have had time to sort and look at your images sometime after the shoot. Ideally you make rough print-outs, about A5 or A4 size, of images you think are interesting and then you literally play with them. Try taking a selection around with you in a plastic wallet and show them to people whose opinions you trust to see what they think.

Often photographers work collaboratively with an editor to select the final photographs; only sometimes is the editor acknowledged, so it is a really difficult process to research and find out more about. An editor might be a gallery curator, a designer, a publisher, gallerist, agency director or magazine editor. Always credit your editing collaborator: brilliance can often be achieved through a collaboration between editor and photographer – bringing an outside influence (one with experience helps) into the mix can shake up the resulting project. In the film business, the editor is acknowledged as a vital part of the project; we need to think about this for photography. A strong picture editor in a magazine can set the tone and style of the imprint.

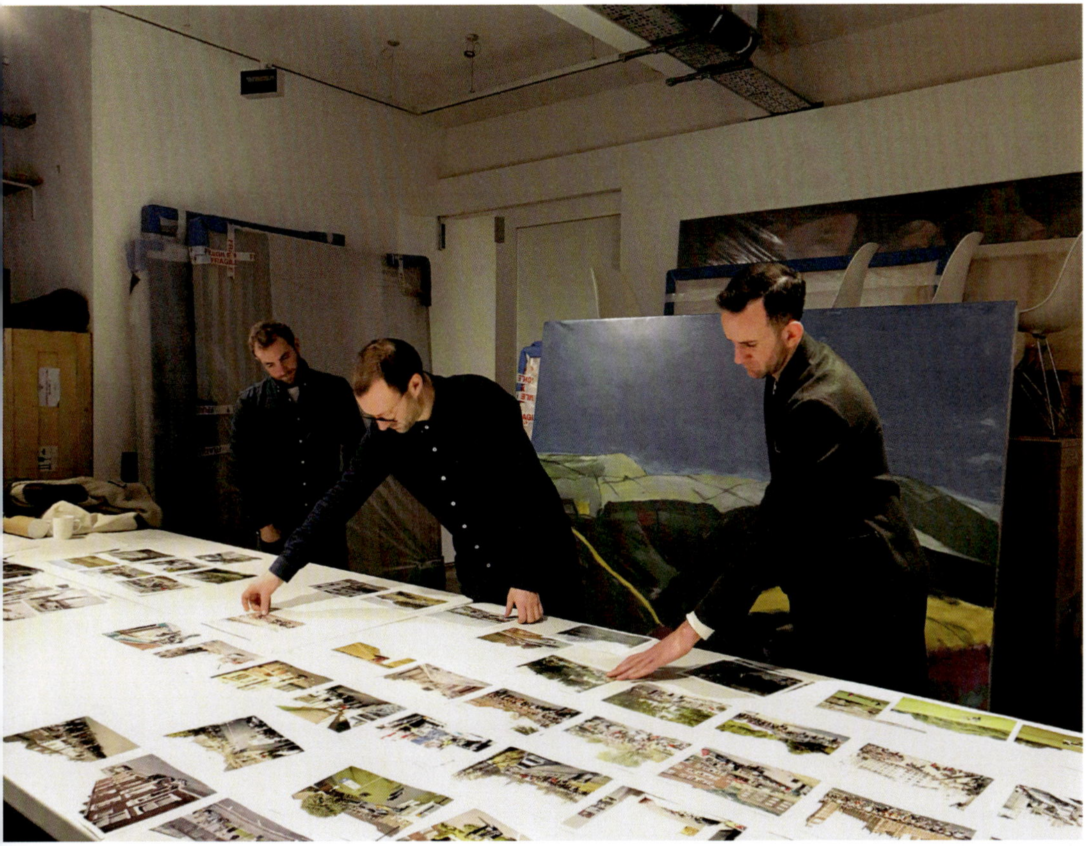

5.6

Title: The editing process for Simon Roberts' monograph *Merrie Albion – Landscape Studies of a Small Island* (Dewi Lewis Publishing, 2017) taken at Flowers Gallery

Photographer: Simon Roberts

Here we can see an important part of the process of the sequencing of photographs for Simon Roberts' latest monograph. Simon enlisted the help of Ben Weaver, who designed the book, and his gallerist, Chris Littlewood (Flowers Gallery, London) to assist with the editing process. Photographers usually work with designers and curators to develop the sequence and narrative for their work – it is vital to know that there is a level of collaboration in the editing process.

Time and changing meaning

Time can have a profound effect on the meaning of photographs. Longer periods of time, such as ten or twenty years, can considerably alter ways in which photographs are read and understood, especially documentary or reportage photographs that depict a particular time or place. As time passes, perspectives on the world change. On the day of a shoot, an outfit or costume will be understood in a particular way, but the meaning of clothing and style can be transformed through the passing of time. It is fascinating to look at style and costume in photographs from preceding decades. Something that may have seemed ordinary at the time may appear exotic; a dramatic costume can become historically significant. An art work can also radically shift in meaning over a period of time, particularly if it was made in response to a particular attitude that was held at one time but not later.

5.7

Title: Cheryl, Sloane Square

Photographer: Derek Ridgers

In the 1970s and early 80s, photographer Derek Ridgers roamed the streets around London's Kings Road with his 35mm camera, looking for punk rockers to photograph. He photographed hundreds of young people during this period and has an extensive archive of the project. These photographs celebrate the inventive dress and style of the period. Ridgers' images from this period have become valuable historical documents as well as being very powerful images in themselves.

Periods of time, such as ten or twenty years, can considerably alter ways in which photographs are read and understood.

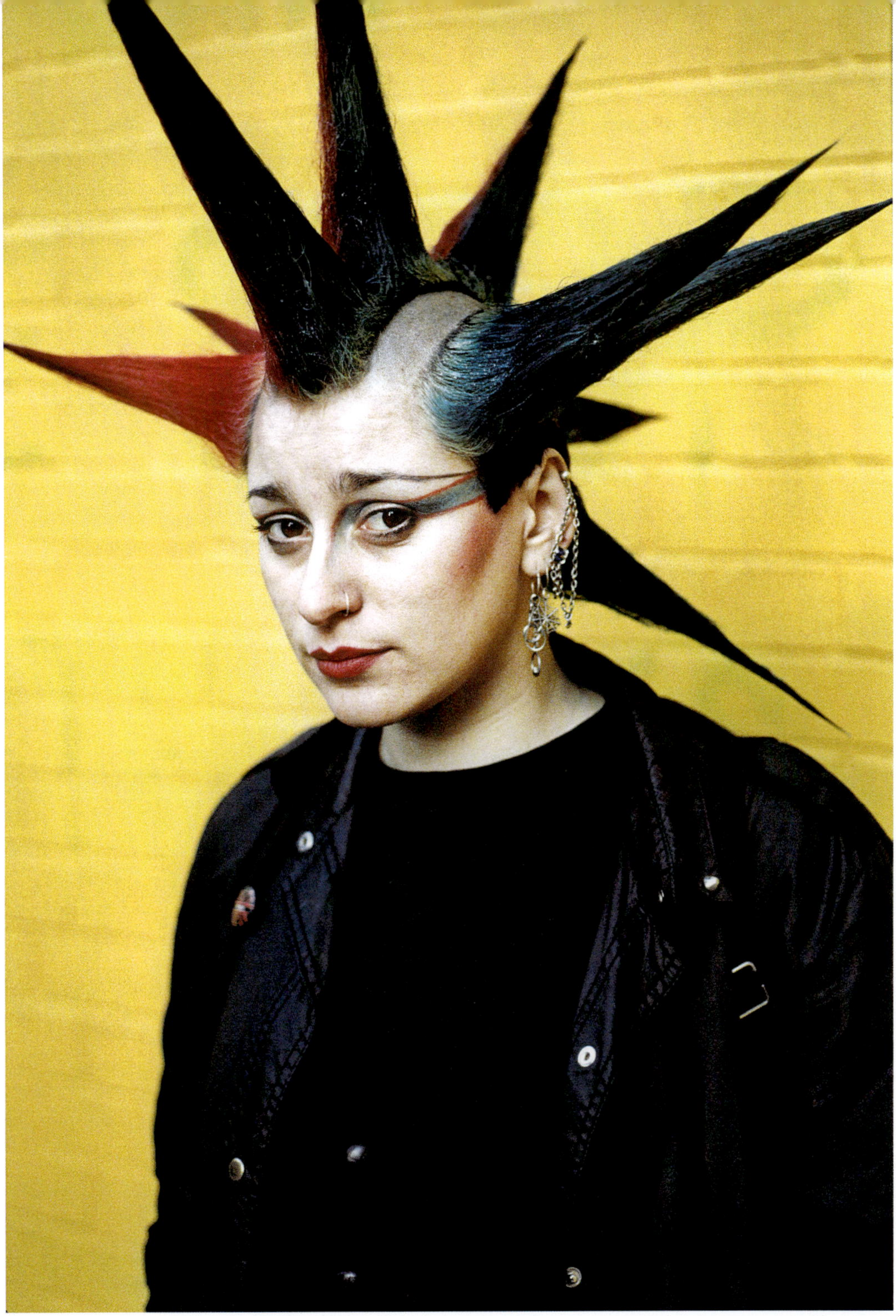

5.7

Numerous issues and ideas may arise during the development of a project, and you are best placed to manage these if you are prepared for change. Keeping a positive attitude is useful when there are setbacks; if a project does not have a degree of flexibility, it may prove very difficult to accomplish. If, for example, an application for funding is rejected, your proposal can be reworked and resubmitted elsewhere.

One body of work can lead directly into another and several small projects can eventually join to make one much larger one. If you start your research thinking that this is a possibility, then the doors are always open for the growth and development of an idea.

As your plan evolves, it should be updated, together with an evaluation of what has changed and why; this is part of your research archive and will assist you in tracking the evolution of the project. It may play a valuable role in future work, as well.

Using change to your advantage

You may find your project evolves differently from the way it was originally planned. You could be shooting outside and bad weather may slow down your progress: rather than feeling behind schedule, modify your shooting plan to take this into consideration. This way you can stay positive and in control. Some changes, such as the weather and poor health, cannot be helped. However, if, during the creative process, you see that your original intention would be stronger with a different resolution, then you must allow space for your plan to naturally evolve with the project.

Wendy Pye has been photographing Beachy Head, on the south coast of England, for more than five years. Making work over this length of time was never her original intention. Pye first planned to explore roadside shrines to the victims of traffic accidents, looking at how society expressed grief. However, being unable to control street lighting frustrated her and slowed her progress. By chance, she came across shrines of a different sort at Beachy Head, known both as a place of natural beauty and as a notorious suicide spot. Pye modified her plan to explore these shrines and has created several successful pieces through this modified approach. Pye's working relationship with this location was only possible because she was flexible and adapted her original plan.

5.8

Title: 'In Memory Of 7. . .' from *Beachy Head*

Photographer: Wendy Pye

In making this work, Wendy Pye explored the floral shrines placed as a memorial for the suicide victims who have jumped from one of Britain's highest cliffs. Through quality of light and feeling for nature, these shrines become symbolic of human fragility and our relationship with loss, tragedy and death.

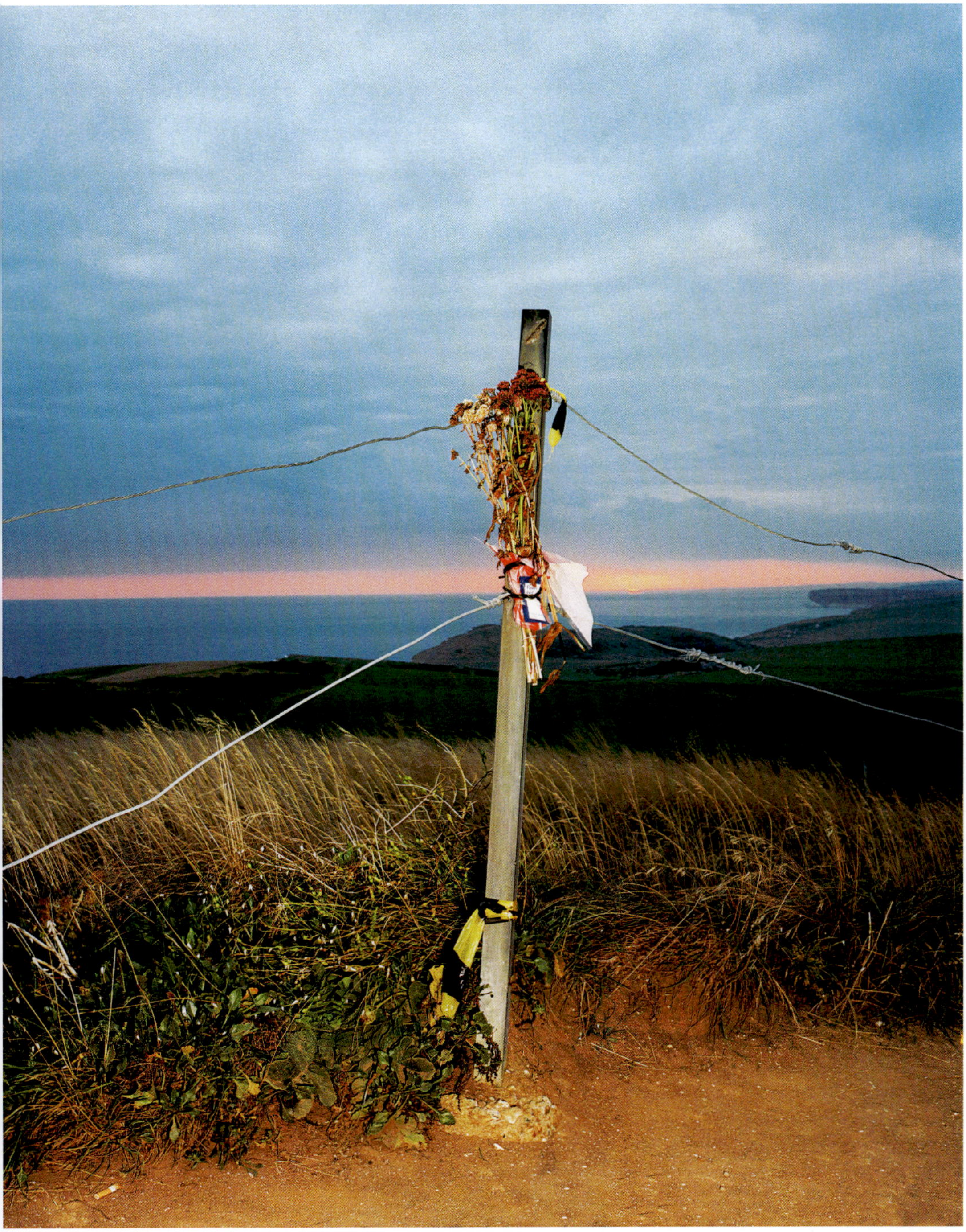

5.8

In the UK during the 1980s, most photography exhibitions tended to be produced in a similar way: prints were usually a maximum of 20 × 24 inches (50 × 61 cm); they were matted and then often framed in simple black or dark wooden frames. There was little to be found that was different in photography exhibitions, except on the occasion when the show had been branded an 'art show', which at that time was rare.

Today, photographers everywhere are interested in exploring the final production and context of their work as an important part of shaping the meaning of their projects. Even details such as the choice of the frame are now considered important.

The growth of the field of photography curation has helped this happen, as well as the acceptance of photography as an art form in its own right (this does vary in different parts of the globe). There now seem to be few limits to what can be achieved in the context of an exhibition, though final production decisions will be constrained by available budget.

5.9

Title: News Truck

Source/Artist: Peter Kennard

Artist Peter Kennard is committed to bringing politics to the fore and he is constantly concerned with inequality and poverty. He uses mixed media, photography, installation and performance in his work. Kennard describes News Truck as a 'rapid response vehicle' that he can wheel out and exhibit as and when he sees fit. His choice of show location for News Truck was always the heart of the city of London whenever there was a shudder on the stock exchange. The truck carries ten giant panels that resemble news stand screens. Each screen is a page from the *Financial Times* with a clearly impoverished hand grasping at it, tearing through it in a gesture representing desperation.

Today, photographers everywhere are interested in exploring the final production and context of their work as an important part of shaping the meaning of their projects.

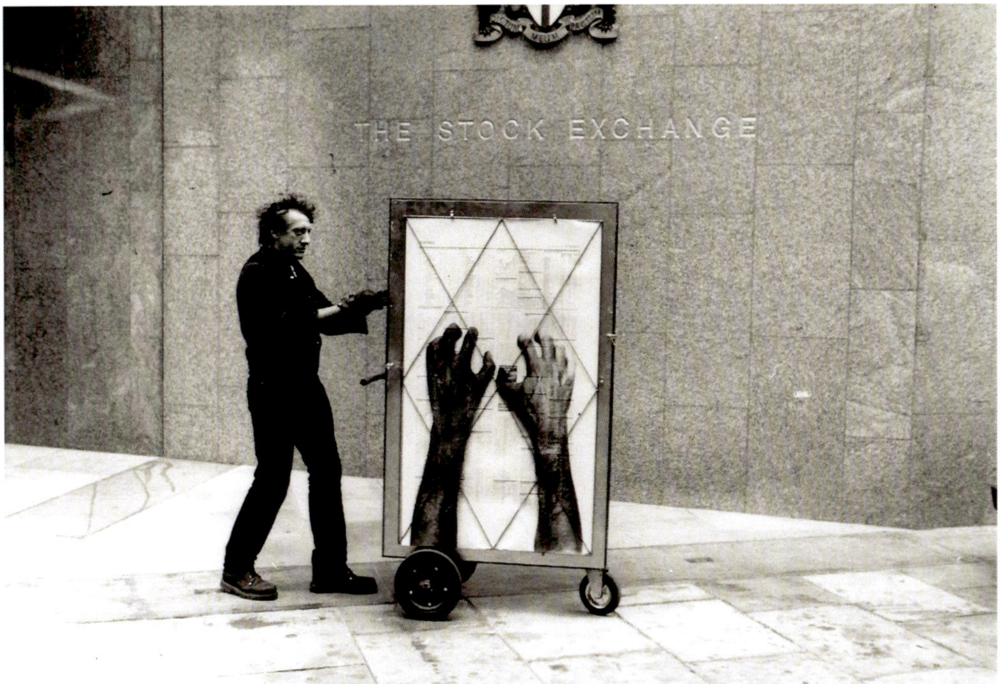

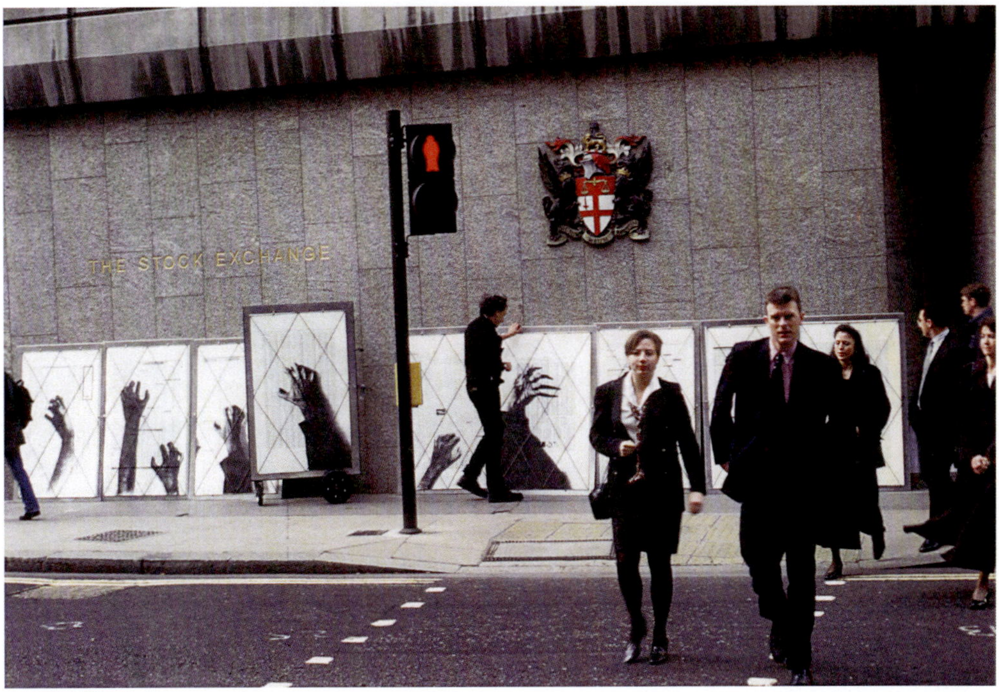

5.9

Photographic books

The design and production of photographic books has developed significantly in recent years. Despite the growth of online publishing, the photography book is redefining itself in a niche market, becoming more specialized and often highly priced. Today, more photography books than ever are being published and both photographers and artists have engaged with the possibilities of designing and producing their own books, either as limited-edition artist works or as online productions through companies such as Blurb (www.blurb.com), where the buyer can pay to print the book on demand.

All of this means that the scope of what a photography book can look and feel like is vast. The physical book still possesses a very special quality in the way that images are read and received: it is an intimate format designed for one person to look at, usually in comfort. Limited-edition publications, in comparison to coffee table books, tend to have a wider range of designs and formats, including newspapers, fanzines, concertina books, books with fold-out pages – the possibilities are almost unlimited. There are specialist bookbinders that can make a whole range of different products worth considering for the final production of your work.

5.10

Title: *The New Town*, book project and detail

Photographer: Mårten Lange

Mårten Lange self-published his limited-edition book, *The New Town*, in 2011, taking total control over the design and format. The project was shot in Milton Keynes, UK, and observes the urban landscape as a post-apocalyptic space. There are no people and only traces of the fabric of the city, photographed as black-and-white details. A set of colour urban landscape images, printed very small on selected pages, function as suggestive spaces that the black-and-white detail images could have emerged from. The book was printed by the online service Ubyu (www.ubyubooks.com).

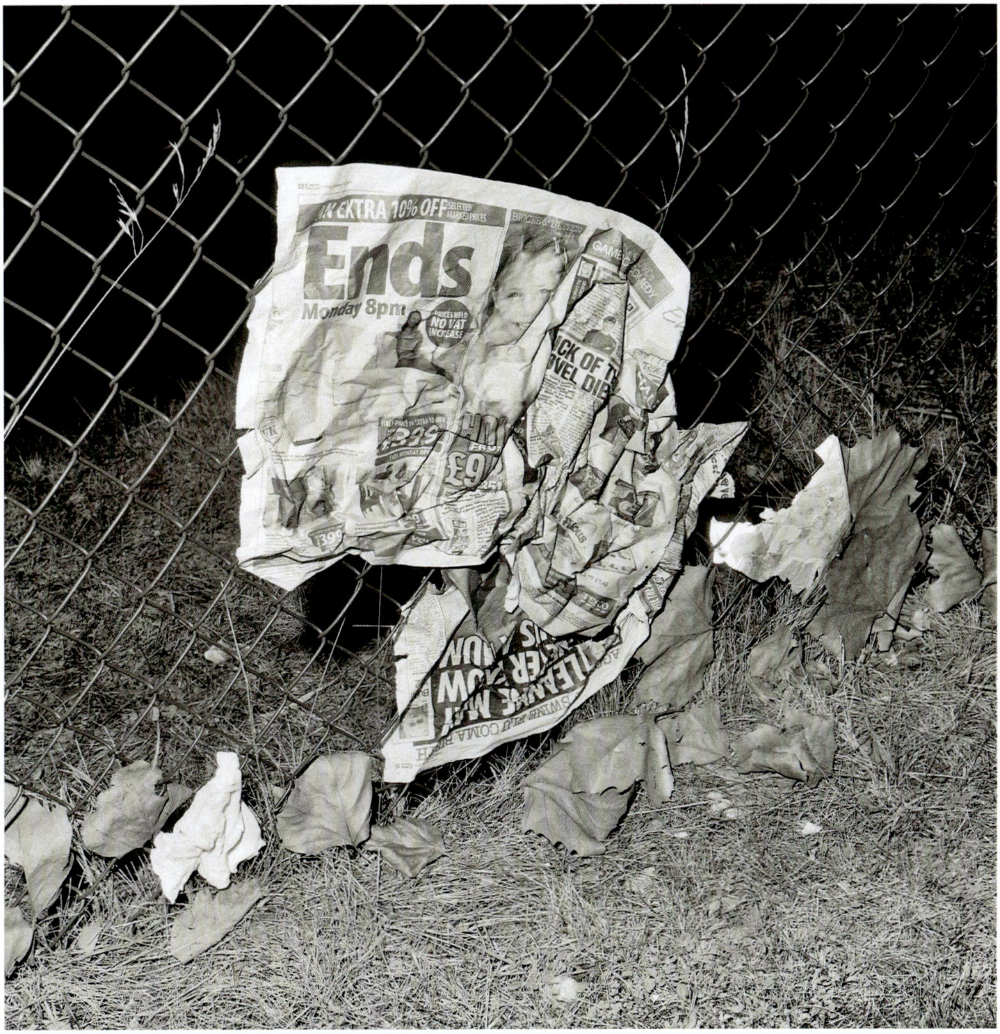

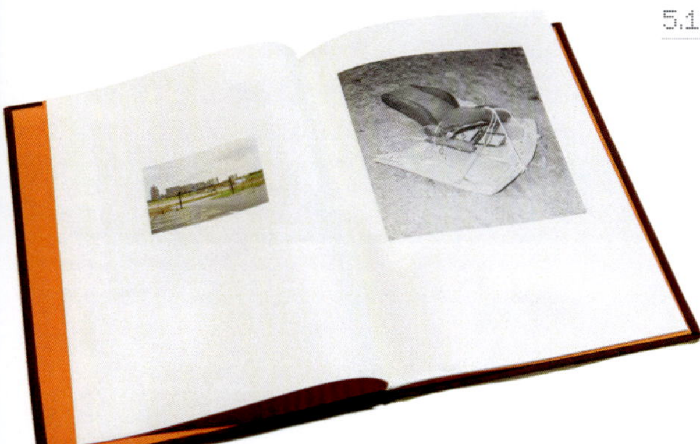

5.10

There are several interesting collections of limited edition photography books – for example, on BookRoom (thebookroom.net) or at SPBH (selfpublishbehappy.com), which is a key resource for self-publishers. SPBH is now a publishing house and a library of over 3000 self-published titles, and it also runs an educational programme and an experimental creative studio. It is also interesting to look at The Photo Book Show (photobookshow.co.uk), which has a library that they regularly exhibit as well as running workshops and talks.

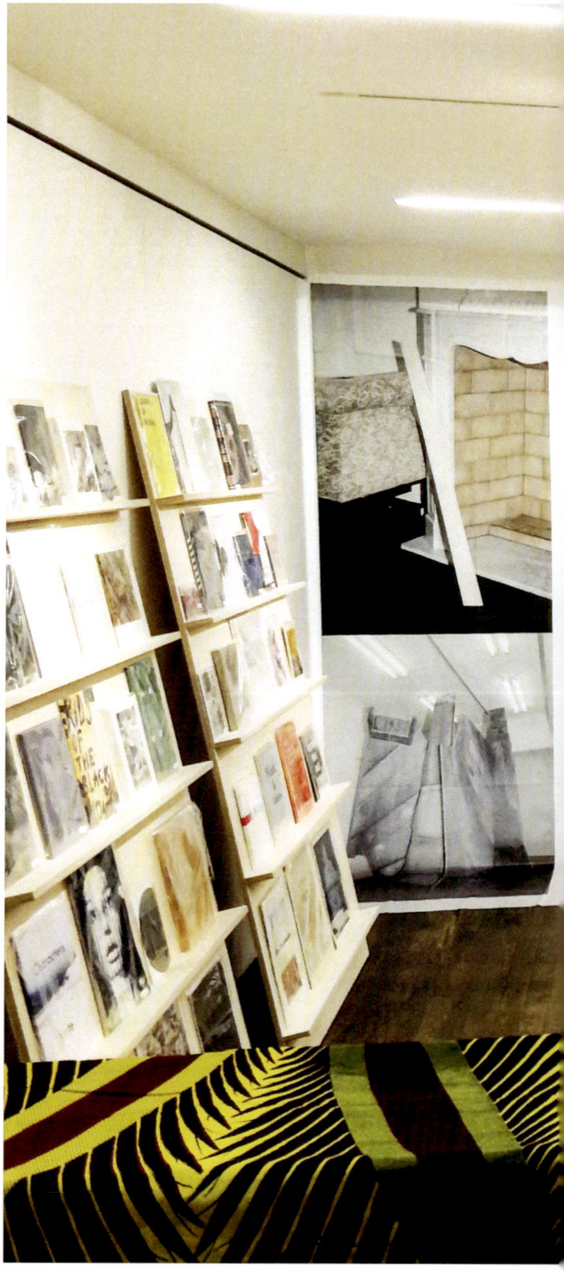

5.11

Title: Self Publish, Be Happy (SPBH) Archive

Source: SPBH

Self Publish, Be Happy (SPBH) was founded by Bruno Ceschel in London in 2010 to promote a new generation of photographers and self-publishers. Through its activities in publishing, education and programming events, it has helped to support and develop photography culture around the world. Self Publish, Be Happy has curated events at museums such as Tate Modern (Britain), Kunsthal Charlottenborg (Denmark), MoMA PS1 (United States) and the National Gallery of Victoria (Australia), and partnered with institutions such as Aperture, Foam and Offprint Projects. It runs its own publishing house, SPBH Editions, and has published books by Lucas Blalock, Mariah Robertson, Lorenzo Vitturi and many others. Self Publish, Be Happy also comprises an education programme, a creative studio and a library of more than 3,000 artists' books from around the world.

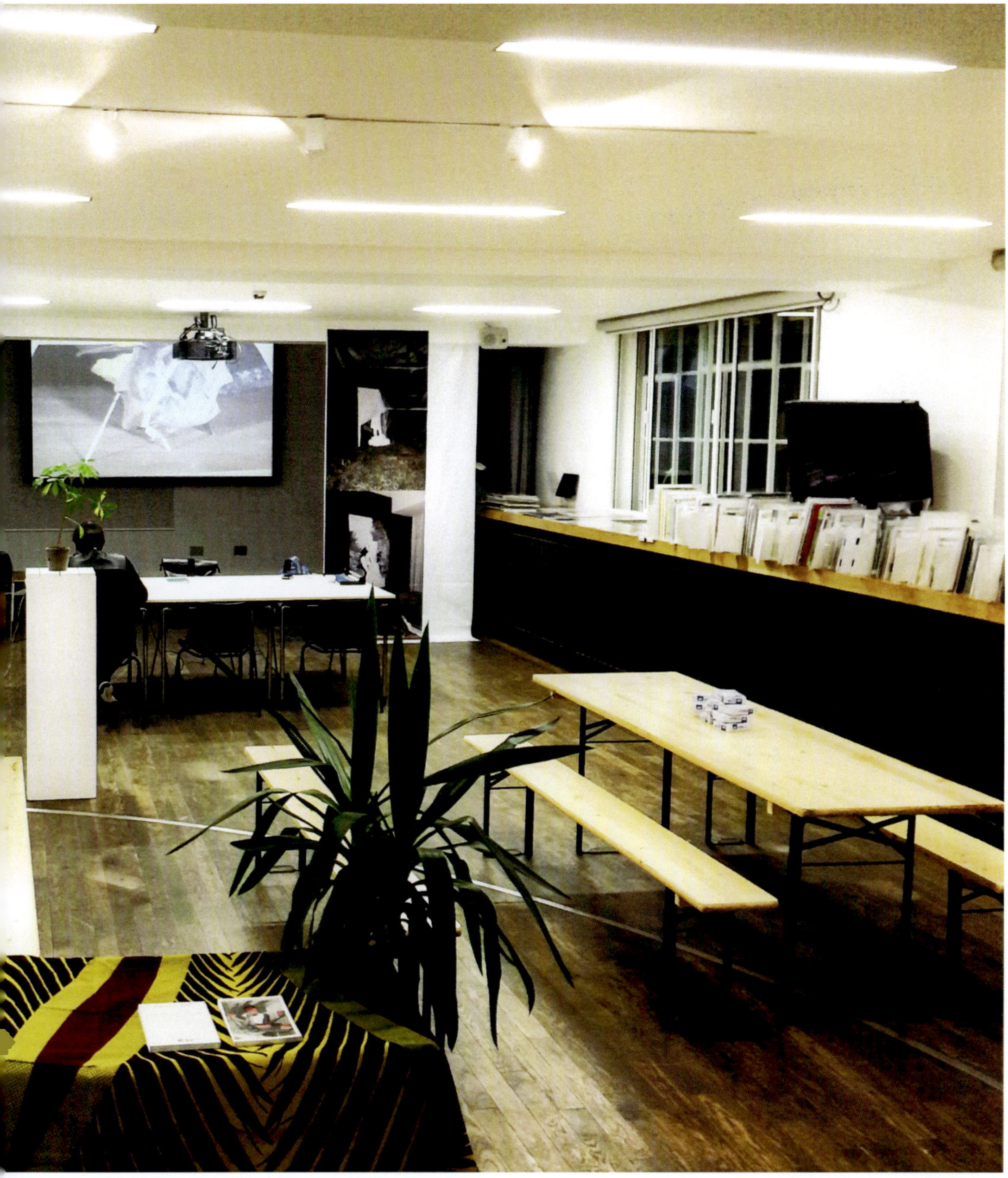

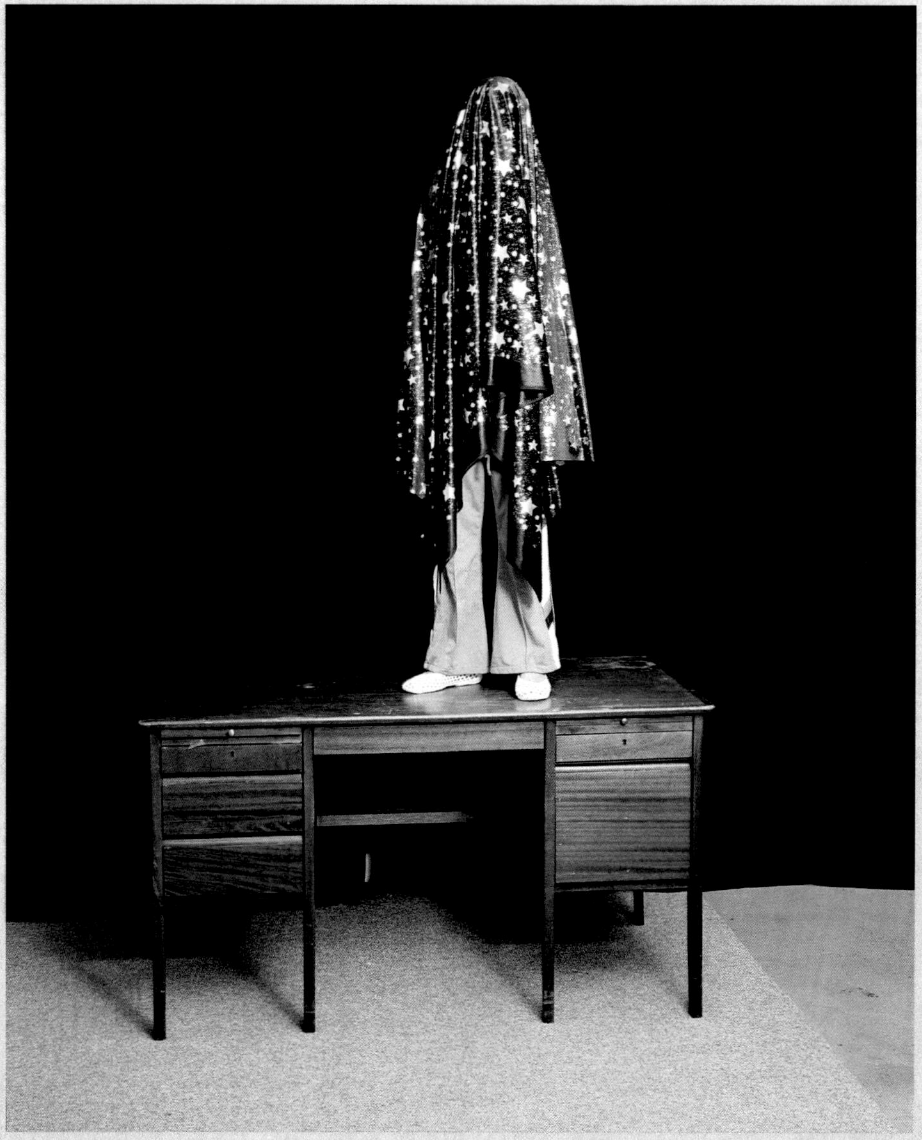

5.12

Title: *The Appearing Lady*

Artist: Clare Strand

Clare Strand views the modes of presentation of her images – the size of an image, the surface of the paper, the way it is framed or mounted, the use of moving image or a sculptured display – as crucial factors in fully realizing the finished work.

Case study 5
Clare Strand

Clare Strand is an artist who has been working with photography for two decades. Her practice has, from the start, been inseparable from her research. Certain images, accrued since her mid-teens, continue to influence her work, and are constantly revisited and reassessed.

Strand studied at the University of Brighton and then the Royal College of Art in London, after which she began to develop her intuitive and personalized approach to image-making. She has continued to evolve her practice into a hybrid art form that draws immense influence from her multifaceted research interests.

Her work is scrupulously planned, researched and executed. Strand has an ongoing passion for utilitarian photography, where the functional overrides the aesthetic. Her past catalogue of work has engaged with the formalism of forensic photography; the mechanics of spirit photography, in which images are manipulated to create ghostly visions; and the conventions of signage in photography used in the everyday delivery of information.

Strand views the process she adopts as being akin to a scientist or a detective at work: attempting to solve a puzzle or a mystery. However, she is not particularly interested in solutions, preferring to formulate new questions in place of answers. By taking into account the possibilities of the evidence gathered, she builds her highly constructed images out of appropriate objects, subjects and locations.

Research, intuition and serendipity guide Strand's artistic process and inform the final resolution of the work, whether on the wall of a gallery, in the pages of a book, on a TV monitor or in a fashion magazine.

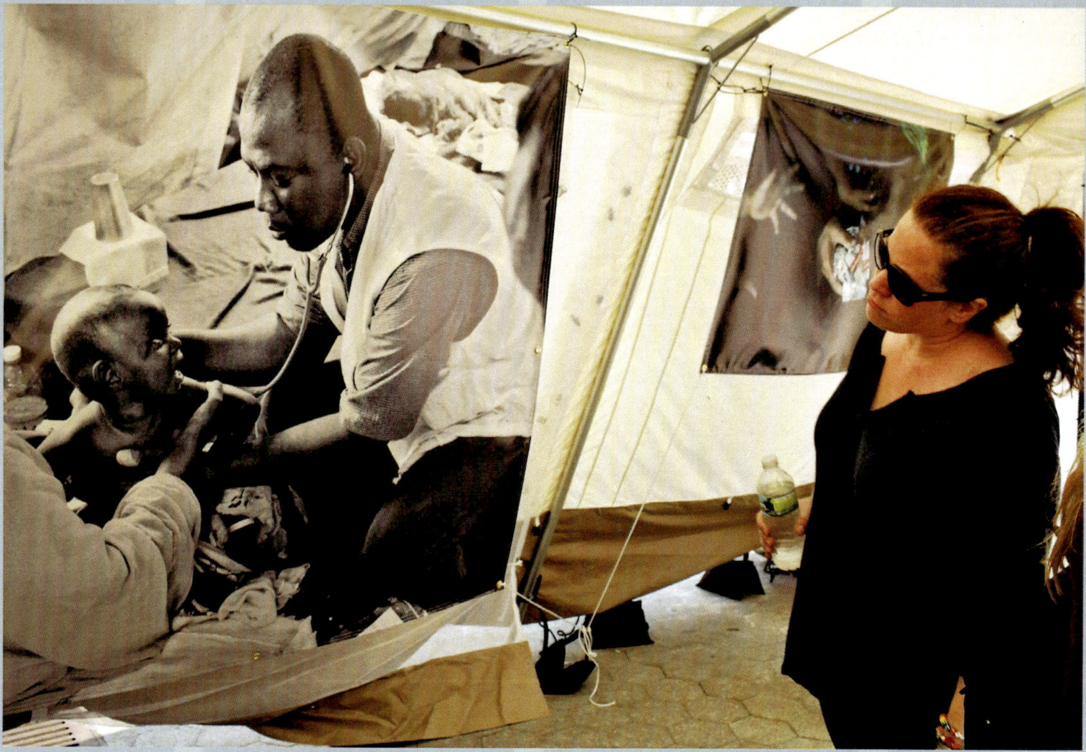

5.13

Title: A field hospital is used as an exhibition in New York, to spotlight childhood malnutrition

Source/Photographer: Getty Images/Spencer Platt

This exhibition was put on by Doctors Without Borders/Medecins Sans Frontieres (MSF) in New York to highlight child malnutrition. The photographs were exhibited in a field hospital which was erected in Union Square.

This put the viewer into the context in which the images of malnourished children were shot. This connection between the images and the exhibition space would have influenced viewers' reactions in a very different way than if the images had been hung on the walls of a conventional gallery.

Activity 5 Context and meaning

To complete this activity, you need to make a series of images that tell a story about a contemporary issue or situation. If you photograph people that can be recognised, you need to get them to sign model releases. The issue can be local or national or even international. Climate change, for example, has become a truly international issue, whereas the building of a new road would be local.

Get permission from your subject/s (if you have people in the images) to exhibit the work in a public space. Then decide on how you can make a very public display of the work.

Your work could be placed on posters on bus stops, or displayed as a night-time projection in the street or in leaflets distributed publicly. It could be displayed in the front window of a shop or on the walls of a café.

Create a platform on one of the social media channels and invite your audience to comment on the work and what it means to them. Leave information at the site of the exhibited works for people to find out how and where to comment. Try to get publicity from local radio or television.

Record what is said in your research workbook or blog and reflect on how the context you have put the work into has brought viewers into the work and affected its meaning. If you feel adventurous, try out the same process in different locations.

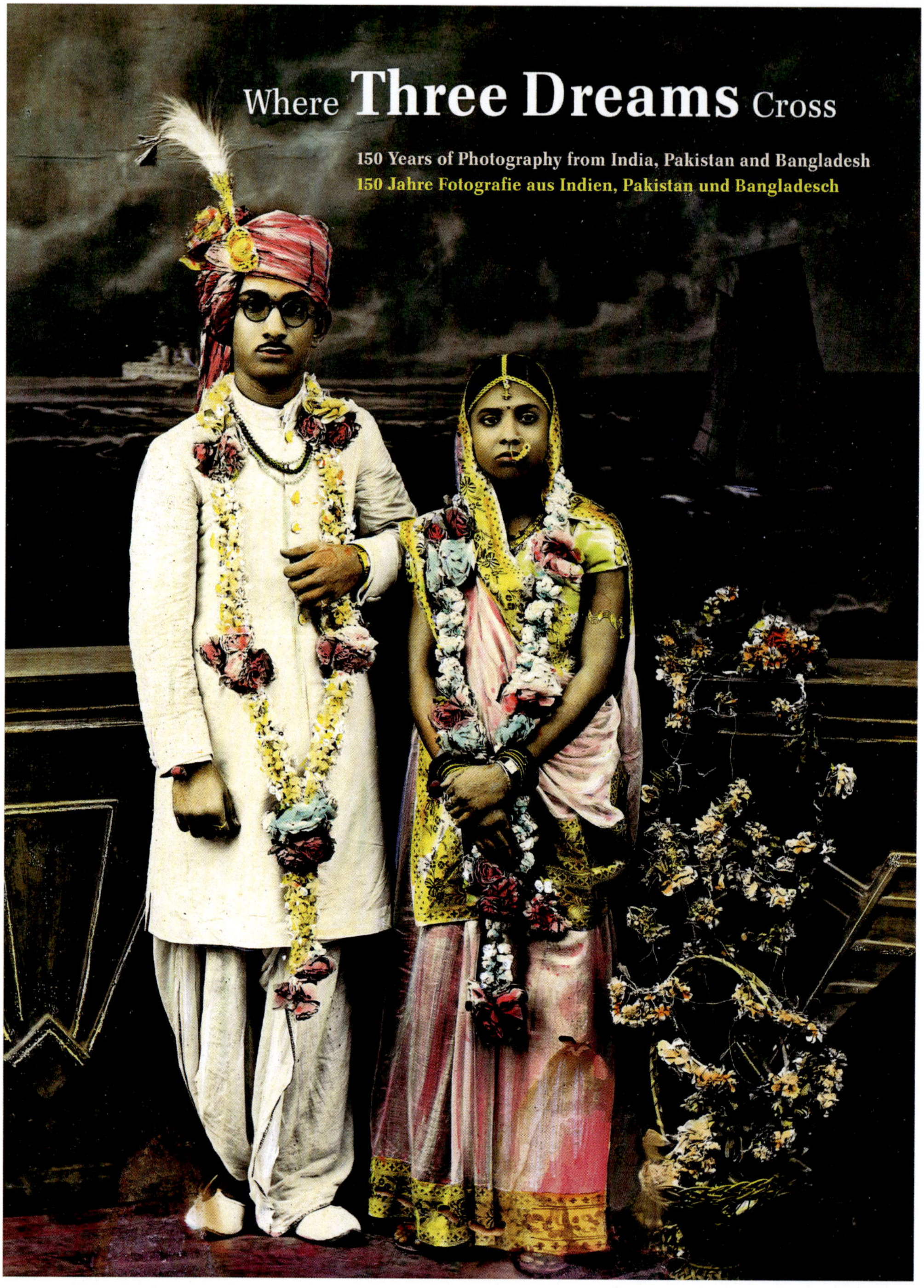
Where Three Dreams Cross
150 Years of Photography from India, Pakistan and Bangladesh
150 Jahre Fotografie aus Indien, Pakistan und Bangladesch

6.1

6 The impact of research

6.1

Title: Cover of *Where Three Dreams Cross*

Source: Steidl/Whitechapel Gallery

This contemporary publication focuses on 150 years of photography from the Indian subcontinent and is just one example of the fascinating research being done around global histories of photography today. As research in photography increases, particularly at post-graduate level and beyond, we are able to expand our knowledge about the wider world of photographic practice.

Research affects all aspects of practice, history and theory – as well as more generally the understanding of the wider context of photographic practice. In order for research to have real impact, the following are vital: access, discussion and thinking, writing and response making. Research needs to reach an audience, as methods of communication and dissemination of ideas play an important role in conveying new knowledge and debate.

Exhibitions can play a key role in the interpretation and dissemination of work, but audiences are sometimes limited to the small community of the gallery-going public. Recently, the rapid expansion of web-based exhibitions and blogging have added a new dimension to the understanding of photography and, most significantly, to the wider dissemination of ideas and knowledge. This democratization of information through the Web has markedly affected photographic practices all over the world. Looking into the future, it is possible to see that we will soon have a far greater awareness of the global histories and practices of photography.

Photographers use research, in all its forms, to aid the development of a project. It is important for practitioners to evaluate and reflect on how their research has supported the progress of a body of work. When research goes unrecorded, its significance can be lost or reduced. By making time to be more aware of both the research process and its influences, you have more scope to reflect on your working process and apply this knowledge to future work.

Gaining perspective

Reflection takes place through a process of monitoring and evaluation, producing distinctive information that can help you improve your photographic practice. It helps you to process new knowledge gained through making a body of work. Reflection allows you to stand back, putting distance between you and your work and frequently increases your awareness of the impact of a body of work. When a photographer has been working intensely on a project, it is difficult to gauge its impact. By standing back, the creator is able to see the work from a fresh viewpoint. This is a vital way of gaining the perspective needed to enable discussion and dissemination of the ideas coming out of your work.

Keeping a journal

Objective reflection is difficult and does not necessarily occur spontaneously: conditions can be structured to encourage it to happen. Reflection is often most successful in the form of a personal journal that can be written without the anxiety of it becoming public information. The development, research and evaluation progress of a project can be tracked, recorded and reflected on.

A personal journal is a 'partner' in the creative process, in which the development of ideas is recorded and considered reflectively. The aim of reflection is to enhance critical thinking that will contribute to the creative process and ultimately add to the dissemination of innovative work that contributes to contemporary debate and new knowledge in the field.

Recording and reflection

Develop your awareness of how you are making your photographic projects by recording your research in detail.

Try to record the ways in which certain aspects of your research have influenced the way you develop a project.

Use these records to reflect on your work and help you expand what you do and how you research an idea.

How have you changed and refined the way you work through the lifetime of the project and why?

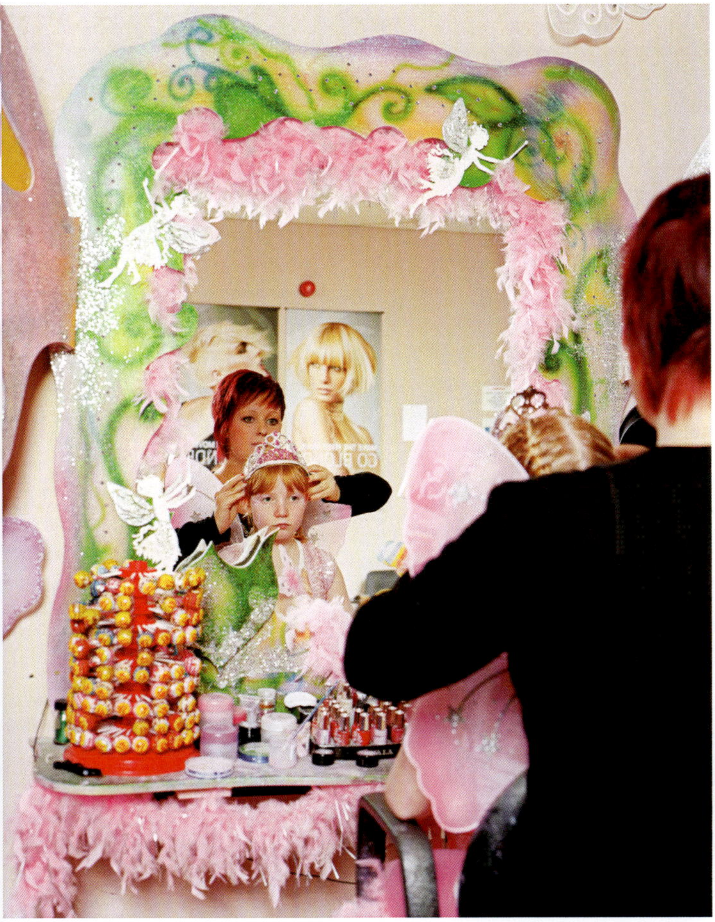

6.2

Title: Hair and make-up shop, from *Resort*

Photographer: Anna Fox

Anna Fox spent two years from 2009 photographing the contemporary face of Butlins, a holiday camp in Bognor Regis, UK. Fox worked through a number of different practical experiments and researched the historical representation of Butlins, as well as the English seaside, before establishing a particular working method. Her final photographs reflect her fascination with the depictions of Butlins made by the John Hinde Studio in the 1970s.

By making time to be more aware of both the research process and its influences, you have more scope to reflect on your working process and apply this knowledge to future work.

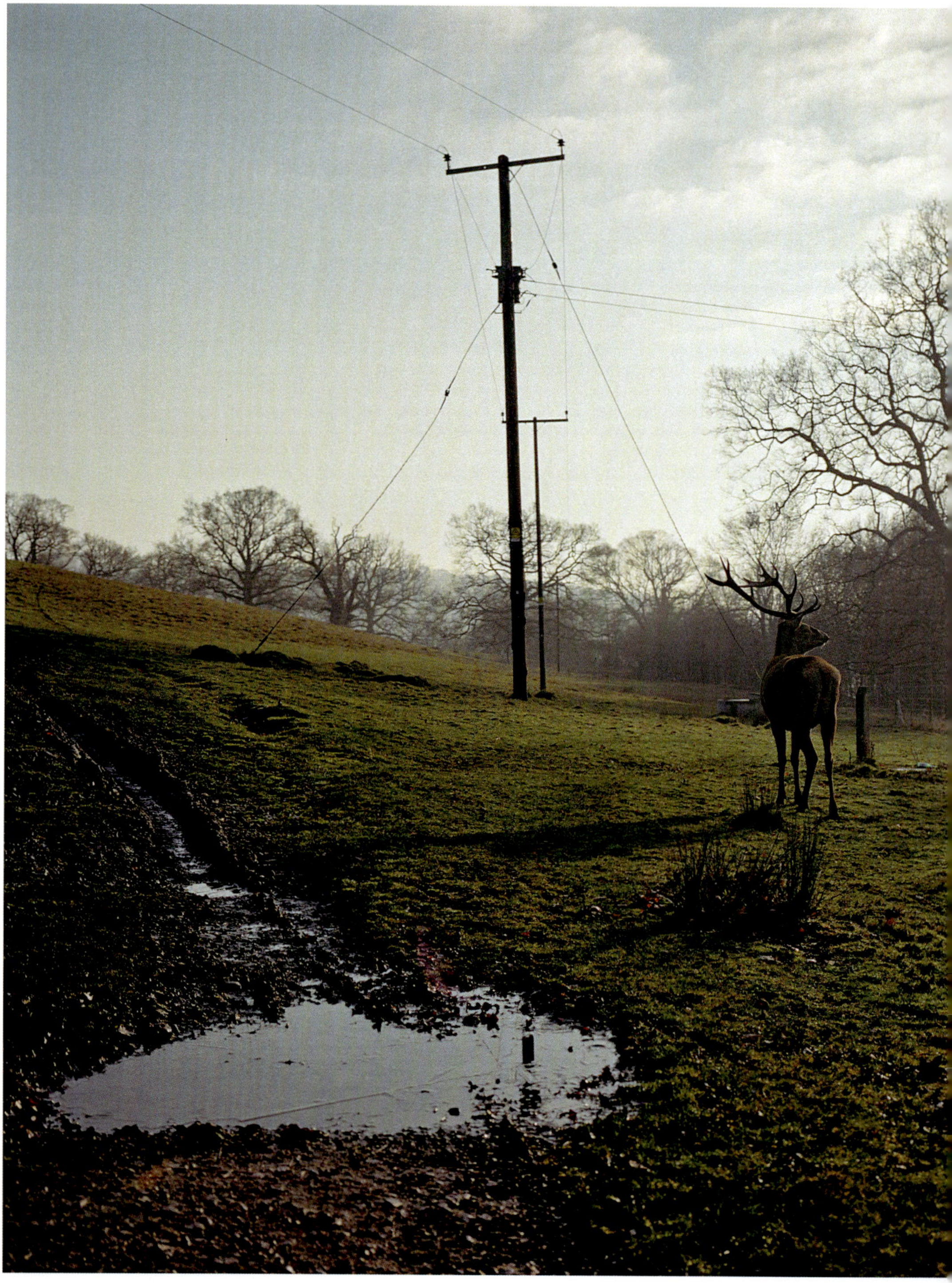

6.3

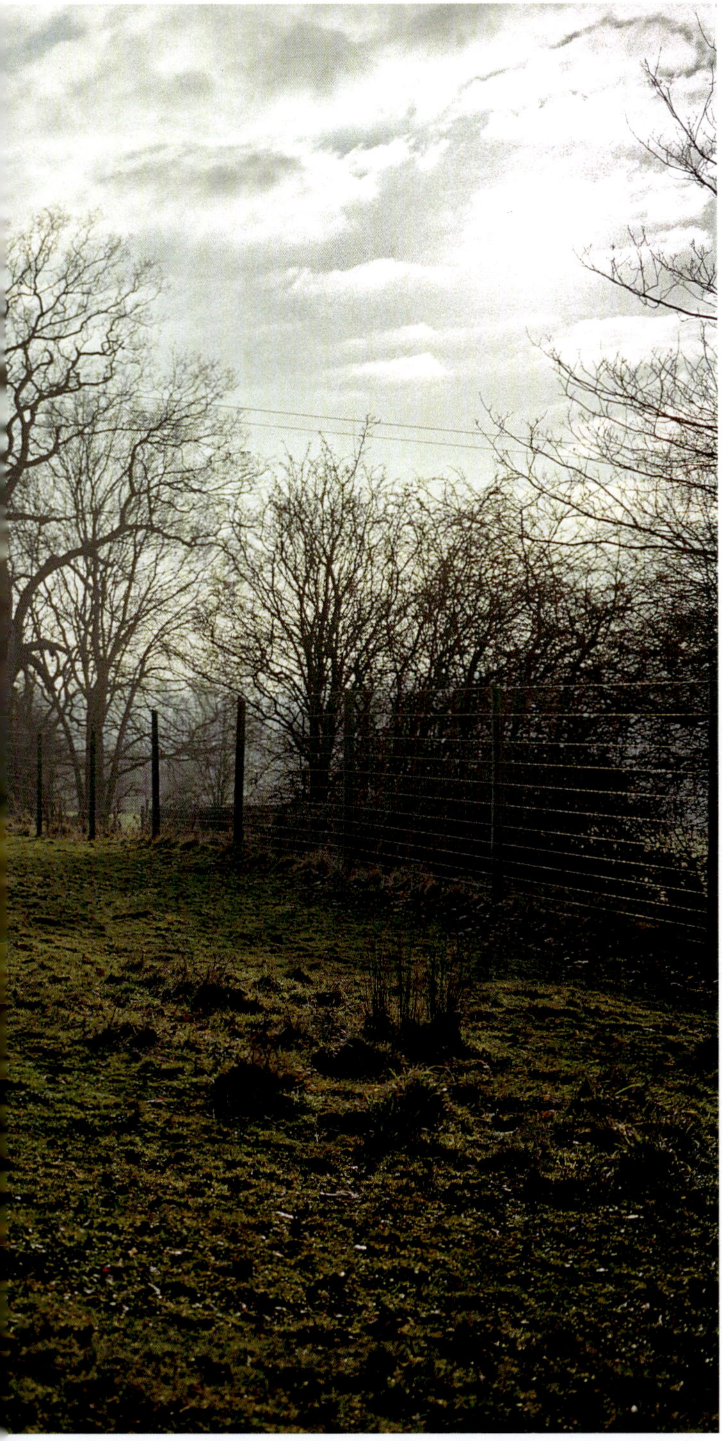

6.3

Title: Untitled, 2007

Artist: Melanie Stidolph

When an image such as this unfolds in front of artist Melanie Stidolph, she is simultaneously thinking about composition, reference and final presentation. For each piece, she always shoots a collection of images, later selecting one or two, and always printing them full frame. She undergoes a process of reflection, both at the time of shooting and at the time of editing, using this process to discover a definitive image that transmits an intensity of looking and acts as a conduit for an emotional experience.

Artists' statements and curriculum vitae

An artists' statement is a place where the artist talks quite generally about their interests, references and approaches to making work. The statement introduces them to the world and highlights their knowledge and understanding, as well as outlining the context that the work has been and made in and for. The statement grows out of the practice and is informed by the research. When writing your personal statement, it is really useful to look back at what you wrote in the proposal and evaluation and draw key phrases from these documents. It is useful to practice doing different word length statements: 150-, 300-, and 500-word statements are valuable to do in advance of when they are needed and then will be ready for any event. They can be used for sending to curators and collectors, entering competitions and putting onto the intro page of your website, as well as for catalogues and introductions to exhibitions. You can always get someone who is good at writing to edit the statement before it goes out into the world.

6.4

Title: Photographers' statements

Photographers: Joanne Coates and Alice Cooke

These photographers' statements were written by students at University for the Creative Arts for their final degree show projects. They were printed both for the wall in the exhibition as well as in the back of the publication they made, *Photo Farnham Showcase 18*. They can also use them in their portfolios when they apply for competitions and on their websites.

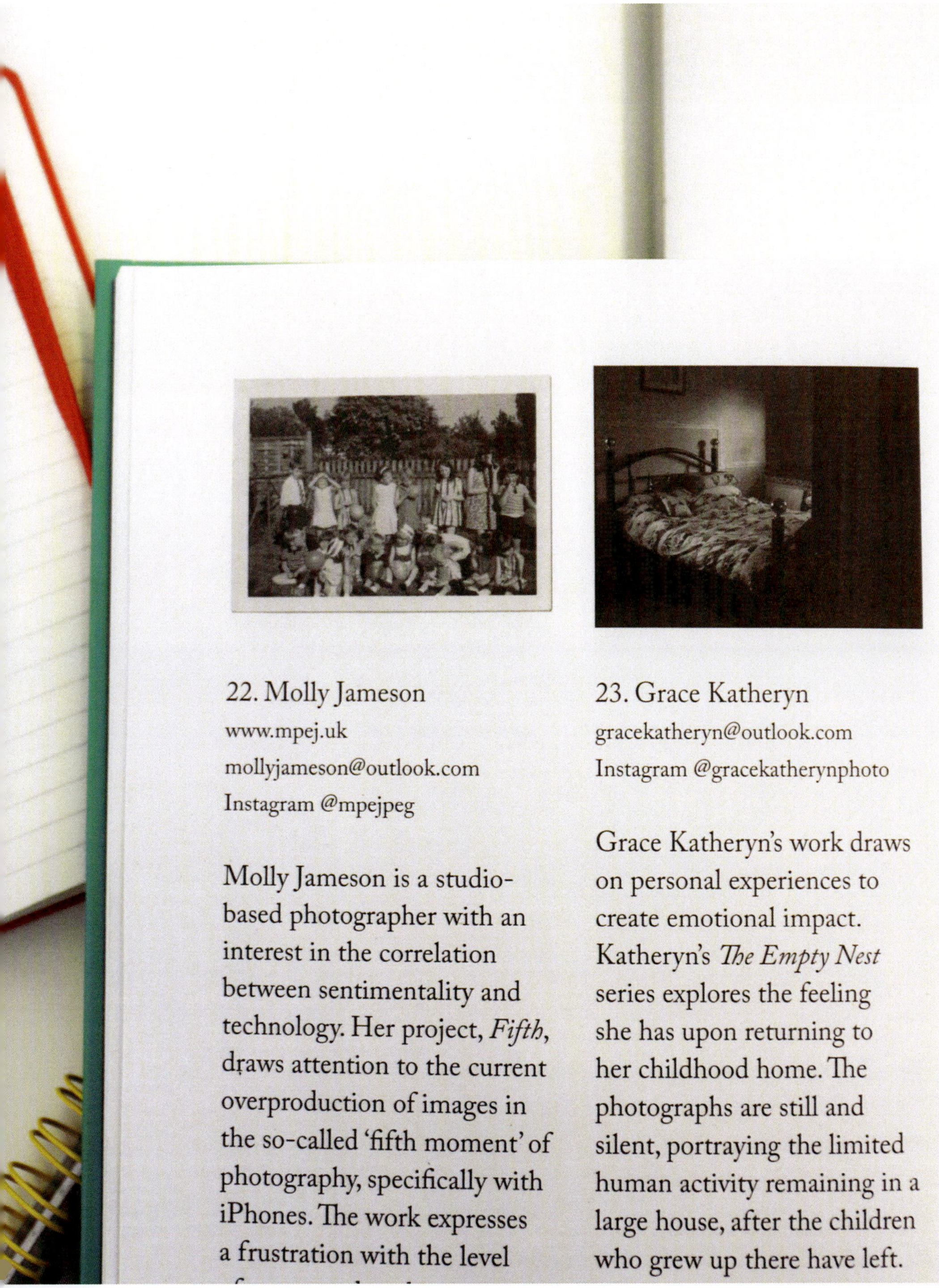

22. Molly Jameson
www.mpej.uk
mollyjameson@outlook.com
Instagram @mpejpeg

Molly Jameson is a studio-based photographer with an interest in the correlation between sentimentality and technology. Her project, *Fifth*, draws attention to the current overproduction of images in the so-called 'fifth moment' of photography, specifically with iPhones. The work expresses a frustration with the level

23. Grace Katheryn
gracekatheryn@outlook.com
Instagram @gracekatherynphoto

Grace Katheryn's work draws on personal experiences to create emotional impact. Katheryn's *The Empty Nest* series explores the feeling she has upon returning to her childhood home. The photographs are still and silent, portraying the limited human activity remaining in a large house, after the children who grew up there have left.

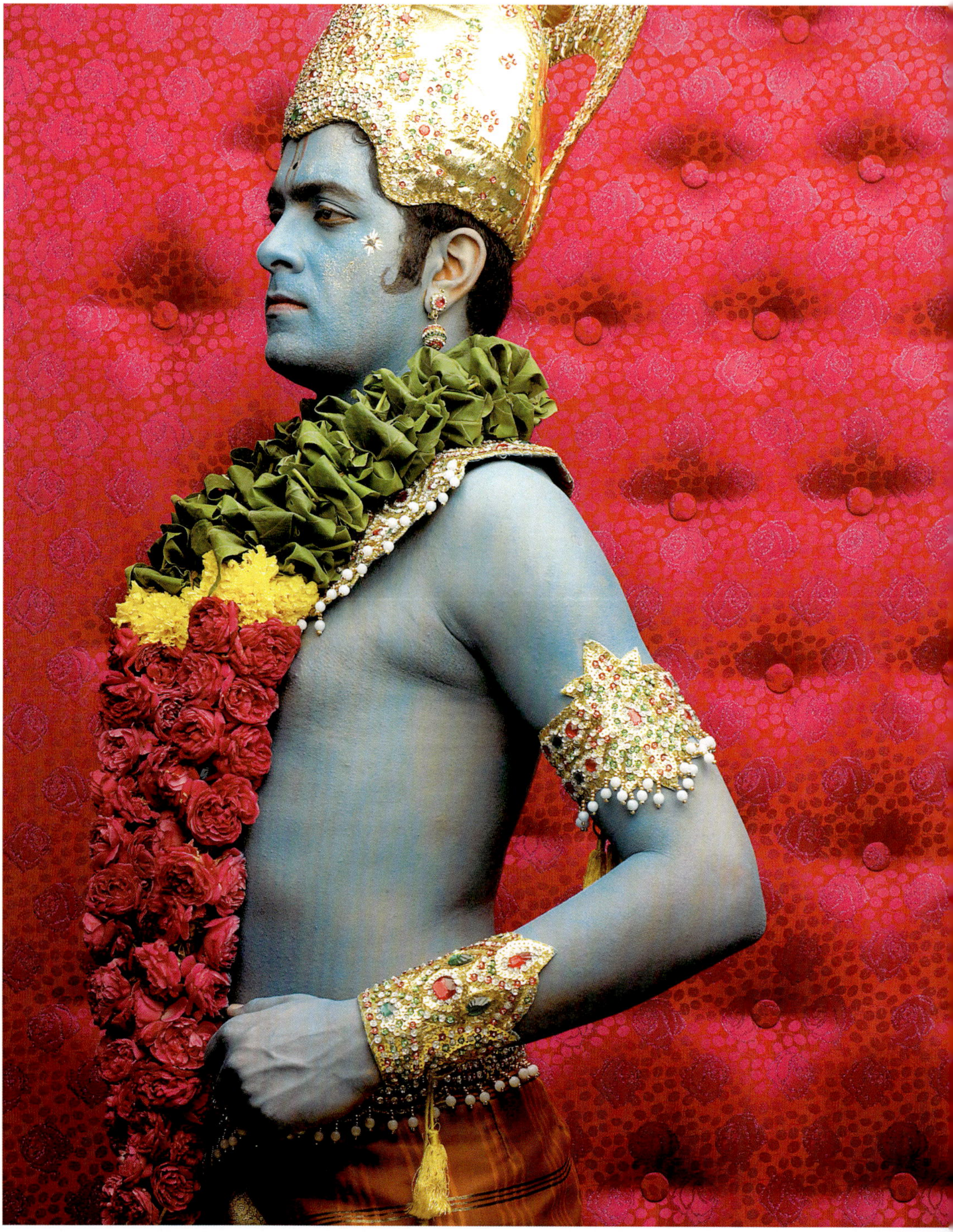

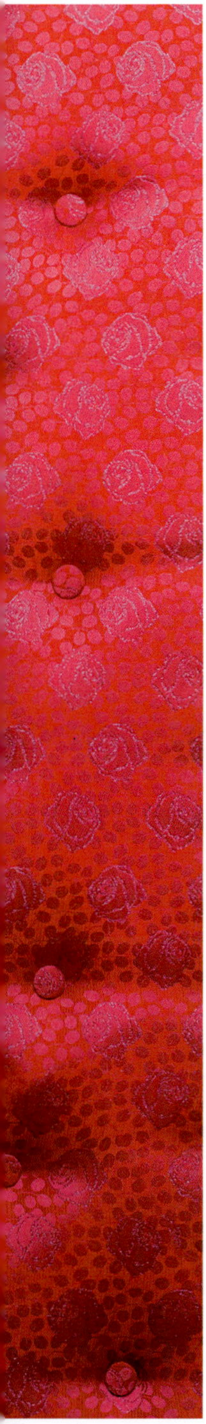

6.5

Title: *Reassurance*, from Definitive Reincarnate

Artist: Nandini Valli Muthiah

This image is from Nandini Valli Muthiah's series in which she juxtaposes traditional depictions of Indian gods with elements of the modern day. Here, a vivid block of colour from the bedroom of a boutique hotel creates the backdrop for her subject.

Historical and cultural contexts

Nandini Valli Muthiah is becoming one of India's key contemporary artists, and her highly constructed photographs rely on the idea of replaying historical ideas within a contemporary context. For her project, *Definitive Reincarnate*, Muthiah took her research references from the traditions of Indian popular art, researching the history of the painted calendar posters that represent Indian gods. These calendars use both traditional painting and painted photographs to create mythical spaces in which the viewer can dream. Muthiah turns around the conventions of this tradition by styling and painting her subjects to resemble the gods in the calendar posters but presenting them in contemporary spaces such as hotel rooms. In this way, the heroism of the traditional poster character is transformed into a more modern myth, allowing the viewer to reconsider the space of the everyday and their relationship to it. Muthiah's research into the history of the painted calendar posters was vital to the realization of her project.

An understanding of global histories and a broad cultural knowledge are invaluable both in terms of understanding photographs and in creating them from an informed perspective. It is becoming increasingly important for the discerning student of photography – and the practitioner – to look further afield in their research and practice than areas they are already familiar with. This exploration and sharing of new ideas will ultimately contribute to the growing awareness of global histories and new directions in photography.

Visiting an archive is a great way to engage with research carried out by other photographers. Personal archives, belonging to photographers, collectors, writers or curators, tend to be private, with access restricted to specialist researchers. Museum archives tend to be more available to public scrutiny, usually through special exhibitions. Access to museum archives outside of exhibitions is usually by appointment only, but you do not always have to justify entry with a bona fide research proposal. For example, students and researchers alike are able to make appointments to look at prints in London's Victoria and Albert Museum photographic print archive. It is a truly fascinating experience to spend time in such a place.

Personal archives

The photographer's archive, appropriately stored, provides a lifelong source of references and potential material for interpretation, evaluation and understanding. The photographer who meticulously creates such a resource is not only creating a rich mine of information for themselves, they are also building a library of information for other researchers, curators and writers interested in their work and the particular period in which they made it. Such archives can be valuable even after as little as five or ten years from their inception. Studying the thinking, inspiration and development process behind a particular photographer's work affects our understanding of how and why their projects or series have been made.

Hidden archives

Archives are a great resource to help you find out about people, places and periods of time, as well as about particular types of photography. Look out for hidden archives—start in your own attic or family album. You could put an advertisement on a notice board at your college or university asking for people to contact you with information about their archives or about a particular type of photograph. Visit car boot sales, second-hand shops and auctions to find old photographs and postcards for sale.

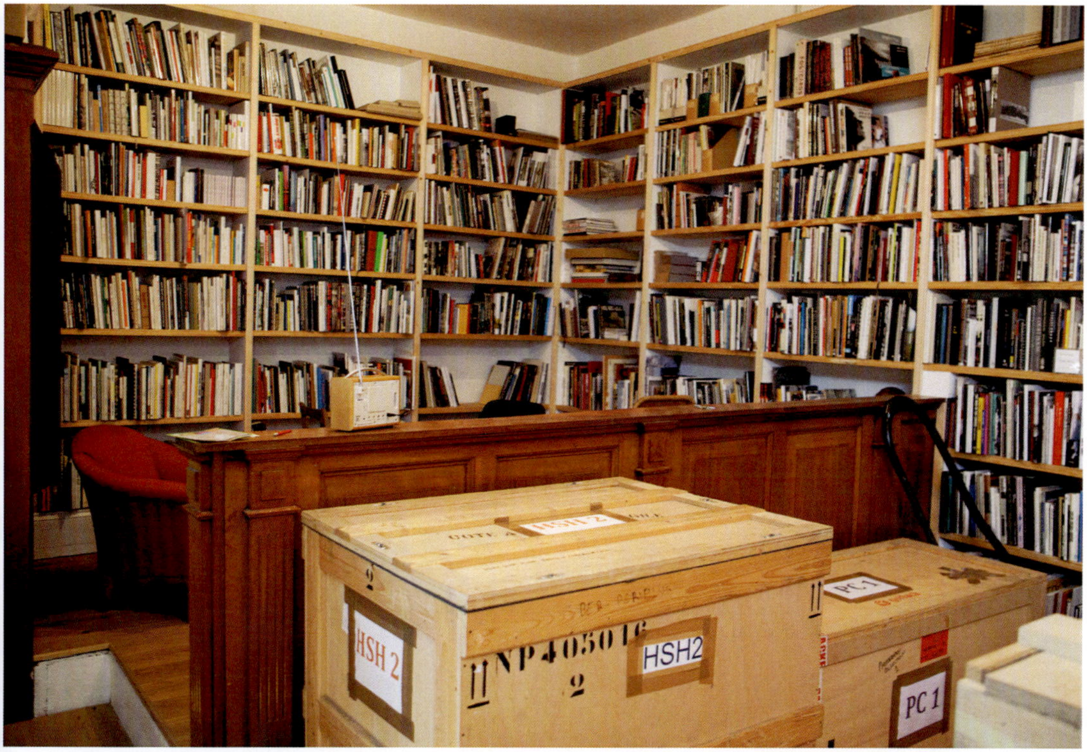

The photographer's archive provides a lifelong source of references and potential material for interpretation, evaluation and understanding.

6.6

Title: *The Bank Archive*

Source: The Martin Parr Foundation

Martin Parr has been collecting books and photography ephemera since the 1970s. His archive contains many hundreds of books from all over the world, numerous artefacts, vernacular photography of all descriptions, book dummies and original prints by various photographers. This is currently a private archive owned solely by Parr, largely used for his own research, although some researchers working on major projects have been granted access to it. Parr has recently opened the Martin Parr Foundation and many of the books from his archive are available there. As well, the Foundation has an exhibition space and hosts numerous events.

Revealing usually unseen background research can put a piece of work in a new context and alter its meaning for the viewer. A number of significant exhibitions, such as the Diane Arbus Revelations show at the Victoria and Albert Museum (London, 2006), have displayed aspects of the photographer's personal archive as part of the show. In this particular exhibition, the viewer was able to see contact sheets, notebooks and letters, giving a unique insight into the photographer's thought processes. It is more typical for photography exhibitions and publications, both contemporary and historical, to simply show the 'great' photographs or the final photographs selected by the photographer or curator. The Arbus exhibit enabled the audience to peer behind the scenes and get a sense of the photographer's character. This revealed details of the context of the work and made the personality and process behind the final pictures as fascinating as the pictures itself.

Writers and curators

When conducting research, it is vital to recognize that the nature of a photographer's work and its meaning have often been affected and shaped by the curatorial process. Discovering how and why curators and writers have conducted their research, and the rationale behind certain curatorial or editorial decisions, is as much a part of the research process as investigating the photographers themselves. Curators and writers are also keen archivists: their archives are often less visible than those of photographers, but they deserve investigation.

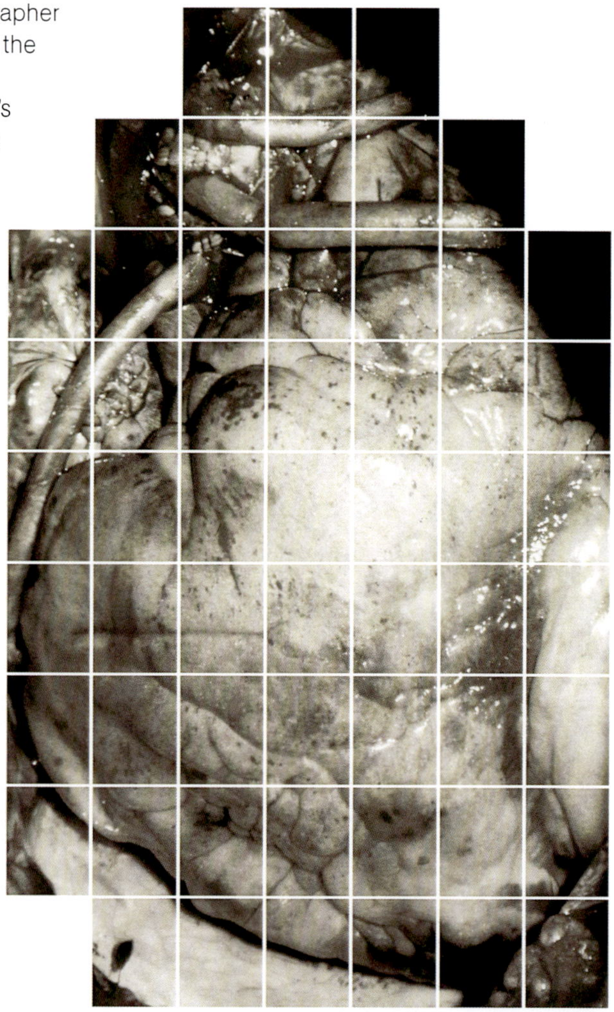

6.7

Title: The Pieces of my Grandfather's Broken Heart, 2018

Source: The Department of Medical Photography, The Texas Heart Institute. Photograph of Lt General Mohsen Mobasser's heart taken during a triple coronary artery bypass – 30 January 1974.

This project uses photographs taken by Mobasser's grandfather, a prominent General in the Shah of Iran's government. He discovered the archive when clearing out his family home in 2016. They are printed by Mobasser as large-scale contact sheets that reveal life in Iran before the Islamic Revolution. The work pays homage to Mobasser's family history as well as speaking about the life of a whole society at a particular time. Some of the contact sheets display damaged photographs, and the final work in the exhibition (also from the rediscovered archive) is a picture of the grandfather's heart divided into sections by a grid (overlaid by Mobasser).

Research centres for photography

Research centres for photography are growing in number. Usually based in universities, they often focus on a particular area of photography research. A research centre is frequently the place where innovation in debate and analysis of research takes place. Conferences, seminars and study days are events regularly hosted, and a research centre may also have a specific collection.

The Photography and the Archive Research Centre (PARC) based at University of the Arts, London, has been steadily collecting posters and invitations from photography exhibitions. PARC has received several major research awards for projects that involved analysing historical material (both written and photographic), alongside commissioning contemporary material. The projects create debate around the relationship between past and present in both vernacular and art-based photographic practices.

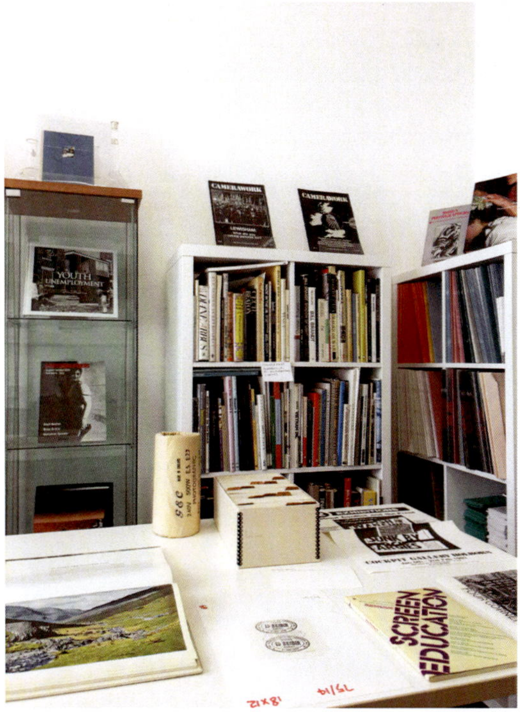

6.8

Title: Photography and the Archive Research Centre, UAL

Photographer: Robin Christian

This image shows some of the materials in the Photography and the Archive Research Centre (PARC), which is part of the University for the Arts, London. The centre specializes in photographic archives, houses special collections and also runs research projects. PARC publishes Field Study twice yearly, which explores issues and ideas connected to photographic archives and artists/photographers who work with archives.

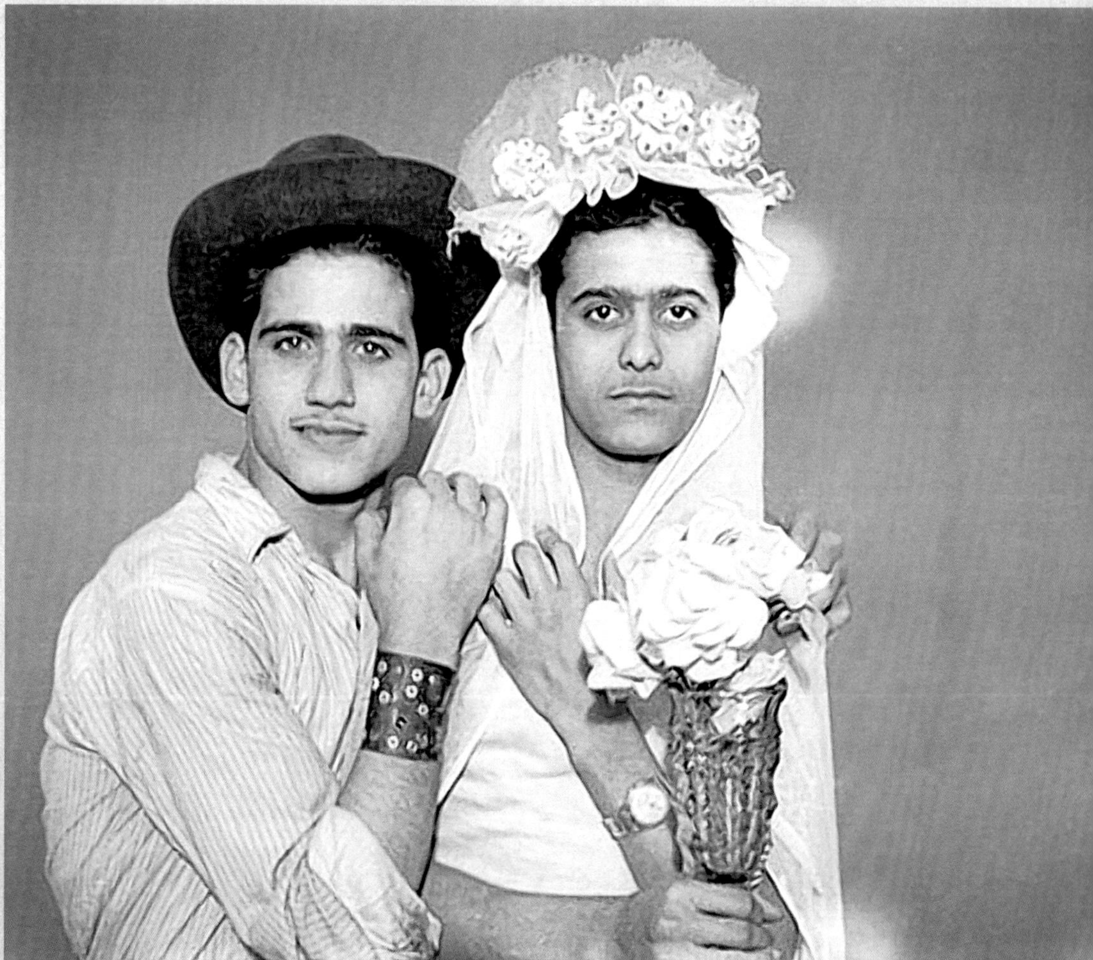

6.9

Title: Najm (left) and Asmar (right)

Source: Arab Image Foundation/ photographer Hashem el Madani

This image shows two of Hashem el Madani's subjects posing in costumes; one as a cowboy, the other as a bride. The photographer said of the shoot, "It was a session of disguise. The bride's dress, the hat and the flowers were part of the studio accessories."

Case study 6
Hashem el Madani

Hashem el Madani is a Lebanese studio portrait photographer. He purchased his first box camera in 1948 and started photographing friends and family. Madani slowly upgraded his photographic equipment by using credit and by selling test images. In 1953 he was able to open his own studio. In the last 50 years, he has taken over 500,000 images.

The studio was in the town of Saida in southern Lebanon, and Madani claims that 90 per cent of the townspeople passed through his studio doors to have their portraits taken. Through his life's work, he has created a collective portrait of one Middle Eastern town.

Inside Madani's photographic studio, people discovered a fantastical environment removed from everyday life, where they could role play and act out their personal dreams. The studio had simple props and Madani used poses cut out of magazines to provide posture guidelines for his sitters to emulate. The people of Saida performed for Madani's camera with humour, honour and sincerity. They acted as themselves, as alter egos, or as superheroes, often posing with objects that were important to them. The work forms an important archive and a social commentary.

Madani's work was brought to public attention by the Arab Image Foundation, based in Lebanon and with the support of the Photographers' Gallery in London. Some of the images from his vast archive can be viewed in the publication *Hashem el Madani: Studio Practices*, published by Mind the Gap/The Arab Image Foundation, in 2005. The layout of the book includes sequences of images illustrating the tests and the preparation leading up to the final portraits. These sequential narratives do not reveal the selected 'final' portraits, so they invite the viewer to imagine the final, prized images that were taken home by the subjects.

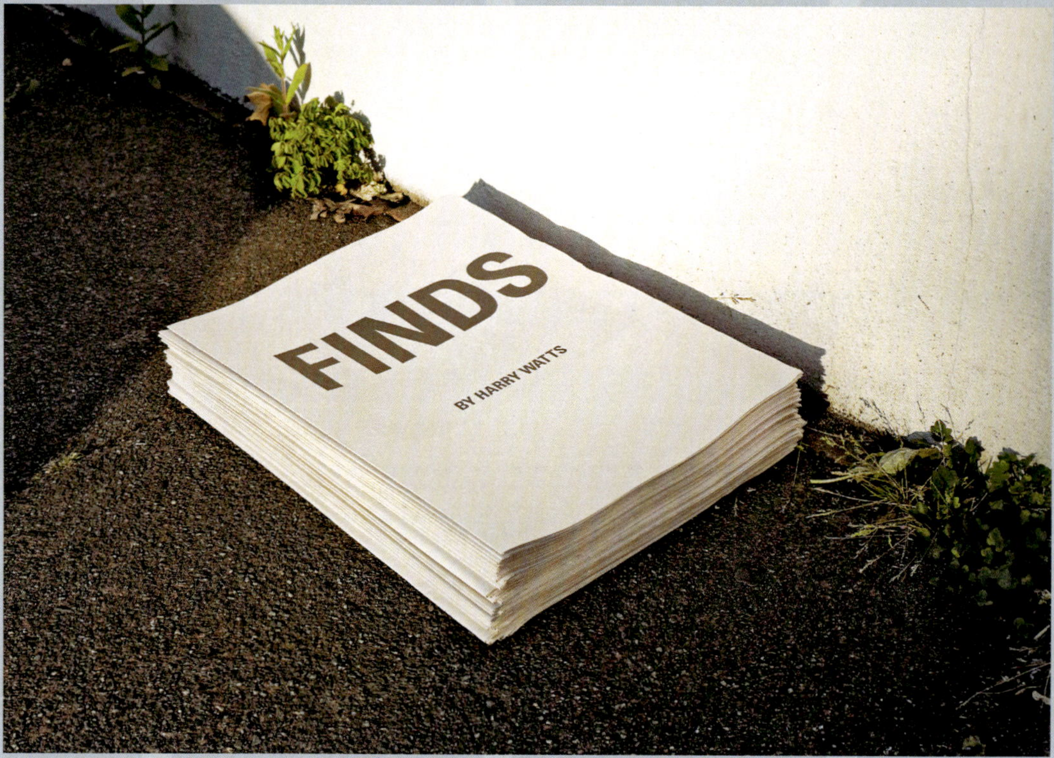

6.10

Title: *FINDS*

Photographer: Harry Watts

Harry Watts' project, *FINDS*, grew from documenting found sculptures left on the streets. His images were then collated and returned to the street in the form of a free printed newspaper. Watts worked with designers to create a professional manuscript to showcase the work. He then placed the newspapers in numerous locations that would target both his key audience and random passers-by.

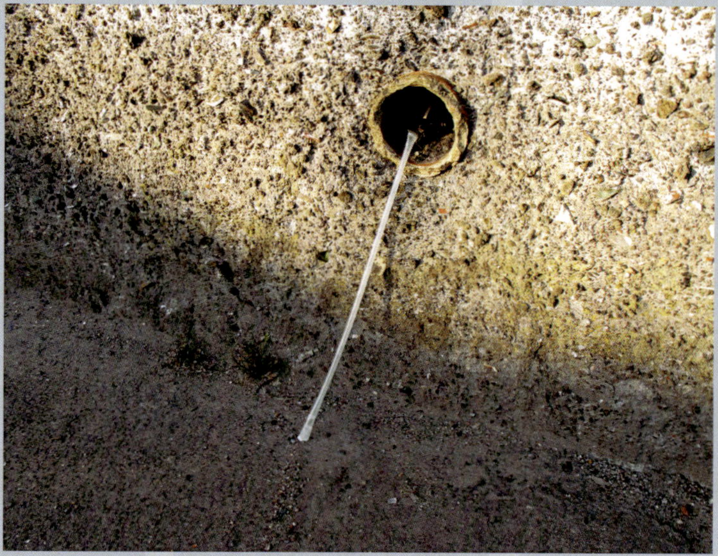

Activity 6 Booklet

For this final activity, you will make an explanatory booklet to accompany your photographic project.

It is common for a gallery or museum to provide a small booklet offering further information about the work of a particular photographer or artist. Guides of this sort often give background information about the photographer's life. They frequently go into considerable detail about how the work was made, what influenced it and how the piece should be interpreted.

Visit two local galleries or museums and pick up an information booklet on a current exhibition from each venue. If there are none on display, ask if a press or information pack is available. Look through these guides and summarize the information that is included. How is it laid out? Which images are used? How is the guide valuable to you, the viewer?

Review your research and development and reflect on the key milestones that have directed your project. Pick out eight images to illustrate this journey – you may want to include scanned pages of your sketchbook or a ticket to an exhibition that you visited.

Write some explanatory text to accompany your images. Remember that what you are writing will need to be in an appropriate tone for a visitor encountering your work for the first time.

Next, use a folded sheet of paper to make a mock-up design and layout for your booklet. Where do you want the text to go? What order do you want your images to be placed in? Making a rough model (a dummy) will help you visualize the final layout. After making the dummy, you can design the layout of photographs and text. This can be done using programs such as Adobe InDesign or Illustrator or Microsoft Word. Good, and usually simple, design is vital to this activity, and you should explore different design options before committing to print.

This exercise will help you to collate and organize your work in a concise, well-designed, manner. The design and editing of the booklet will allow further reflection and, most importantly, direct you to consider how an audience will be introduced to your work.

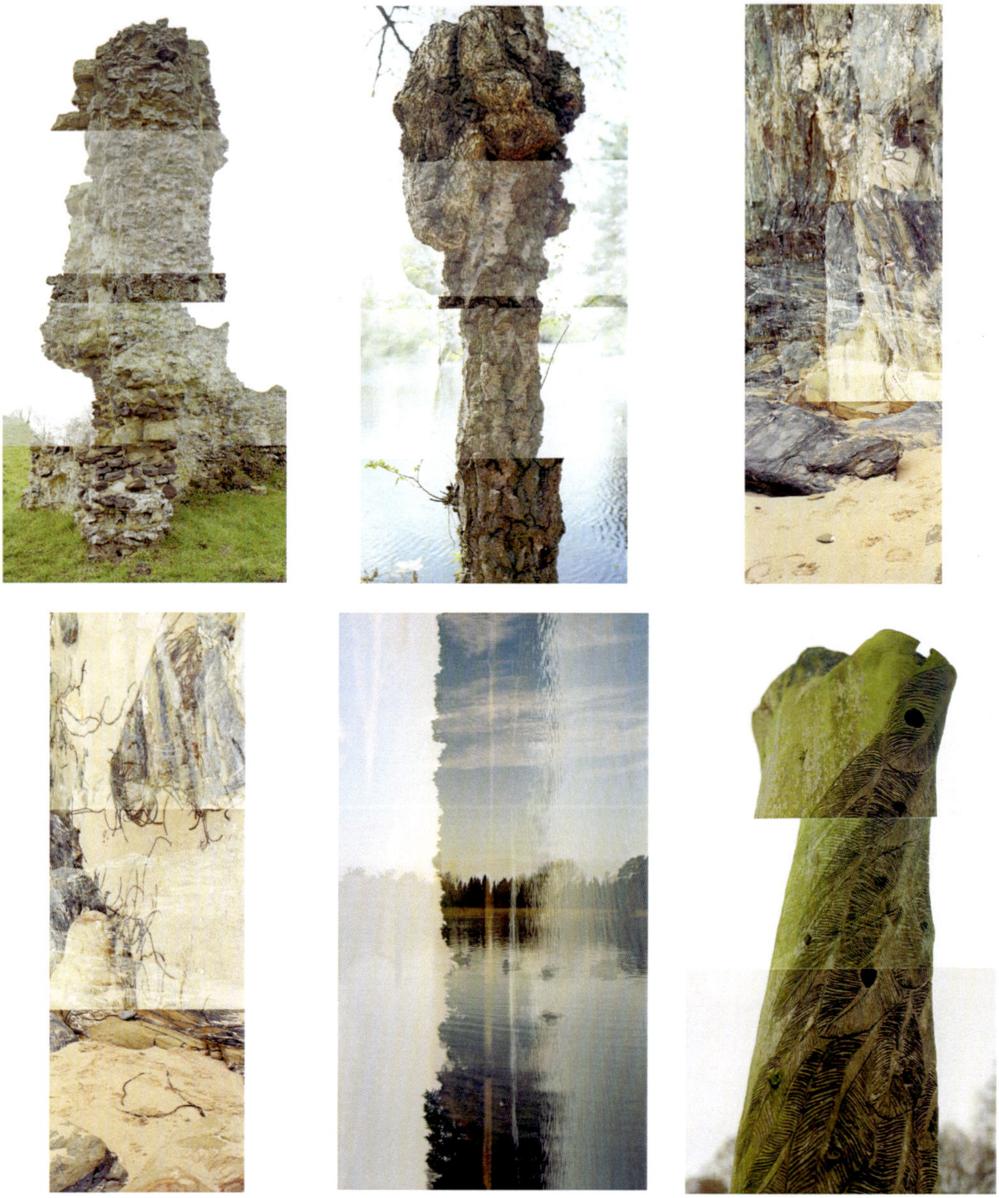

7.1

Title: Looking for a Way Out

Source/Photographer: Xiaoran Xu

When Xiaoran Xu travelled to the UK to study for a Masters in photography after her undergraduate studies at Zhejang University, she did not anticipate how homesick she would be nor how in awe of the British landscape she would become. For the first time she discovered analogue photography, and, through a process of trial and error as well as multiple accidents, she discovered a way of working with film and an old five series Hasseblad camera that involved overlapping frames and then looking at them from different perspectives (e.g. rotated) and then relating them back to an idea of Chinese painting that not only gave her a connection to home but allowed her to re-imagine the English landscape from the perspective of an outsider.

7 Conclusion

The emphasis of this book has been on understanding, acknowledging and recording the research process in a way that enables critical reflection and evaluation, creating a rich and vibrant resource archive for continual use in the production of new work.

We have talked primarily from the perspective of the practitioner and have avoided categorizing different approaches as types of research method (valid within pedagogic discourse). The point of the discussion throughout this book has been to inspire, and enable, reflective photographers.

Photography has an extraordinary history and numerous theories have been applied to its history and practice as part of an analytical research process contributing to the understanding of the medium. One of the most fascinating areas, yet to be extensively researched and written about, is the global history of photography. Most academic enquiry into photography, to date, is based on the history of North American and European (particularly western European) photographic practice, and photographic education is developing quickly in other parts of the world. In the future, this imbalance of knowledge will be redressed, and the researcher should always be aware of the lack of primary information available in relation to an international understanding of the practices of photography.

In this book we have brought in some references to that international history, thanks to those members of the global photography community that we have been fortunate enough to have discussion with. It is down to you as future researchers to travel and discover new histories: each time you have the opportunity to visit a new country, try investigating its photography, both contemporary and historical.

Research is always limited by current knowledge and the most exciting investigations bring new knowledge into the field; innovation in research instigates inspiration for future photographers and artists.

We have looked at the fields of both art and commerce, and referred to both throughout the book, though the bias has been on arts-based practices. Knowledge gained in the field of art can be transferred to any other type of photographic practice: commercial photographers, journalists and artists alike all look to a wide range of references for the creation of their work and employ strategies for creating images that are discovered through a practical and theoretical research process.

Knowledge is empowering, and the scope of any project or idea expands alongside the development of an understanding of photographic practices, histories and theories.

Acid-free material – Acid-free material has a neutral pH that makes it ideal for preserving documents. Many items in photography such as paper, negative boxes and masking tape can be purchased acid free and it is important to be aware of this to ensure the archival stability of your work.

Agent – An agent is someone who represents the work of a photographer to a commercial market.

Anthropology – The study of human societies and cultures and their development.

Art director – The person who directs a commercial shoot for moving and still imagery. The art director is the person who communicates between the client and the photographer.

Camera-less photography – A photograph does not necessarily have to be made with a camera; in fact, the first photographs ever made were produced without cameras. It is possible to create images using photosensitive materials and different techniques (such as the photogram).

Contact sheet – A photographic record of all the images on one roll of film (analogue photography) or a record of all the images on one shoot (digital photography). The images are usually actual size and so an analogue 35mm film has 36 shots on it and will fit onto a 10 × 8-inch sheet of photographic paper when printed as a contact sheet.

Curator – This term can be applied to a freelance person or gallery employee who organises, designs and creates an exhibition. It is also a person who manages and organises a collection of work in a museum.

Darkroom – A darkroom is a room that can be made completely dark to allow the processing of light-sensitive photographic materials, including photographic film and photographic paper. Analogue printing with an enlarger is carried out in total blackness if printing colour, or with a red 'safe light' if printing black and white.

Diaspora – Diaspora is the spread of peoples (any peoples) who have moved from their home (land) to other places.

Digital production suite – The digital production suite, or 'digital darkroom', is wherever the photographer prints their work or spends time manipulating the image in post-production. Equipment may include computers, scanners, printers, drawing tablets and hard drives.

Diptych – Two images that are either hung together or printed on the same sheet of paper to act as one work. The artist/photographer would not want the images in a diptych to be separated.

Fieldwork – Going out (i.e. out of the home or work place) to make work.

Forensic photography – Forensic photography (also known as crime scene photography) is a field in which photographs are used for their accuracy in recording a scene, so that record may later be used in court or to aid an investigation. Photographs of this kind often use certain lighting, viewpoints and scales in order to give the most accurate representation of the scene.

Formalism – Formalism is the concept that the most important element of an image is its form – that is, its purely visual aspects, as opposed to its context or narrative content. Certain photographers may say that they are interested in referencing the formalism of an artist or aesthetic movement, meaning that they wish to reference the 'form' or look of that work.

Glass negative – Glass photographic plates preceded photographic film and were used in early photographic methods of the 1800s. A light-sensitive emulsion was applied to a glass plate and then used in a large-format camera (such as with the albumen process).

Hasselblad camera – A Swedish manufacturer of high-quality medium-format cameras. The popularity of these small and well-built cameras means they have gained an iconic status and have a dedicated following of artists, enthusiasts and professionals using them today with both analogue and digital capture.

Juxtapose – To put two different things next to each other. This can often create a new meaning.

Large-format cameras – Large-format cameras take film sizes from 5 x 4 inch (12.7 x 10 cm) to 10 x 8 inch (25.4 x 20 cm), and even up to 20 x 24 inch (51 x 61 cm). These cameras are heavy and slow to use, so they are unsuitable for some applications. However, the added perspective controls, large negative, and quality that comes with that often makes them preferable, especially for producing large, detailed prints.

Lighting Designer – is someone who directs and designs how the lighting will be in a photographic shoot. They are in charge of the lighting system and on a big shoot may have assistants.

Linguistics – Linguistics is the scientific study of human language. Linguistic enquiry can generally be broken down into the study of language structure, language meaning and language in context. Many photographers are interested in the relation between language and photography and also in photography as a language itself.

Medium-format camera – Medium-format cameras record images on film or a digital sensor that is larger than the 24 × 36 mm of 35mm film, but smaller than the 5 × 4 inch (12.7 × 10 cm) size which is considered to be large format. Generally this is 6.45 cm, 6 x 6 cm, or 6 × 7 cm on 120 film. Medium-format cameras are often considered the ideal mix between quality and portability and are favoured by photography professionals looking for an especially high-quality image.

Montage – A composite image produced by blending multiple photographs or text (either digitally or in the darkroom) to create a fully realized final image.

Paradox – A paradox is a self-contradictory statement or event.

Photogram – A photogram is a photographic image made without a camera by placing objects directly onto the surface of a photosensitive material such as photographic paper and then exposing it to light.

Photographic film – Photographic film consists of a sheet of plastic coated with a light-sensitive emulsion. Film comes in a range of sizes, from small-format roll film to large-format sheet film. Print film turns into a negative when developed, while colour reversal film (otherwise known as slide film or transparencies) yields a positive image.

Picture editor – A picture editor is a term used to describe the person who works in a magazine or newspaper choosing images and deciding where they go into the publication. A photographer makes an appointment to meet the picture editor in order to promote a series of work or get further work by showing a portfolio.

Pinhole camera – A camera that uses only a tiny 'pinhole' instead of a glass lens. Images made by these simple cameras are typified by distortion and aberrations that can be used for creative purposes. The longest ever photographic exposures have been made with pinhole cameras.

Polaroid – The pioneering company that introduced instant film in 1948. The film itself contained all of the chemicals needed for developing and fixing the photograph, so the image was usually visible just 30 seconds after the exposure.

Proposal – A proposal is something you write to explain what you are doing. You may be asked to write a proposal before you start a commission or a University project. The commissioner or university should provide guidelines regarding content and word length.

Psychoanalysis – A branch of psychotherapy developed in the late 1800s and early 1900s by Austrian neurologist Sigmund Freud. In psychoanalytic theory it is understood that a large part of human behaviour is determined by irrational drives. Many photographers and artists are interested in delving into the workings of the mind, and psychoanalytical theory has been hugely influential in the way we understand art and photography.

Reportage – Photojournalistic photography.

Rorschach psychodiagnostic test – A psychological test in which subjects' perceptions of inkblots are recorded and then analysed.

RSS reader – Blogs and online magazines often utilize RSS channels. Using an RSS reader (such as Google Reader), you can keep track of all of the blogs and websites that you 'follow' or are subscribed to, and see new posts as soon as they are published. This is the easiest way of keeping track of a large number of sources and quickly and concisely keeping up to date with current ideas and work.

Screen printing – A process that forces ink onto a surface through a prepared screen of fine material so as to create a picture or pattern. A screen print can be made from a photograph.

Small-format cameras – In the early 1900s when the first cameras were designed to take the perforated 35mm roll film that was used in motion-picture cameras, these were by far the most compact cameras that had ever been seen. Cameras such as the legendary Leica altered the way people held the camera, the angles that people could point their camera and the way the camera was perceived. 35mm soon became the most popular film format due to its compact size and ease of use. In 2000, digital cameras with sensors smaller than 35mm gained in popularity until digital cameras became the standard, from small but high-quality compact cameras (with sensors usually only measuring about 6mm diagonally), to high quality 'full-frame' digital SLRs with sensors the same size as 35mm film.

Stylist – A stylist works with the photographer to style the models and/or the objects and environment in a shoot.

Trade show – A show where people in the photographic industry can display and show off their products for photographers to look at and buy.

Triptych – A piece of work that includes three photographs that need to be seen together in the design/layout specified by the photographer.

Vernacular photography – Ordinary photography not attributed to artists or well-known photographers. Vernacular photography may be created by high street studios or amateur photographers; it can also be snap shots.

Vintage prints – These are historical prints made soon after the photograph itself was taken, often by the photographers themselves. Vintage prints are amongst the most valuable and highly sought-after photographs in the art market and will often be signed and dated by the photographer to prove authenticity. They can reveal a lot about the vision of the particular photographer and the time they lived in.

Bibliography and webography

Further reading

Bate, David (2016). ***Photography: The Key Concepts*** (2nd edition). Bloomsbury

Cotton, Charlotte (2009). ***The Photograph as Contemporary Art***. Thames & Hudson

Davidmann, Sara (2016). ***Ken. To be destroyed***. Schilt

Issa, Rose (2008). ***Shadi Ghadirian: Iranian Photographer***. Saqi Books

Lange, Mårten (2011). ***The New Town***. Ubyu

Langford, Michael (1990). ***The Darkroom Handbook***. Ebury Press

Langford, Michael; Fox, Anna; Sawdon Smith, Richard (2010). ***Langford's Basic Photography: The Guide for Serious Photographers*** (10th edition). Focal Press

Madahar, Neeta (2010). ***Flora***. Nazraeli Press

el Madani, Hashem (2005). ***Hashem el Madani: Studio Practices***. Mind the Gap/The Arab Image Foundation

Roberts, Simon (2017). ***Merrie Albion – Landscape Studies of a Small Island***. Dewi Lewis Publishing

Savage, Tim (2016). ***Understanding Digital Black and White Photography: Art and Techniques***. Crowood

Singh, Dyanita (2010). ***Dream Villa***. Steidl

Wells, Liz (2009). ***Photography: A Critical Introduction*** (4th edition). Routledge

Magazines and journals

Aperture
Fine-art photography magazine, featuring the work of high-profile photographers alongside academic articles.

PHOTOWORLD
Contemporary Chinese photography magazine run by Xinhua News Agency. The magazine shows art-based, documentary photography and the latest equipment. It is published on the first day of the month.

EXIT
Arts-based photography magazine published in Spain twice per year. It publishes leading art and fashion photography from across the world.

Foam
International photography magazine. Each issue is themed and split into eight photographic portfolios.

Photography & Culture
Peer-reviewed journal, featuring research papers and critical writing on photography.

Photoworks
Features the work of new and established photographers, critical writing, and reviews.

Blogs and online resources

alecsothblog.wordpress.com
US photographer Alec Soth's archived blog.

atacarnet.com
Company that arranges travel carnets for photographers taking their own equipment into a different country.

blurb.com
Self-publishing company where a buyer can pay to print a book on demand.

davidcampany.com
David Campany is a writer, curator of exhibitions and an artist who shares over a hundred essays from a range of projects to read on his website.

flakphoto.com
Flak Photo is an online photography magazine.

happyharleyproductions.com
Happy Harley Productions is a group that will assist the photographer to get access to what they want to photograph.

laurahynd.com
Laura Hynd is a photographer who works across art and commerce. This website features *Lady into Hut* and other projects.

lightstalking.com
Light Stalking offers guides and tips on the practical elements of photography.

littlebrownmushroom.wordpress.com
US photographer Alec Soth's publishing company.

offprint.org
Art publishing fair periodically held in London and Paris.

otmfc.com
Company providing trucks and assistants to carry studio kit and lighting equipment for location shooting.

photobookshow.co.uk
Photo Book Show offers a library of photography books, workshops and talks.

robertwyatt.net
Fashion photographer who has worked for numerous high-profile clients, including Prada, Valentino and British Airways.

selfpublishbehappy.com
Website showcasing self-published books.

thebookroom.net
Collection of limited edition photography books.

wanderingbears.co.uk
Online creative community with international guest bloggers.

work-show-grow.com/blog
Insider guide to photographic professional practice focusing on how to get ahead.

Page references in italics denote illustrations.

21st Century Types, 60

Abteilung Nr/L, 117
activities
booklet, *208*, 209
context and meaning, 190–1
illustrated story, *72*, *73*, *74*
making a mood board, 164–5
pioneers of photography, 131
recording ideas, 33–4
Adam, Nik, 160–3
Adams, Douglas, 165
advertising, 156
Aeppli, Simon, 119
After 'Invisible Man' by Ralph Ellison, The Prologue, 34
'Agnieszka' from One Month, 97
Alkazi Foundation of the Arts, 52
analogue photography, 102
An Angel Appears, 104
Andrew Bruce at work in India, 74
Anna with Magnolias, 70
The Appearing Lady, 188
Arab Image Foundation, 206, 207
Archive Research Centre, 53
archives, *50–2*, 50–5
accessing, 52
hidden, 202
history of, 53
personal, 202
photographer, *125*, 202, *203*
research, 108
Self Publish, Be Happy (SPBH), *186–7*
storing, 124
vernacular photography, 54
art-based photography, 7
artists' statement, 198
art practice, 96
Arts and Humanities Research Council (AHRC), 66
Arts Council, 66, 114
arts funding, 114
Assisted Self-Portrait of Charmian Edge, 89
Association of Photographers (AOP), 138, *139*
Atlas Group, *166*
audiences, 14, 170
Ault, Emory, 160

background research, 36–45, 60, 204
backgrounds, 86
The Bank Archive, 203
Basement Archive, 124
Bate, David, *27*
Because your eyes won't see, 147
The Beijing Silvermine, 128
Beyond the View 5, 97
Bilder von de Strabe No. 832, 55
blogging, 47, 120, *121*, 122–3
Blurb, 184
booklet activity, *208*, 209
bookmarking, 46
BookRoom, 186
books, 26, *27*
The Bowery in two inadequate descriptive systems, 108–9
Breed, 76–7
Brian Dowling, BDI, 103
Bright, Susan, 54
British Library, 36, *37*
Bruce, Andrew, *49*, 74, 140, 142, 164
budget proposal, 18, *19*
Bull, Stephen, 54
Buts, Ernie, 171

Calypso, Juno, 143
Campany, David, 123
Carletta, Lisa, 146
Caruana, Natasha, 18, *19*, 32, 112, 115, 143, 144
Cat (Cyan 0, Yellow 60, Magenta 81), 100
Centre for Contemporary Photography, 42
The Chase, 100
Cheryl, Sloane Square, 179
Christian, Robin, 205
Churchill, Vicki, 70, 150
Clark, Edmund, *8*, 9
The Clown, 115
clowns, 115
Coates, Joanne, 198
collaborations, 16, 21, 41, 42, 176, 177
between models and photographers, 142
with researchers, 62, 66
with subjects, 84, 88
collections and collectors, 44
commercial photography, 7, 134
editorial, 154
fashion and advertising, 156
fields of, 158
compiling research, 116, 118
blogging, 47, 120, *121*, 122–3
keeping workbook/sketchbook, 116, 118, *119*
storing an archive, 124
'Consider Falling', *45*
consent, getting subjects', 16, 84
context, 7, 14
audience and, 9, 170
for finished work, 16, 114
historical and cultural, *200–201*, 201
and meaning, 190–1
putting research into, 204–5
Cooke, Alice, 169, 198
Cotton, Charlotte, 96, 127
Creative Camera (journal), *136*, 137
Creative Review, 148, *149*
Crisp, Fiona, 117
curators, 204
curriculum vitae, 198
cyanotypes, 105

The Darkroom Handbook (Langford), 102
darkrooms, 17, 75, 100, 102, 103, 104
Davey, Sian, 95
Davidmann, Sara, 62, *63*
Davies, Ellie, *10*
Davies, John, 93
Davison, Dolin, 42, *43*
Dead Water, 66, *67–9*
Definitive Reincarnate, 201
Design production house, 159
Diane Arbus Revelations, 204
Diary by Andrew Bruce, 49
digital
photography, 102
post-production, 106
workbooks, 118
The digitisation studio at The Postal Museum, 140
Dizzy the Clown, 115
Doctors Without Borders/Medecins Sans Frontieres (MSF), 190
documentary photography, 94
Dots, 138
Double exposure, 99
Dreamers, 171
Dream Villa (Singh), *25*

Edge, Charmian, 88, *89*
editing, 110, 152, 176, *177*
editorial, 154
Ellison, Ralph, 34
Emergency Briefing Room, 14, *15*
ethics, 170
evaluation, 112
Evans-Pritchard, E. E., 40
Ever After, 3
Evidence/Evidence Image 3, 79

Facebook, 48, 118
Family Portrait, 52
fashion, 156
Fast Forward, *135*
Fenton, Roger, 130
Ferreira, Ângela, 59
A Field Hospital is Used as an Exhibition, 190

film, 16, 18, 34, 41, 166
format, 92, 96, 98, 102, 103, 106
makers, 119, 141
thinking time, 174, 176
Financial Times, 182
FINDS, 208
Flak Photo, 123
Fletcher, Gem, 148
Flickr, 141
Flight to Freedom, 106–7
Flora, 70, 71
Forte Sisters, 155
Fotomuseum Winterthur, 38–9
found photographs and postcards, 72
Fox, Anna, *20–1*, 84, 125, 142, 164, 175, 195
Fox, Louis, 101
Franck, Erik, 50
Freelance Club, 142
Freelancer Club, 138

Gaby, Hanne, 156, *157*
galleries, 42, *43*
genre, medium and technique, 92, *93–5*, 94, 96, *97*, 98, *99–101*
art practice, 96
documentary and reportage photography, 94
fashion and advertising, 156
landscape photography, 92, *93*
Gentlemen, 172
Getty Research Institute, 50
Ghadirian, Shadi, 25
Gibson, Melinda, 126, 127–9
Girl Thing, 105
glossary, 212–13
Goddesses series, 71
Gomi, Yuri, 51
Google Images, 141
Goto, John, *171*
Graham, Paul, 54
Gregory, Joy, 42, 105
Guantanamo: If the light goes out, 8
Gucci. Cruise. Cannes, France, 141

Hackney Eyes, 119
Hair and make-up shop, *195*
Harrodsburg, 86
Hasselblad HX1D II 50C, 98
Haynes, Peter, 160, 162
High Summer, 171
histories, *22–3*
global, 193, 201, 211
oral, 36
refining results, 24
understanding, 22
Hitchcock, Sasha, 154
Hollowood, Dean, 100
Horst, Horst P., 71
Howe, Sarah, 45
Hurrell, George, 71
Hyman, Claire and James, 44
Hyman Collection, 44
Hynd, Laura, 132
Hynd, Simon, 132
Hyper Passive, 117

ideas, 11
creating a mood board, 143, 164–5
deciding on subject matter, 76
directing, 148, 150, 152
editing and production, 152
equipment and techniques, 150
guiding through, 78
location hunting, 140–1
mind map, *32*, 33
model spotting, 142
notebook, *32*, 33
recording, 33–4
team, 148
testing, 146
illustrated story activity, *72*, 73, *74*
images
shooting in early stages, 77
toning, 104
impact of research, 9, 193
archives, 202, *203*, *205*
Madani's work, *206*, 207
putting research into context, 204
reflection, 194, *195–7*, 198, *198–201*, 201
research centres for photography, 205
Inside Out Upside Down, 163
Instagram, 48, 138
Interior Wellcome Collection, 41
Internet, 46–8
research source, 138
social media, 48
interviewing tips, 57
interviews, 57
Invisible Man (Ellison), 34

Jacobs, Michael, 39
journal, keeping, 194
journal, photography, 26, *27*, 116
judgments, 114

Kapajeva, Maria, 97
Kennard, Peter, 182
Ken. To be destroyed, 62, *63*
Klenz, Steffi, *13*
Knorr, Karen, 106, 172

Ladies, 172
Landmark-European Tour, 51
landscape photography, 92, *93*
Lange, Marten, 184, *185*
Langford, Michael, 102
Langford's Basic Photography, 102, 140
Last One Out, Please Turn on The Light, 103
Lau, Grace, 60, *60–1*
Laura Hynd at work, *132*
lectures, 56
Leister, Wiebke, 2, *3*
Let's be honest, the weather helped, 166
Leverhulme, 66
Levie, Victor, 21
libraries, 36, *37*, 38
Light Stalking, 123
lighting, 16, 75, 78, 92, 134
natural, *130*, 131, *132*
in street photography, 86, 88
in studios, 80, 82, *83*, 140
Linaker, Chris, 111
Linderstam, Anna, 81, 83
listening, 58
Little Black Dress, 105
Little Brown Mushroom, 123
Littlewood, Chris, 177
location hunting, 140–1
Loisirs, 174–5
London College of Communication, 53
London Metropolitan University, 38
Longhurst, Jo, 76
Looking for Alice, 94–5
Looking for a Way Out, 210
Lunar Caustic, 126, 129
Luvera, Anthony, 88

Madahar, Neeta, 70, 71
el Madani, Hashem, *206*, 207
magazines, 24, 136, *137*, 162
Maidan – Portraits from the Black Square, 90–1
Maier, Vivian, 87
The Making of Anna Linderstam's 'Triptych', 83
Martar, Diana, 79
Martin Parr Foundation, 203
Mary Ellis, 70
Masters photography, 64
Match Day contact sheet, *111*
Material Girl Mag, 146
Mathews, Chloe Dewe, 28–9, *30–1*
Mazaccio & Drowilal, 82
McBean, Angus, 70, 71
McConnell, Gareth, 127
meaning of photographs, changing, 178
Meek, Nick, 150
In Memory of 7, 181
Metropoli, 93
mind map, *32*

mirrors and windows, 86
Mobasser, Ali, 124
Mobasser, Mohsen, 204
Model Mayhem, 142
model spotting, 142
mood board, 143, 164–5
Mood board for Cold Cases, *143*
Moore, David, 14, *15*
Muse Magazine, 156, *157*
Museum of Modern Art (MoMA), 40
museums, 40, *41*
Muthiah, Nandini Valli, *200–201*, 201

Najr (left) and Asmar (right), *206*
National Exhibition Centre, 135
National Institute of Design, 96
National Media Museum, 71
natural light, *130*, 131, *132*
Nazraeli Press, 71
networking, 134
New Street Station, *93*
News Truck, *183*
The New Town, 184, *185*
New York Magazine, 160
Nicholson, Richard, 103
Nick Meek Beetle Campaign, 150
Norman, Luke, 160–3
notebook, *32*
Nummianus, *12–13*

obituaries, 23
O'Kane, B., 36, *37*
Old Police Cell Museum, 143
Oral History of British Photography, 36
Orrantia, Rodrigo, 132
OTMFC – 'Their Little Black Truck', *150–1*
Out of the Box commission for *New York Magazine*, *160*

Painted Cow, World War II, *53*
painted photographs, 52, 201
Parr, Martin, 54, 127, 203
past research, 172
People per Hour, 138
The Photograph as Contemporary Art (Cotton), 96, 127
photographers
  agreement, 144, *145*
  oral histories of, 36
  pioneer, 131
  researching, 22, 23, 24
  statements, *198–9*
photography
  art practice, 96
  final production, 182, 184, 186
  histories, 22, 23–4
  pioneers of, 131
  research centres for, 205
Photography (Bate), *27*
Photography & Culture, *27*
Photography: A Critical Introduction, *27*
Photography and the Archive Research Centre (PARC), 205, *205*
The Photography Show, 135, *135*, 150
photojournalism, 94
Photoworks, 123
Photoworld (journal), *137*
Pieces of my Grandfather's Broken Heart, *204*
Pinterest, 48, 138, 143, 165
pioneers of photography, 131
Pitt Rivers Museum, 40
planning, 7
  histories of photography, 22, 23–4
  magazines, 24
  photographs as research, 78
  photography blogs, 123
  photographic books, 184
  photographic journals, 26, *27*
  photographic theory, 26
Platt, Spencer, 190
Portfolio reviews, *59*
Portrait of Rhys, *101*
The Postal Museum, 140
post-production, 102
  darkroom, 102
  digital, 106
  editing, 152
  example of, *153*
  toning images, 104
Power Suit, 156, 157
practice and research. *See* research and practice
practice as research, 7, 75–125
  applying research to practice, 108–10, *111*, 112, *113*
  blogging, 120, *121*, 122
  commercial projects, 134, 136, 138
  compiling your research, 116, 118
  deciding on subject, 76, *76–7*
  guiding an idea through, 78
  making judgments, 114
  photographs, 78
  post-production, 102, *103*, 104, *105*, 106, 107
  project evaluation, 112, *113*
  shooting images early in project, 77
  storage archives, 124, *125*
  street photography, 84, *84–7*, 86, 88, *89*, *90*, *91*
  studios, 80, *80–3*, 82
  style, genre, medium and technique, 92, *93–5*, 94, 96, *97*, 98, *99–101*
  using own images for research, 78
practice-based PhDs, 64, 66
Pye, Weny, 180
PYLOT (magazine), 142, 164

Raad, Walid, 166
Ray, Man, 156
reading, 6, 11, 14, 22, 24, 26, 57, 108
Reassurance, *200–201*
reflection, 110, 112, 194, *195–7*, 198, *198–201*, 201
Remake of Fenton original (2010), 130
reportage photography, 94
research
  arts funding, 114
  background, 36–45
  commercial projects, 134, 136, 138
  developing ideas through, 7
  framework for practice, 62
  framework in action, 62
  impact of, 9
  interactive forms of, 56–8
  Internet, 47
  writing for, 64
research and exploration, 6
research and practice, 9, 24
  ethics, 170
  final production, 182, 184, 186
  methods of testing, 168
  modifying a plan, 180
  revisiting past research, 172
  thinking time, 174, 176, 178
research councils and bodies, 66–67
research ethics, 170
research informing practice, *60–1*, 60–9, *63*, *65*, *67–9*
research proposals, 12–20
  approach and methods, 16
  audience of, 14
  budget example, 18, *19*
  cover designs for project 'Resort 1', *20*, *21*
  getting in, 16
  proposals for funding, 18
  references, 18
  timetable and budget, 18
  title, 12
  topic or theme, 14
  writing, 144
research sources
  Internet, 138
  magazines, 136, *137*
Resort, 195
Resort 1, cover designs for, *20–1*
resource websites, 123
Restaurant at the End of the Universe, 165
reviewing work, 58
Ribeiro, Marilene, 66

Ridgers, Derek, 178
Roberts, Simon, 177
Rosler, Martha, 109

Sagmeister & Walsh, 159
Sauvin, Thomas, 126, 128, 129
Savage, Tim, 152
scale, testing, 168
Schmid, Joachim, 55
Schwarzenegger, Arnold, *54*
Sealy, Mark, *22*, 23
Sear, Helen, 96
search engines, 46
Self Publish, Be Happy (SPBH) Archive, 186–7
selenium toning, 104
sepia toning, 104
SF Camerawork, 42
Shadi Ghadirian: Iranian Photographer, 25
Shanghai Centre for Photography, 42
Shot at Dawn, 28–9, *30–1*
Singh, Charan, 65
Singh, Dyanita, 25
sketchbooks, 116, *119*
Smith, Richard Sawdon, 104, *104*
Snapchat, 48
social media, 48, 191
Soth, Alec, 123
Steller Stories, 48
Stidolph, Melanie, 197
Still Life with Fruit, 130
storage, 124
story activity, illustrated, *72*, 73, *74*
Strand, Clare, 188, 189
street photography, 84, *84–7*, 86, 88, *89*, *89–91*
  available backgrounds, 86
  changing perspective, 88
  equipment, 88
  privacy and permission issues, 84
  windows and mirrors, 86
studios, 80, *80–3*, 82
subject matter, 76
A Suicide Constellation, 17

Tank (journal), *137*
Tate Britain, 54
Taylor-Lind, Anastasia, 90
team, 148
technical aspects, 16, 98
  colour film, 92, 98
  double exposures, *99*
  experimenting with, 104, 106, 108, 127–8
  for landscape photography, 92, *93*
  photograms, 17
  toning images, 104
testing
  methods, 168, *169*
  work, 146
Thames & Hudson, *22*, *23*
themes, 14, 18, 24, 33, 108, 165
theory, 26
thinking time, 174, 176, 178
Those Who Fear, 173
Tilley, Aaron, 148
Tillmans, Wolfgang, 127
time, 109
  analogue and digital, 174
  changing meaning, 178
  editing and, 176, *177*
  thinking, 174, 176, 178
'Timely Tale' budget example from, 18, *19*
toning images, 104
topic, 14
Town and Country Magazine, 154, *155*
Triptych: In Unheard Contractions, 80–1
truth, concept of, 35
Twitter, 48

Understanding Digital Black and White Photography (Savage), 152
University for the Creative Arts, 161, 198
Untitled 1, 65
Untitled, 1953, 87
Untitled, 2007, 196–7
Untitled, from Basingstoke 1985/86, 84–5
Untitled XII, 129

Vantage Point 1, 10
vernacular photography, 54
Vero, 48
Vicente, Pedro, *17*
Victoria & Albert Museum, 50, *50*, 202, 204

Walker, Tim, 141
Wall, Jeff, 34
Wallace, Dougie, 86
Wandering Bears, 162
waste photographs, 55
Watson, Camilla, 99
Watts, Harry, 208
Waxworks, 54
Wearing, Gillian, 96
Weaver, Ben, 177
Website of Association of Photographers (AOP), 138, *139*
We Chat, 48
Weiner Library Institute of Contemporary History, 124
Wellcome Trust, 41, 66
Wells, Liz, *27*
Where Three Dreams Cross, 192, 193
Whitechapel Gallery, 193
Whiteread, Rachel, 96
Wild Style, 82
Williams, Val, 54, 62
Winterthur Museum of Photography, 40
Witkin, Joel-Peter, 104
Women's Library, 38
workbooks, 116, 118
Work-Show-Grow, 120, *121*, 123
The World of Interiors (journal), *137*
World Press Exhibition, 94
World Wide Web, 35
writers, 64, 204
Wyatt, Robert, 156

Xiaoran Xu, 210

Yevonde, Madame, 71
Youpic, 48

Zaine, Taro, 99
Zhejang University, 210

We would like to thank all those people who have supported us in the making of this book through sharing their ideas and research knowledge. We also thank all those photographers and artists who have generously contributed their images.

With special thanks to Felix Fox, Sarah Howe, the University for the Creative Arts at Farnham and the London College of Communication, University of the Arts London.

Thanks also to Felicity Cummins and Courtney Coffman, and to all the Bloomsbury staff directing and working on this production.

p3: Wiebke Leister, from the series 'Ever After' (2008).

p8: © Edmund Clark

p10: Image by Ellie Davies. *www.elliedavies.co.uk* All rights remain with the artist.

p12: Steffi Klenz, courtesy of the artist.

p15: David Moore, from the series, 'The Last Things' (2008).

p17: Pedro Vicente.

p22 (above): Thames & Hudson

p22 (below): Mark Sealy and Lawrence & Wishart

p23: Thames & Hudson

p25 (above): Dream Villa, by Dayanita Singh, published by Steidl, 2010.

p25 (below): *Shadi Ghadirian: Iranian Photographer*, by Rose Issa Projects/ Saqi Books, Westbourne Publishers Ltd. Reproduced with permission of The Licensor through PLSclear.

p27 (top left): Photography: The Key Concepts, by David Bate, published by Bloomsbury Publishing Plc.

p27 (top right): PHOTOGRAPHY, A CRITICAL INTRODUCTION, 5th Edition by Liz, Wells, published by Routledge. © *Liz Wells, 2015, reproduced with arrangement with Taylor & Francis Books UK. Cover image of Malik Sidibe's Studio, Moi, un blanc.* © *Jose Pedro Cortes (2011).*

p27 (below): Photography & Culture, Volume 3, Issue 1, 2010, reproduced with arrangement with Taylor & Francis Group UK.

p30: © Chloe Dewe Mathews 2014

p34: Courtesy of the artist, Jeff Wall, and Marian Goodman Gallery, New York.

p37: B. O'Kane/Alamy.

p39: Photo by Michael Jacobs/Art in All of Us/Corbis via Getty Images

p41: Courtesy of Wellcome Collection

p43: Colin Davison

p45: Sarah Howe

p49: © Andrew Bruce

p50: © Victoria and Albert Museum, London.

p51: Yuri Gomi.

p52: © The Alkazi Collection of Photography.

p53: © Alpha Press.

p54: Stephen Bull.

p55: Joachim Schmid.

p59: Format

p60-61: Courtesy of Grace Lau.

p63: Photographs by Sara Davidmann, © Sara Davidmann

p65: Courtesy of the Artist/SepiaEye

p67–69: © Marilene Ribeiro 2016

p70 (above): Angus McBean photograph (MS Thr 581). © Harvard Theatre Collection, Houghton Library, Harvard University.

p70 (below): Courtesy of the artist, Neeta Madahar.

p74: © Andrew Bruce

p76–77: Jo Longhurst. Four photographs on aluminium disks, 2005.

p79: Diana Matar

p81 and 83: © Anna Linderstam.

p82: She's Out Of My Life, The Dog's Best Friend, 2013, Mazaccio & Drowilal

p86: Dougie Wallace

p87: Photo by Vivian Maier / Courtesy of Maloof Collection.

p89: Charmian Edge / Anthony Luvera.

p90–91: Anastasia Taylor-Lind

p93: © John Davies 2000.

p94–95: Sian Davey

p97 (above): Maria Kapajeva.

p97 (below): © Helen Sear, Courtesy: Klompching New York.

p99: Taro Zaine

p100: Dean Hollowood

p101: © Louis Fox

p103: © Richard Nicholson.

p104: © Richard Sawdon Smith.

p105: © Joy Gregory 2002.

p107: © Karen Knorr.

p108–109: © Martha Rosler / courtesy of Mitchell-Innes & Nash, New York.

p111: Chris Linaker.

p117: © Fiona Crisp, courtesy of Matt's Gallery, London.

p119: Simon Aeppli.

p121: Work-Show-Grow

p124: Courtesy of Ali Mobasser.

p126: Melinda Gibson & Thomas Sauvin

p129: Unknown

p139 (above): SCALA / Roger Fenton

p139 (below): Photography students, UCA, Farnham, UK

p132: Simon Hynd

p135: The Photography Show

p139: The AOP

p140: © Andrew Bruce

p141: Magnum Photos/Martin Parr

p142: © Andrew Bruce and Anna Fox

p143: Juno Calypso

p147: Lisa Carletta

p149: Cover image art direction by Gem Fletcher. Photography by Aaron Tilley.

p151: © vickichurchill

p153: Tim Savage

p155: Sasha Hitchcock

p157: Robert Wyatt

p159: © Marco Scozzaro 2013. All Rights Reserved

p160–163: Model: Emory Ault; Assistant: Peter Haynes; Photographers: Luke Norman & Nik Adam

p164: © Andrew Bruce and Anna Fox

Acknowledgments and picture credits

p166: The Atlas Group/Walid Raad. Let's be honest, the weather helped. © Walid Raad, courtesy Anthony Reynolds Gallery, London.

p169: Alice Cooke

p171: Photo courtesy of Ernie Buts.

p173: © Karen Knorr.

p177: © Simon Roberts

p179: © Derek Ridgers.

p181: © Wendy Pye 'In Memory of 7. . .'

p183: Peter Kennard

p185: Mårten Lange, 2011.

p187: SPBH

p188: Courtesy of Clare Strand.

p190: © 2011 Getty Images.

p192: *Where Three Dreams Cross: 150 Years of Photography from India, Pakistan and Bangladesh*, by Whitechapel Gallery, Fotomuseum Winterthur. Published by Steidl & Partners/www.steidlville.com.

p196: Courtesy of the artist, Melanie Stidoloph.

p199: Joanne Coates and Alice Cooke

p200: © Nandini Valli Muthiah

p203: Courtesy of Martin Parr.

p204: The Department of Medical Photography, The Texas Heart Institute. Photograph of Lt General Mohsen Mobasser's heart taken during a triple coronary artery bypass – 30 January 1974.

p205: Robin Christian

p206: Studio Shehrazade, Saida, Lebanon, 1950s. Excerpt from Akram Zaatari's 'Objects of Study' project, 2006. © Arab Image Foundation.

p208: Harry Watts.

p210: © XuXiaoran

All other photographs and images are courtesy of the authors, Natasha Caruana and Anna Fox:

www.natashacaruana.com

www.annafox.co.uk

All reasonable attempts have been made to trace, clear and credit the copyright holders of the images reproduced in this book. However, if any credits have been inadvertently omitted, the publisher will endeavour to incorporate amendments in future editions.